# LIFE AFTER FAVRE

The Green Bay Packers and their Fans Usher in
the Aaron Rodgers Era

Phil Hanrahan

SPORTS
PUBLISHING

This book is dedicated to my parents.

Sports Publishing books may be purchased in bulk at special discounts for sales promotion, corporate gifts, fund-raising, or educational purposes. Special editions can also be created to specifications. For details, contact the Special Sales Department, Sports Publishing, 307 West 36th Street, 11th Floor, New York, NY 10018 or info@skyhorsepublishing.com.

Sports Publishing® is a registered trademark of Skyhorse Publishing, Inc.®, a Delaware corporation.

www.skyhorsepublishing.com

10 9 8 7 6 5 4 3 2 1

Paperback ISBN: 978-1-61321-020-8

Library of Congress Cataloging-in-Publication Data

Library of Congress Cataloging-in-Publication Data

Hanrahan, Phil.
  Life after Favre : the Green Bay Packers and their fans usher in the Aaron Rodgers era / Phil Hanrahan.
    p. cm.
  Originally published: c2009.
  Includes bibliographical references and index.
  ISBN 978-1-61321-020-8 (alk. paper)
  1. Green Bay Packers (Football team)--History. 2. Football fans--Wisconsin--Green Bay. 3. Favre, Brett. 4. Rodgers, Aaron, 1983- I. Title.
  GV956.G7H36 2011
  796.332'640977561--dc23
                            2011020905

Printed in the United States of America

# Contents

# CONTENTS

"There is no script for this."

> —Packers head coach Mike McCarthy, July 26, 2008


"Some dreams don't come true."

> —lyric by Adam Schlesinger, for the band Ivy

# PROLOGUE:
# "ROOKIE" HAS A MELTDOWN

"**R**OOKIE" **COULDN'T TAKE** it anymore. He'd had enough. Four straight months of callers bashing Packers management for not welcoming Brett Favre back. Week after week it was *Brett this, Brett that,* two hours of listener calls a day. This Green Bay sports radio station was on the front lines when it came to fan feedback. What had the Favre Horns—that's what Rookie called 'em—all riled up this Friday morning was the previous night's thrilling 34–31 Jets victory over archrival New England. Favre had gone 26 of 33 for 258 yards, with two touchdowns and no picks. In overtime, he took his team 64 yards in 14 plays, connecting on 5 of 6 passes. He looked like the Brett of old. Or make that the Brett of 2007, as callers were oh-so-quick to remind Rookie. The Brett who led the Packers to 14 victories and a near Super Bowl berth. That Brett.

"This one ranks right up near the top," Favre told reporters after the game, a quote that put a little ding in the hearts of Packers fans. After Jets kicker Jay Feely booted home the winning 34-yarder, Brett raised his arms in grinning triumph, just like he'd done so many times for the Pack. Through ten games, Favre was leading the AFC in completion percentage. The New York Jets had won four straight. At 7–3, they were alone atop the AFC East for the first time since 2001.

Rookie had been at WDUZ longer than anyone—hence the nickname. They didn't call him Iron Man—they saved that for Favre—but the fact remained that Rookie was sturdy, durable, a radio grinder doing twenty-five hours of sports talk weekly with his partner, Bill Rabeor. Weekdays from 6–9 A.M. they hosted "The Fan Nation Morning Show," a drive-time program broadcast on 107.5 FM and 1400 AM The Fan, a.k.a. *Northeast Wisconsin's Sports Authority* and *Your Source for ESPN Radio*. At 9 A.M. they kicked off their two-hour call-in show, "Fan Line with Bill and Rookie." Guess what people wanted to talk about today?

Normally the last twenty minutes on Friday morning formed the best part of Rookie's radio week—and not only because his weekend more or less started at the top of the hour. It was the "Friday Fish Fry" segment of the show, one in which listeners called or e-mailed to salute or slam some person in the sporting world. If you were a caller offering kudos, you asked Rookie and Bill to "pop a top" to the person. They cued the carbonated opening to Jim Ed Brown's 1967 country hit "Pop a Top," a tune that starts with possibly the world's greatest recording of a pull-tab can being opened.

If, conversely, you were calling to rip someone, you told Rookie and Bill to "dunk 'em in the hot fryer!" With the push of a button, they'd promptly cue a sound effect of lake perch dropping into a vat of sizzling oil.

Guess who was getting kudos today?

Guess who people wanted to fry?

"Pop a top to Brett!" hollered Scott from Sturgeon Bay. "Brett's on the train to the playoffs!"

That was a twofer. Well done, Scott from Sturgeon Bay. A plug for Brett and a not-so-subtle dig at Packers head coach Mike McCarthy, who the previous summer had famously said, "The train has left the station," meaning the team was moving on without Favre. "Watching the Iron Man last night was awesome!" exclaimed Eric from Appleton. "He still has tons of fans out here. We want him to go to the Super Bowl and win it for the Jets!" And now Brian from Neenah was on the line. "Crack open a tall cold one for number 4!" he trumpeted. "Brett knows how to win the close ones! To think we could have had him for another year!"

Rookie and Bill popped a top. Multiple tops. *Whoosh!*

Mike from Green Bay called with payback on his mind. "Get that deep fryer going!" he shouted. "You saw what Brett did last night. I wanna deep-fry all those Favre bashers! Cook 'em up!"

*Sizzle, sizzle, fry.*

Todd from Oshkosh had it in for the Packers general manager. "Let's deep-fry Ted Thompson!" he crowed.

At this point Rookie finally lost it. After sixteen weeks, ten hours a week—160 hours of his life—hearing the same thing over and over, he had his Howard Beale from *Network* moment. He wasn't so much mad as hell, he just didn't want to take it anymore.

"It's driving me crazy, listening to this every day!" he said into his mike. "When's it gonna end?"

"Not till January," said Bill.

"For two days before the Pats game, everyone was bashing Brett," Rookie continued. "Now because of last night all the Favre Horns call in and blow! 'Brett this, Brett that, if only we still had Brett.' Well, we don't! The Jets spent $140 million in the offseason—no wonder their record's better than last year! Let's see how the Packers and Jets do over the next three years. It's been like this since August! People who just can't get over it. When are they gonna move on? It's so tiresome, speculating what it would be like if Favre was here! He's not! Can't we talk about the guys who *are* here!"

Rookie paused for breath. Scanning some e-mails, he groaned.

"Oh my God, it's all just more of the same! It's never gonna stop. Five hours a day, it's all we talk about. Brett's been gone three months! He's not coming back! People gotta start dealing with reality. When are we gonna put this to bed? *Do we ever get to talk about anything else?*"

The show went to commercial. "Drop by Brett Favre's Steakhouse on Brett Favre Pass for lunch or dinner," said the chipper radio voice in Rookie's headphones. It was the first ad of the break. There was no escaping No. 4. Rookie held his head in his hands.

# INTRODUCTION: "WE'RE AT THE GAME"

I **T HAD HAPPENED** before. Twice. Lambeau and Lombardi—two men synonymous with the Green Bay Packers, winners of eleven NFL championships between them, faces of the franchise—suddenly gone. Curly Lambeau, a hometown football star back from Notre Dame, had the idea to start a semi-professional team. It was 1919. He founded the Packers, coached them, managed operations, and played, taking snaps at halfback and throwing passes when he didn't run. He played through the 1929 season and coached and managed the team for another twenty years after that. Thirty years as Packer Incarnate. Then just like that, he was gone. After toxic feuds with the team's board of directors he departed for, of all places, Chicago, becoming head coach and vice president of the Chicago Cardinals. "I don't see how the Packers can last without him," said one of Lambeau's former offensive linemen, Charles "Buckets" Goldenberg. "He *was* the Packers."

Lambeau spent two years in Chicago then headed east to coach the Redskins. Washington is also where Vince Lombardi, the savior of the franchise, went too, in 1969. After a bloodless year serving as Packers GM, Lombardi wanted to coach again. And he liked that the Skins gave him a small team ownership stake.

Lambeau resigned. Lombardi asked the Packers to release him from a five-year contract. Both times it was the frigid start of February. And both times, Packer fans mourned the departure of a man who had turned their tiny Midwestern city into a place of champions, of glory.

This book began when Brett Favre announced his retirement on March 6, 2008. After sixteen seasons as a Packer, three league MVP awards, a Super Bowl victory in '97, a Super Bowl loss in '98, a near-trip to the big game ten years later, NFL records for career touchdown passes, passing yards, completions, and attempts, and a mind-bending, record-breaking streak of 275 consecutive starts by a quarterback commencing in a time when George Bush's *father* was in the White House, it was over. A lifelong Packer fan raised in Wisconsin, I watched Favre's tearful press conference from my apartment in Los Angeles. The world as Packer fans knew it had changed. A new era—a whole new *reality*—had arrived. It seemed like this might be a book. The story of the first season A.B. *After Brett.*

I left California for Wisconsin in early July.

Eight days later we learned Favre wanted back. Things just got more interesting. They didn't get any less interesting when the Packers traded their iconic quarterback to the New York Jets for a conditional fourth-round draft pick. Like Lambeau, like Lombardi, Brett Lorenzo Favre would come striding out of some other team's tunnel onto some other team's field for the September home-opener of some other NFL team. A big-city team. A team from New York.

Wow.

All season long—you just knew it—Packer fans would have one eye on Green Bay, the other on Brett and the Jets. Quarterback performances would be compared, win-loss records compared, team rosters compared. Cheeseheads would go deep into the weeds of quarterback ratings, QB deployment, importance of the signal-caller to game outcomes. In a weird way, it would almost be like the Packers were *playing* the Jets each week. There would be that much dual scrutiny. Fun for Aaron Rodgers, Favre's 24-year-old successor. Fun for Packers management.

But what kind of season would the Favre-less Packers have in 2008? Considering that they went 13–3 in 2007, came one play from reaching the Super Bowl, had nearly all their players and the same coaching staff back, the year figured to be a pretty good one. Nine or ten regular-season wins and a playoff victory or two—that was my guess. But it could be even better. It could be Hollywood-movie better. Rodgers, Favre's untested Cal-Berkeley understudy, could seize his big chance, stand firm under the pressure of succeeding a legend and lead the Pack to a spectacular season—all the way to Tampa Bay and the Bowl that is super. Could happen. And this book would be along for the ride.

Then again, maybe it wouldn't be a movie. Maybe the team would struggle. Pro football is like that—clubs up one year, down the other, for reasons we all can rattle off: injuries, personnel misfires, coaching stumbles, a tipped pass here, a stuffed run there, a doinked field goal. It wasn't a cliché the first time someone said that football was a game of inches. It was wise, the first time someone said this. Very wise.

I spent training camp evenings devouring books that chronicled an NFL team for a single season. Not being a pro sportswriter (just a passionate sports fan/ESPN junkie with a background in writing and love for summer softball and pickup basketball), I needed some examples. It was interesting noting how some authors hit the jackpot and chose teams that went all the way to the Super Bowl, while other authors hitched their wagons to teams that began their seasons with high hopes but then went south. Dick Schaap had the golden touch. He teamed with Packers guard Jerry Kramer for the 1968 classic *Instant Replay: The Green Bay Diary of Jerry Kramer*, taking readers inside the Packers' third straight championship season in '67. Returning to Green Bay almost thirty years later, he followed the Favre-led 1996 team in *Green Bay Replay: The Packers Return to Glory*. Maybe he goes with a different subtitle if the Packers don't end up beating the New England Patriots in Super Bowl XXXI.

John Feinstein's *Next Man Up: A Year Behind the Lines of Today's NFL* chronicled the 2004 Baltimore Ravens. Though their fate wasn't decided until the regular season's final hour, the 9–7 Ravens missed the playoffs. For *A Few Seconds of Panic: A 5-Foot-8, 170-Pound, 43-Year-Old Sportswriter Plays in the NFL*, Stefan Fatsis of the *Wall Street Journal* spent the summer of 2006 training as a placekicker with the Broncos, then checked in with the team during the season. Like the 2008 Packers, Denver was coming off a 13–3 year and trip to the conference championship. They started out red-hot at 7–2 but lost five of their last seven games, including a Week 17 heartbreaker in overtime, to finish 9–7 and out of the playoffs.

Then there was Roy Blount Jr.'s rollicking account of the '73 Steelers, *About Three Bricks Shy of a Load: A Highly Irregular Lowdown on the Year the Pittsburgh Steelers Were Super but Missed the Bowl*. Blount—no relation to Steelers defensive back Mel—was a *Sports Illustrated* staff writer at the time and followed the colorful Steelers during a 10-4 season in which they made the playoffs, but lost in the first round to Oakland.

As the 2008 season started, I promised myself that no matter how the Packers did, I was going to write a certain kind of book, one that never gets too heavy of touch, one mixing coverage of the games and players with Packer Nation travels and a look at Packer fandom in this time of change and disunion. Also, I wanted a book in tune with the joy of Packer game days in Green Bay, a joy beginning three or four hours before kickoff, the tailgating and street parties for a dozen blocks around Lambeau reaching Mardi Gras–like levels of merriment. People eat, drink, dance, laugh. They paint their faces green and gold. They wear Packer-colored beads. *No matter what,* I vowed, *I'm keeping the joy.* I kept the joy.

Like the Kramer/Schaap, Fatsis, and Blount books, *Life After Favre* is written in the first person. I moved from L.A. to Green Bay in 2008 to follow the Packers. I caught all eight home games at Lambeau. I hit all eight tailgate extravaganzas. By chance, not design, the one game I watched from the comfort of the Lambeau press box—the Houston contest, December 7—turned out to be the coldest of the season. Three degrees with whipping winds at kickoff. I did thermal penance by shoveling snow from the Lambeau bleachers on another brutally cold December day—me and 300 others.

I journeyed to Green Bay, but journeyed away from it as well. I ended up logging 5,000 road miles and 4,000 through the air following the team and pursuing adventures in Packer Land. I attended road games at the Metrodome and Superdome. I caught other away games in small-town Wisconsin taverns 200 miles from Green Bay. I watched the Tennessee Titans game in a bar and grill owned by rookie receiver Jordy Nelson's parents in rural Kansas. I caught the second Bears game in Mabel Murphy's, a year-round Packers bar in Scottsdale that's the proud home of the Arizona Pack Fan Club. Until diving into this book, I hadn't understood the full scope and breadth of Packer

Nation. Not only does it extend to every corner of Wisconsin, it thrives in cheesehead outposts from coast to coast.

The team granted me locker room access, let me watch a late-season practice, helped arrange interviews with Aaron Rodgers and teammates, and assisted in numerous other ways during my three months in Green Bay. They did not hand me an all-access pass, however. Nor did I expect them to. Even in a normal year, the Packers, like all NFL teams, are sparing when it comes to giving writers access to their inner workings, wanting to protect game strategies, player privacy, the free flow of team communication, and more. Even in a normal year, the Packers say no to some would-be chroniclers, as they, along with several other NFL teams, did in 2005 when approached by Stefan Fatsis for his book. And this was no normal year. No, not one that saw the team hire former Bush White House press secretary Ari Fleischer to advise on media strategy during what some came to call "Favre-Gate," the controversy surrounding the team's divorce from Brett Favre. I worried the Packers might turn me down altogether. But they did not, and for that I was grateful.

* * *

*It's not whether you get knocked down, it's whether you get up.*

*The title of champion may from time to time fall to others more than ourselves, but the heart, the spirit, and the soul of champions remains in Green Bay.*

*The Green Bay Packers never lost a football game. They just ran out of time.*

Vince Lombardi. Words to motivate, words to swell a Packer fan's heart. More than once during the season, especially late in the season, I found myself thinking of his words, his famous words. The line about *never losing, just running out of time* came in handy a couple times. So did something I heard in Lambeau Field the day the Packers played the Carolina Panthers. It was November 30, an overcast day threatening snow. I was seated in row 54, section 115, six aluminum bleachers from the top of the stadium's bowl. Sitting two rows below me was a rosy-cheeked, convivial guy in his thirties wearing a grass-green ski hat with a tiny tassel. He sat with four beer-drinking friends. He was the comedian in the group, cracking his friends up. But he also said something that stayed with me, words I remembered that night after the game. They came in handy, too.

"Whatever happens," he said to his friends before kickoff, raising his beer in a toast, "we're at the game." A few minutes later he said it again, and toasted again. He ended up saying it four or five more times, including once or twice during the game when something bad happened from a Packers perspective. "Hey, we're at the game." He said it with a smile. He said it with humor in his voice. He knew it was funny the way he kept repeating himself, and he may have been a little drunk, but you also felt he meant what he said. And you thought you knew what he meant. Something along the lines of: Here we are at Lambeau Field, with beverages, watching a game between our beloved Pack and a very good team in the Panthers, and we don't know what's going to happen in the end. There's a lot in life and in the world to worry about right now, but being here, right now, all of us, watching the Pack, at Lambeau—this is not one of those things.

That was the meaning of his mantra.

I try to take that attitude in this book.

We're at the game.

# PART ONE: ORIENTATION

# CHAPTER 1:
# LOMBARDI WAS HERE

"**THE PACKERS USED** to have their offices right down there," said Jason Vanden Heuvel, pointing floorward and a little to the left. We were standing in a beige-toned Quality Inn & Suites extended-stay studio apartment overlooking Crooks Street just off the corner of Washington Street in downtown Green Bay. It was a sunny day in late September. Light streamed in south-facing windows looking out over a corner tavern toward the Mason Street Bridge.

Did he just say what I think he said?

"Yeah," Jason affirmed, his stocky frame clad in a dark green Quality Inn golf shirt and khaki pants. Jason was 26, with a neatly trimmed G.I. Joe beard and ever-present glint of humor in his eyes. "Lombardi, coaches, film room, ticket office—everything was right here until they moved across the river to Lambeau in '63. Or what became Lambeau. They were still calling it City Stadium then."

I nearly cartwheeled. I'd had no idea. I picked this place because it offered three-month leases, free breakfast, a fitness room, and a pool. I liked being a football's toss from the Fox River. I also liked being downtown, though downtown Green Bay is barely ten square blocks. Lambeau Field was three miles away. I was already looking forward to jogging over there a few times a week, imagining myself running across the Mason Street Bridge up to Oneida Street then down Oneida to Lombardi Avenue and the mecca of football. At night, the stadium would be a welcome sight. Plus, I could quickly replenish the burned calories with a half-pound cheeseburger and mug of beer at Curly's Pub inside the Lambeau Atrium, its wall of windows overlooking the fenced-in team parking lot nicknamed "The Cage."

But to learn I'd be living in more or less the same spot Vincent T. Lombardi spent so many workdays during the years in which he game-planned his first two NFL championships—that had to be good luck, right? It might even carry more mojo than the Wilson NFL football signed by Bart Starr in 1974 that I was going to put on my writing table for inspiration. "To the Hanrahans—With Best Wishes—Bart Starr," wrote the great Lombardi-era Packers quarterback and soon-to-be Packers coach. The occasion was a Packers evening at the Milwaukee Athletic Club. I was ten. I got to shake Bart's hand.

"Lombardi met Hornung here for the first time," continued Jason, referring to Hall of Fame Packers halfback Paul Hornung. "The team even used to bunk some players in rooms down the hall." Jason Vanden Heuvel was only the latest unofficial Packers historian I'd met in the past two months coming up here weekly from Milwaukee, 120 miles south. I'd already met Ray Nitschke's former paperboy, a friend of the farmer whose cow pasture became Lambeau Field, and a guy whose dad used to fish with Curly Lambeau. The same guy who used to deliver papers to Nitschke also "peddled pop" from a crate fixed to his one-speed bike. He said one day a man called out, "Hey kid, how about a soda!" He turned around and it was Paul Hornung sitting in his white 1959 Cadillac DeVille.

I also met a young woman who shared a story about a more recent former Packer, the "former" something we were all still getting used to. Her name was Becky Van Kauwenberg. We were seated along one side of the square bar at the center of the Stadium View, a sports fan's paradise located a block from Lambeau Field, around the corner from Brett Favre's Steakhouse. "One day Brett came by my parents' dairy farm to get some hay for his deer blind," recalled Becky, 24, her brown eyes glowing with the memory. "The farm's in Seymour, about twenty miles from here. Brett was going hunting. He asked the Packers equipment guy if he knew where to get some bales. This guy knows my brother—that was the connection. Unfortunately, I wasn't home that day! Only my mom was there. She said Brett pulled up to the barn in a white pickup. He was wearing an old *NYPD Blue* T-shirt and those shorts he always wears. It was either 2003 or 2004. The year he had the broken thumb."

I probably just could have yelled, "Hey, when did Brett break his thumb?" and forty people would have shouted "2003!" As a Packers fan I should know this information, however, so I didn't yell. While I wish I was, I'm not one of those cheesehead *Rain Man* types who even behind six beers can tell you the fourth-string running back from the 1984 Forrest Gregg–coached 8–8 Packers squad. (It was Ray Crouse, by the way. I looked it up.) It's a lame excuse but I missed some osmosis opportunities spending all but five of the past twenty-five years outside of Wisconsin, living in Vermont, England, and North Carolina before New York and California. When I got home I checked the date of the Favre fracture. It was October 19, 2003. Favre slammed his thumb on a Packer lineman's shoulder pad early in a game at St. Louis and toughed it out, completing 23 of 32 passes for 268 yards in a 34–24 loss. Eschewing surgery, he furthered his Iron Man reputation by playing the rest of the season with a broken, splinted thumb, recording his best-ever completion percentage at 64.5 and throwing a league-leading 32 touchdown passes.

"Because of the thumb, Brett had to be careful grabbing the bales," Becky continued, finishing her story. "I guess he made some jokes about being a wimp. After he got the bales in his pickup, my mom gave him something to drink in our farmhouse. We have a picture of Brett Favre standing in our kitchen!"

It's only a slight exaggeration to say everyone you meet in Green Bay or the surrounding environs has some personal Packers story or link to Packers history. A few days after moving into the hotel, I'd meet Jason's colleague Peter Burkel, 28, a sunshiny lobby presence with round, gray plastic glasses and a brush-cut. Like Becky, Peter grew up on a dairy farm. Besides knowing the longtime Catholic chaplain to the Packers, the Reverend Jim Baraniak—"Father Jim" to Peter and the Packers, he holds services for the Packers the morning of every game—Peter is also the grandson of an early Lambeau-era Packers water boy. His granddad, Louis Conard, was a high school classmate of Curly Lambeau's at Green Bay East. Right there at the start of Packers history, Curly hired Louis to keep those leatherhead Packers hydrated.

Before Jason and I headed back to the front desk at the other end of this low, block-long hotel, he asked what kind of book I was writing. I filled him in, mentioning the travel and focus on fans along with games and players. "Should be fun," I added. "Just be a total cheesehead for three months." Memorably, Jason replied, "Kind of like gonzo journalism—with the Packers." I believe I barked out a laughing semi-yes. I hadn't been expecting a nod to Hunter S. Thompson in a Green Bay hotel room, especially since we'd just been talking about Lombardi, a.k.a. "St. Vince." Jason, it turns out, is a big reader and might go into writing himself. I suggested that the book probably wouldn't be *Fear and Loathing in Green Bay*, but that I would certainly be open to the unplanned, and would also have to "research" a few Packer bars.

"Can I just say," said Jason, growing serious a moment, "that despite what the national media seems to be saying, not everyone in Green Bay is running around with FIRE TED THOMPSON and BRING BACK BRETT signs." Thompson, the Packers general manager since 2005, is the individual who, in the end, had the final say regarding whether or not Favre remained a Packer. There was—there is—no love lost between Thompson and Favre backers.

"You're going to talk about that, right?" Jason asked. "I mean, there are plenty of Packer fans—plenty of people in this town—who are glad Aaron Rodgers is our quarterback and think Thompson made the right decision. It's just that Favre people make the most noise."

I told Jason that, yes, I would definitely be talking about this.

We left the second-floor apartment. We stepped out rear doors used mainly by the extended-stay residents and patrons of the new hotel restaurant, Cheffetta's. Jason had already told me that one of the Cheffetta's dining rooms used to be Lombardi's office during his first four years as Packers coach. It was here the great Brooklyn-born motivator came each workday promptly at 9 A.M. after attending 8 A.M. Mass at St. Willebrord's Catholic Church two blocks away on Adams Street. Standing on sunny Crooks Street with our backs to the South End Pub & Grill, the corner tavern my apartment windows would overlook, we regarded the elegant two-story red-brick edifice occupied by the Packers from 1950 until 1963. Built in 1914 as the Marvin Building, the compact corner structure became part of the hotel some years back. It's a quiet corner, and it would become even quieter a few weeks hence when the Green Bay Chamber of Commerce moved from its home across Washington Street in a former riverfront train depot, all round-arched windows and brown-brick facades, to a new glass-and-steel development three blocks north. But when the Packers were here, this was a happening place. The thoroughfare named for our first president (presidents and trees gave downtown Green Bay its street names: Adams and Walnut, Monroe and Pine) used to be the city's main drag—its shopping street, restaurant street, theater street, parade street. The Meyer, Green Bay's grandest theater, an art deco former movie palace now used mainly for concerts and stage productions, is pretty much all that's left from Washington Street's heyday. Unless you count, and I do, diminutive Al's Hamburgers five doors down, a squat, stucco-faced diner about the size of a mobile home.

EAT commands Al's neon sign in big gold letters, its date of establishment, 1934, in smaller gold numerals below. "Lombardi used to eat lunch there," Quality Inn manager Deb McAllister would tell me as I signed my lease. I stopped by Al's as part of my subsequent explore-the-neighborhood walk, and sure enough, there was a small framed photo of Lombardi on the wall along with a Lombardi sketch. Three wooden booths, eight counter stools, and a menu of burgers, chops, fried chicken, and hash—that was Al's. The ghost of Edward Hopper would feel welcome. "In the Holmgren years some Packers used to come here," said floral-bloused Judy Rank, 70, as she topped off my cup of coffee at the counter. "Especially if they needed to bulk up. Gilbert used to come in," Judy added, referring to 350-pound former Packers nose tackle Gilbert Brown, a run-stuffing behemoth from the '96 Super Bowl team. "Breakfast and lunch. He could really put it away."

Between Al's Hamburgers and my new hotel home a block south was another sign bearing a year of origin, though this one went back a little further than FDR's first term. "On the river shore directly west of this marker about the year 1745," began the inscription on an old bronze plaque set in a low brick wall on the west side of Washington Street. It told of a French Canadian fur trader named Augustin Langlade who with son Charles built a house and trading post here. The plaque calls them "the first permanent settlers of Wisconsin." That explained Langlade Street five blocks from Lambeau. I'd come to learn that the younger Langlade is considered nothing less than "The Father of Wisconsin." I'm sure I learned this in grade school, but like the year Favre broke his thumb, it had dropped out of my head. Writing this book helped restore some data.

Train tracks no longer exist on the east side of the river (in place of the rails is a riverfront jogging path), but they remain on the west bank, and slow-rolling freight trains would be a regular sight as I gazed across the river or jogged across one of the three downtown bridges. Train horns were common, too. The *click-click* rumble of the cars served as a reminder that Green Bay was still an industrial city, though not as much as it was in the early Packer years of Curly Lambeau. In the 1920s, the railroads and the river and the bay leading into Lake Michigan and beyond, in concert with Wisconsin's pastureland and forests, made this small city the world's leading producer of milk, cheese, and toilet paper. Luckily there was some meatpacking, too, or Lambeau's pigskin startup might have been tagged with a dairy-themed moniker, or even something TP-related. Think that's a stretch? Thirty miles downriver, the Kimberly High football team is called the Papermakers. A state power in football that enters the 2009 season on a 28-game winning streak, Kimberly's mascot is a paper wasp, an image with more sting than a guy churning a vat of newsprint pulp.

While this east riverbank no longer has an industrial footprint along the eight-block length of downtown, warehouses and factories still line the west bank. And just south of the Mason Street Bridge rise pyramids of piled coal, huge black planetary dunes that become something else entirely when it snows, transforming into white pastoral hills. These coal mountains were around when Lombardi was here. He drove past them every time he took the Mason Street Bridge from his Crooks Street office to the stadium where he built his legend.

Ivory plumes of steam rise from the manifold smokestacks poking heavenward alongside steeples in this town of churches and bars, just as in Lombardi's day. Cottony cumulus on blue, they do something almost sublime to a cloudless winter sky when it's frigid, best viewed from a bridge.

No doubt there were fewer crystalline winter days then, though, with more smoke, more smell, coming from those stacks along with steam. And when Lombardi looked out the window of his Crooks Street office, he didn't see riverfront parkland with a running path, gazebo, and small wooden docks for pleasure craft visiting the Fox Harbor Pub & Grill opposite the former Marvin Building. He saw riverfront railroad tracks. The train depot itself, built in 1898 in a Flemish renaissance style, had been shuttered by the Milwaukee Road in 1957 but it would be decades before the river frontage became green and the river itself began to revive.

On permanent display at the Neville Public Museum located on the west riverbank just south of the Ray Nitschke Bridge is an exhibit—encompassing a whole wing of the museum—called "Hometown Advantage: The Packers and the Community." It's highlighted by five short films mixing interviews and archival footage ranging over nine Packer decades. Together, the films vividly illustrate the team's intimate connection to the city. "There's been a history of the community saving our team," says former Packers chief operating officer John Jones, referring to a series of decisive moments when public monetary support got the team back on sounder financial footing: 1922, the Depression-era early '30s, 1949, the 1997 Packers stock sale, and most recently the county-wide referendum in 2000 approving a half-cent sales tax that raised millions for the Lambeau upgrade. Bankruptcy loomed three times in this citizen-owned, not-for-profit franchise's first three decades until the community rallied. The Packers, in one telling historical footnote, were the only small-town professional football team to survive the Great Depression.

Some day down the road, it's conceivable the Neville will devote a whole exhibit to the Favre years, and to No. 4 himself—his mark on the team, place in Packers history, importance to the community, and painful departure, one that sharply divided the Green Bay community. History was made when the Packers traded Favre, when Brett became a Jet. For now, museumgoers can only reflect on perspectives offered in regard to the previous dramatic departures in Packers history, those of Curly Lambeau and Vince Lombardi, while recognizing that these parallels are imperfect, as these men elected to leave and Favre . . . well, it was more complicated.

"After Lambeau defected to Chicago, the Packers went eleven years without a winning season," says then 81-year-old Lee Remmel in one of the exhibit's films. A former *Green Bay Press-Gazette* Packers reporter turned longtime Packers public relations director, Remmel is perhaps our greatest living repository of Packers knowledge. Remmel goes on to refer to an "eleven-year famine" that followed Curly's leave-taking, a deprivation ending only when, in 1959, former New

York Giants offensive coach Lombardi arrived in town after a pitiful one-win Packers season. A second, longer deprivation followed after Lombardi's exit—29 years without a championship. Some of the post-Lombardi seasons were downright ugly, years some Packers fans refer to as "The Gory Years" when compared to the Glory Years Lombardi rang in.

How did Green Bay feel when their savior coach himself defected for a big-city team? "It was very devastating when Lombardi left," Remmel says. "It was a shock to us all."

These two Packer skids—green and gold droughts—that followed the departures of two men who brought world-class winning to Green Bay had to be in the back of the Collective Cheesehead Mind when Favre was traded to New York. Would another famine follow?

# CHAPTER 2:
# MAGICAL HISTORY TOUR

**T**AKING THE "Legends of Lombardi Avenue: Old School Tour" the weekend the Indianapolis Colts came to town, I met Santiago Gardner of San Diego. It was October 18, a crisp, cloud-scudding Saturday with temperatures in the low 50s. At 11 A.M. on nine separate occasions between early August and November 2008, a yellow Lamers school bus left the parking lot of the Greater Green Bay Convention & Visitors Bureau across from Lambeau Field loaded with Packer-accessorized tourists, a few fans of Packer opponents during the season, and a tour guide with a microphone. On this particular morning, our guide was an irrepressibly jolly, round-faced gentleman about forty years old, a blue-sweatered Chamber of Commerce employee making a little extra scratch on the weekend. He had a gift for Packers schtick—he made it feel fresh.

"Anyone from more than a thousand miles away?" he asked as we rumbled toward Lambeau. He'd already elicited raised hands and shouts from four Packer fans up from southern Illinois and a family of five in for the weekend from Indianapolis to watch their Colts play the next day. Since I was a Green Bay resident now, I didn't raise my hand. But a dark-haired man in a Packers ball cap sitting alone three seats in front of me did. "Where'd you come from?" the guide asked. In slightly accented English, the man said cheerily, "San Diego, California."

This was Santiago Gardner, I'd learn after the tour when we talked. A native of Tijuana, Mexico, he's a Nextel technician, 39 years old. During the tour, I noticed he listened very closely to everything the guide was saying, no matter how historical it got, while some of the other tour takers tuned out a little, chatting with each other. He wore a reflective, quietly content expression as he took in the Green Bay sights.

As we neared the stadium, our guide warmed things up with a softball Packers trivia question. "Who invented the Lambeau Leap?" he asked. "LeRoy Butler!" chorused a dozen different voices. The people up front, Packers fans in their sixties and seventies, sets of husbands and wives, were the most vocal. They also rocked the most team gear, coming equipped with Packers caps, jackets, sweaters, jerseys, tote bags, gloves, scarves, and seat cushions. They were boisterous from the get-go, and our guide was feeding off their energy.

"Bingo!" he exclaimed. "LeRoy Butler. December 26, 1993. L.A. Raiders. Zero degrees that day. Fourth quarter. Packers up fourteen to nothing. But who can tell me who got an assist on the play?"

"Reggie White!" shouted nearly everyone who'd first shouted Butler's name.

"Right again! LeRoy comes up from his strong safety position, lays some wood on a Raiders receiver, ball pops loose. Reggie scoops it up, rumbles, stumbles down the sideline, then right before he's about to go down flips it to LeRoy and the rest is history."

Applause filled the bus.

We pulled around to the Lombardi Avenue side of Lambeau and stopped. We regarded two bronze figures towering outside the Lambeau Atrium.

"Now I suspect the gentleman on the left needs no introduction," said our guide, referring to the twenty-foot-high statue of Lombardi (fourteen feet for Vince, four for his black granite base, plus two more for two white stone steps at bottom). The statue and its bronze partner command the entrance to the fabulous five-story Atrium, the crown jewel of a 32-month, $295 million stadium redevelopment completed in 2003. Lombardi is captured in a familiar sideline pose, his gloved hands behind his back, head tilted slightly, small appraising smile, clad in his trademark fedora and overcoat. From our vantage, he was backdropped by the Atrium's 85-feet-high, 70-yards-wide wall of glass. Multiple entrance doors run along its base, terminating on the left at more glass-paned doors leading into the two-level Packers Pro Shop. "But who's the guy pointing at Vince?" quizzed our guide, tossing another softball he knew would call forth instant shouts.

"Curly Lambeau!"

"None other!"

Lambeau's statue is the same height as Lombardi's, on an identical six-foot base. Sweatshirted, his stance square, he stands with his left hand holding a football low off his thigh, like he's ready to hand it off, while the rest of him is directed Lombardi-ward, right arm fully extended, forefinger pointing in a "You da man" way toward a bemused Vince. A couple hours hence I'd be right back here on the Robert

E. Harlan Plaza, towered over by these figures, on a walking tour of Lambeau Field. Tom, our white-haired guide, was just as energetic, just as entertaining as the much younger bus guide. For an hour he'd lead us briskly all over the stadium, his crisp look and upright bearing suggestive of a four-star general who begins his day with 100 push-ups and ends with a story, a good joke, and a single beer with the fellas before heading home to his wife.

"Some people say it should be Lombardi pointing at Lambeau," said Tom, swiftly, "since Curly got this whole thing started. Interesting point. But I don't think the statues suggest any kind of pecking order. And all you have to do is look at . . ." Tom pointed to the broad sign topping the 85-foot glass wall, the one reading LAMBEAU FIELD ATRIUM.

"Can't do any better than having the whole place named for you."

The Packers renamed City Stadium "Lambeau Field" when Curly died in 1965. The city renamed Highland Avenue "Lombardi Avenue" two years later. A quarter century after that, the Packers commissioned the Chicago-based husband and wife sculptors responsible for the Michael Jordan-soaring-for-a-dunk statue in front of Chicago's United Center to work their bronze magic in honor of the two Packer colossi. They finished in nine months, producing 4,400 pounds worth of art at a cost of $400,000-plus. Julie Rotblatt-Amrany, a Chicago native and daughter of a football-fan father, tackled Vince, while her husband Omri Amrany, a native of Israel, handled Curly, someone he didn't know from Adam going in. Then Packers president Bob Harlan, the Energizer Bunny behind the Lambeau renovation, gave Omri a photo of Curly in that ball-holding, pointing pose. Julie found her inspiration for Lombardi's small smile in the photo gracing the cover of David Maraniss' monumental Lombardi biography *When Pride Still Mattered*.

Appropriately, Lombardi gazes toward his namesake avenue. And it's good Julie and Omri didn't have Vince pointing at Curly or otherwise acknowledging him as it's a matter of record that the pride of Lombardi *did* matter when it came to sharing the spotlight with the Packers founder and first coach, winner of six NFL titles. As Maraniss reveals in his 1999 book, Lombardi was less than delighted when the editor of the 1965 Packers yearbook scrapped the original cover shot of a Packer player and replaced it with a photo of Lombardi and Lambeau shaking hands down on the stadium field. The idea was to honor the Packers patriarch who'd died that June. But there'd been a side to Curly that Vince was never sure he liked—the high-living, Hollywood actress–dating, Malibu beach house–living side. Moreover, Lambeau was the Packers' past. He—Vince Lombardi, coach of Hornung and Gregg, Nitschke and Thurston—was the present. Lombardi chewed out the yearbook editor, wouldn't talk to him for months. The feisty coach's mood didn't improve when the Packers board of directors voted to bestow the ultimate posthumous honor on Green Bay's most famous son. Now, for as long as Vincent Thomas Lombardi coached the Packers, he would have to do it inside . . . *Lambeau Field*.

Our school bus paused before the Neufeld Street home once occupied by Packers linebacker Ray Nitschke. In the Neville Museum there's a 1964 photo of four Norman Rockwell–looking kids gathered at the open door of the brick ranch house. Before them stands Nitschke's smiling wife, Jackie. The caption reads, "Please Mrs. Nitschke, can Ray come out and play?"

We moved on to a Catholic high school attended by Lombardi's son, Vince Jr. We considered a storefront once home to a lawn-care company owned by Hall of Fame 1940s running back Tony Canadeo, "The Gray Ghost of Gonzaga." Today you can still get your lawn cut by the Canadeo Mowing Co., and can tool down a street named Tony Canadeo Run. Remaining on the west side of the river, we carried on to a modest, verging-on-shabby two-story apartment complex where African-American players and their families congregated in the 1950s and early '60s. Not every area landlord was willing to rent to black Americans back then, not even black Green Bay Packers.

Crossing the Fox River on the Ray Nitschke Bridge, we rolled onward to the birthplace of Curly Lambeau. Built of red brick in 1866, it's one of the oldest houses in Green Bay. Now a state historic landmark owned by a charitable foundation, you can rent out the garden for a get-together or even spend the night inside, with proceeds going to a school across the street. A bronze plaque on the wall between two paned, arched front windows records the 1898 birth of Earl Louis Lambeau, first child of Marcel and Mary Lambeau. Marcel was of Belgian extraction, Mary of French. Earl Louis went on to earn the nickname "Curly" for the thick black curly hair that topped his head at the time he was starring for the Green Bay East football team. As the plaque notes, he then "briefly attended Notre Dame University, scoring the first touchdown ever for Notre Dame's first-year football coach Knute Rockne." As a Golden Dome freshman, Lambeau played with star halfback George Gipp, destined to die of strep throat in 1920 not long after his last game senior year. Later, of course, Ronald Reagan immortalized "The Gipper" in the 1940 movie *Knute Rockne, All-American*. Lambeau himself contracted a severe case of tonsillitis during Christmas break and never returned to Notre Dame. If he had, the Packers might not have formed.

Our next stop was the Cherry Street bungalow where the Lambeau family lived for most of Curly's boyhood. They attended St. Willebrord's, the same church Lombardi would one day frequent so regularly that locals still refer to it as "Vince's Church." Our guide conjured a vision: young Curly kicking and throwing a football fashioned from "an old salt sack stuffed with sand, leaves, and pebbles" on adjacent, unpaved St. Clair Street. We didn't tour St. Clair but I worked it into a jog later. It seemed important to visit, as it was here that Curly discovered the joy of playing football. And given how little money there was in the game at its inception, nobody was devoting their life to it unless they truly loved it. Not to get too Ken Burns on you, but without that old stuffed salt sack, maybe the Packers don't happen, either.

Just a couple blocks east we stopped to check out the original City Stadium site. The Packers played their first games in a factory sandlot, switched to a field adjacent a brewery, then set up here alongside Green Bay East High School. Original bleacher capacity was 6,000. By the 1950s, the stadium could hold 25,000. That was possibly a few too many people, as former Packers receiver Max McGee, who played his first three seasons here, remembered an ominous "creaking" sound coming from the packed stands. *Get a new stadium or become the Milwaukee Packers*, the NFL more or less told the team in the mid-1950s. The down-home charms of a bleacher-ringed neighborhood field went only so far with teams like the New York Football Giants, Chicago Bears, and Los Angeles Rams, who were used to playing in grand venues like the Polo Grounds, Wrigley Field, and the Los Angeles Coliseum.

Today, replica gates and turnstiles join an ornamental iron fence, stone marker, and bronze plaque as monuments to the historic acreage, the field itself used by the Green Bay East Red Devils football team. An elegant red sandstone garage and one structural wall built of the same red stone recycled from the old East High building are all that remain of the original City Stadium. In July 2007, the contemporary Packers—Brett Favre's last Packers team—held a public practice here to commemorate the fiftieth anniversary of moving from the old to the new City Stadium. And Lombardi's ruffled feathers notwithstanding, going with "Lambeau Field" was a good idea. Because let's face it, *The . . . Frozen . . . Tundra . . . of . . . City . . . Stadium* just doesn't have the same ring.

"Who knows why they're called the Packers?" our guide queried as we rolled west on Walnut Street toward downtown. It was a semi-trick question and today the trick worked.

"Because they were sponsored by the Acme Meatpacking Company!" shouted a snow-haired woman in full Packers regalia. "Are you sure?" the guide teased. The woman bit her lip, looked at her husband. "Anyone else?" asked our merry inquisitor. The attentive listener from San Diego raised his hand as if to answer but just then another Packer-capped woman of years called out, "It wasn't Acme, it was Indian! The Indian Meatpacking Company!"

"Ding, ding, ding!" sang our smiling guide, proceeding to dip into some more Packers history. Curly Lambeau, having chosen not to return to Notre Dame, took a job as a shipping clerk at the Indian Meatpacking Company. After he and beer-loving *Green Bay Press-Gazette* sports editor George Calhoun dreamed up the idea of a football team (conception happened on a street corner, in a bar, or in the *Press-Gazette* offices, depending on the story), Curly asked his employer to sponsor the team. Before long, Indian Meatpacking was bought out by Acme Meatpacking, who maintained the team sponsorship. In 1921, when the club joined the 22-team federation that would re-form as the National Football League a year later, they joined as the Acme Packers. They were the Acme Packers in iconic early photos,

ACME PACKERS emblazoned in big white letters across jersey chests. As for the name Packers, early on the team trial-ballooned the Green Bay Blues, the Big Bays, and the Bays (hey, it worked for the Lakers) but public opinion rallied behind Packers, and today the moniker stands as the NFL's most enduring.

As we reached downtown, our guide pointed out the *Press-Gazette* offices and a couple other buildings where course-setting early franchise meetings happened. We came to a stop before the former Hotel Northland, a grand eight-story stone-and-brick edifice constructed in 1924 in a Tudor revival style. Now called the Port Plaza Towers and home to residential apartments, this was the hotel favored by visiting NFL teams. The New York Giants stayed there when they came to Green Bay to play the 1961 championship game and got whupped 37–0, earning Lombardi his first ring as head coach of the Packers. And it was here three years earlier where forty-five directors on the Green Bay Packers Inc. governing board voted to approve the seven-member Executive Committee's decision to hire Vince Lombardi, passing over Curly Lambeau, who'd lobbied for a return to Green Bay.

Our tour's last stop was my new home. Crooks Street off Washington. Glancing up toward my apartment windows, I suppressed an urge to tell everyone on the bus that's where I lived.

"That was Vince's office," said our guide, pointing to a street-level casement window with salmon-colored trim dressed inside with a white lace curtain and potted plant. "Now it's a room in Cheffetta's Restaurant. The glass trophy cases are still there but the trophies aren't. Up until recently, there was a sports bar in there called The Glory Years. It had all kinds of Lombardi memorabilia, including Vince's actual coat rack."

Next we eyed a neighboring window sealed with tobacco-brown boards.

"And that was the old Packers ticket window. Back then, the people of Green Bay would get all dressed up to buy their Packers tickets. During game weeks you'd have a long line of well-dressed people on the sidewalk, men in fedora hats and blazers, women in their finery."

My kitchenette window looked right down on this spot. During the next ten weeks I'd have moments where I'd imagine these fans in their hats and dresses, overcoats and furs. It must have been nuts here the week of the '61 NFL championship game. And I'd imagine Vince Lombardi down there, too, arriving after Mass, in his camel hair coat and hat, about to use the coat rack. This is where he broke down game film. This is where he perfected the Packer Sweep.

Five minutes later we were back in the parking lot across from Lambeau. I spoke to one of the livelier, snow-haired Packers couples— they hailed from Burlington, Wisconsin, where Cowboys quarterback Tony Romo grew up—then approached the Packers fan from San Diego as he was getting into his rental car. Large-framed, maybe six feet tall, his face broad and open, Santiago Gardner wore a red windbreaker, pressed gray trousers, black leather shoes, and sunglasses along with his Packers ball cap. He took off his shades as we started talking.

"How'd you become a Packer fan?" I asked.

His answer topped any I would hear in three months of asking this question.

"By investigating their history," he said. Santiago smiles a lot—he has a big smile—but he was solemn answering this most essential of questions. "I didn't know anything about the NFL growing up in Mexico," he continued, "but after moving to San Diego in 1994, I started learning. I read about the Green Bay Packers. All their championships. Lombardi. I learned as much as I could about Packers history. That's how I became a Packer fan. Doing research."

I asked if he had an opinion on the Favre matter.

"Well, it's sad," he said, "but at least I got to see him again this year. I went to the Chargers–Jets game three weeks ago. I wore my number 4 Packers jersey. I got yelled at a little bit. But it was good to see him playing. He did pretty good. But the Jets lost."

I asked him if he liked the Chargers, too.

"Oh yeah," he said. "I watch every game. I've been to Qualcomm many times," he added, referring to the stadium where the Chargers play their home games.

"Okay," I said, "but if it's Packers–Chargers in the Super Bowl, who are you rooting for?"

The very thought made his face light up—with about as much light as a face can carry.

"The Packers," he said. "They're my number one."

He'd flown out solo from San Diego to watch the Packers play at Lambeau once a year since 2004, he told me. "Cowboys, Saints, Rams, Bears," Santiago recited, listing in order the teams he'd seen play the Packers since his Lambeau tradition began. "At first I thought I was good luck!" he remarked, recalling that the Packers handily beat Dallas 41–20 in 2004, then clobbered New Orleans 52–3 in 2005. "The Saints game was a little sad," he continued. "It was right after Hurricane Katrina. Maybe I didn't cheer as much."

But his winning streak ended at two. He watched the Packers lose 23–20 to the Rams in '06, and 27–20 to the Bears in Favre's last year. "So right now," said Santiago, "my record's .500. But I think we're gonna beat the Colts tomorrow!"

I asked him when he got into town.

"Wednesday," he answered.

When I asked why so early, he gave a small smile. "Because I wanted to see every little bit of Green Bay," he replied.

"Santiago, man, you're like a Chamber of Commerce dream!"

"Okay, but I did drive down to Milwaukee yesterday," he added with a grin. "I wanted to see Miller Park." Miller Park is the retractable-roofed home of baseball's Milwaukee Brewers.

If I ever got to San Diego, Santiago told me I should check out the Australian Pub. "That's where Packers fans go. They have Packer stuff on the walls. It feels like Green Bay on game days!"

Except it's three blocks from the ocean in the sun-splashed Pacific Beach neighborhood. I looked it up when I got home. "Wisconsin sports fans love this bar during Packer games," wrote one online reviewer in August 2008. "Cheeseheads go crazy. This year the Packers are playing without Brett Favre. It could really get crazy." The Australian is the unofficial headquarters of the San Diego Packers Fan Club. Their slogan? "Cheeseheads in paradise." Owned by a guy from Sydney, the pub serves chicken wings and other American staples along with Aussie meat pies, Vegemite sandwiches, and burgers with egg, bacon, beets, and pineapple. The blend of Down Under visuals and Packers tchotchkes puzzles some online reviewers. "Tons of Packers memorabilia. Beats me why," wrote one. "Adorned with, oddly enough, a photographic mix of the Green Bay Packers and Australia," another observed. "Green Bay, Wisconsin and Australia. Only in America," hailed a reviewer for the *San Diego Union Tribune*.

Apropos of Oz, I asked Santiago if he'd heard of the Australian man who quit his job, sold his house, and took his wife and two young sons from Sydney to Green Bay a year ago last September so he could follow his beloved Pack. Attending all eighteen games, he burned up much of his life savings in the process but realized his biggest dream. And he won the lottery in terms of season selection: 14 total wins, a conference championship game, and Favre's last year as a Packer, with No. 4 setting a couple more NFL records in the bargain.

"Yeah, they talked about this guy in the Australian," Santiago said. "Then I heard about him again when I was here. Great idea! We were both at the Bears game together!"

I hadn't heard of Wayne Scullino, Australia's biggest Packer fan, until I got to Wisconsin, but he came up fairly often in conversations with Packer fans, especially here in Green Bay. The community welcomed Wayne and his family, opened their homes to them, assisted him in acquiring tickets and arranging travel. Green Bay— all of Wisconsin—fell in love with the story of this thirty-year-old Aussie dreamer who'd never even seen snow or experienced freezing temperatures before traveling 8,000 miles to Titletown with his better half and boys (two years old and nine months old) in tow. "Once in a lifetime" was the phrase that resonated most when he thought about pursuing his long-held dream, and he ended up using this phrase for his blog, www.TheOnceinaLifetimeFan.com. Wayne Scullino's Packers love began at age 15 when, like Santiago, he learned about the team's existence, the town of Green Bay, the championship history, and the singular bond between team and town. Next thing you knew, he was subscribing to the *Packer Report*, though the magazine took weeks to reach Australia.

Wayne Scullino. Santiago Gardner. All pro sports teams have passionate fans, and some have legendarily devoted followers (the Red Sox and Steelers, for example), but there's something about the romance of the Packers story that seems to strike a special chord. The cynic in me arrived in Green Bay prepared to resist this chord, as a matter of principle, but within a couple weeks resistance began to seem silly. Why it began to seem silly is part of what this book is about.

Web sites devoted to informing cheeseheads where to find the nearest Packers bar list outposts in nearly every state and major

American city, six Canadian cities, two German cities (Frankfurt, Munich), Bangkok, and Dublin. Check out www.packer-bars.com and feast your eyes on the multiplicity of listings. Not all of these establishments are as festooned with Packers stuff as San Diego's Australian Pub, but the majority of them are populated with at least some rowdy cheeseheads on Packer game days. Not surprisingly, given their number of "Sconnie" transplants, California, Arizona, and Florida are the big winners in terms of Packer-friendly bars, all with numbers into the dozens. But far-flung cheeseheads, you can find green-and-gold brethren in bars in Alaska, Alabama, and Idaho, too.

And Packer fan clubs dot America's map. I've already mentioned the Arizona Pack. Their ranks are joined by fans in the SoCal Packer Backers, the Cheddarhead Pack of Houston, the Heartland Packer Backers in Oklahoma City, the Tulsa Packer Backers, the Indy Packer Backers, the Georgia Packer Backers, the Greater Baltimore Chapter of Packer Backers, and more. Some of these fans are Wisconsin transplants, but a good number are simply people who, like Santiago Gardner and Wayne Scullino, respond to the Packers story.

Will fan-club membership drop off in the post-Favre era? I'm guessing not much.

Before Santiago and I went our separate ways, he told me how hard he'd taken it nine months earlier when the Pack lost the NFC championship game 23–20 in overtime to the New York Giants at subzero Lambeau. After Giants kicker Lawrence Tynes shanked a 36-yarder at the end of regulation, the Packers won the overtime coin toss. Two things had just gone their way. But then Favre underthrew an out route to Donald Driver on the second play of overtime. Giants cornerback Corey Webster picked it off and before you could say

"Goodnight, Irene," Tynes hit a 47-yarder to send the Giants to the Super Bowl.

"We were that close," lamented Packers linebacker Nick Barnett in the locker room afterward. "One play away. One drive away. One series away. One game away from the big one . . . from what you dream about."

"Wow, was I upset," Santiago told me in the now empty parking lot. "You know what I did? I went into my bedroom and punched my bed. That's how mad I was. After that, I was depressed for like a week. I didn't want to talk to anyone. My friends, my sister, they said, 'Santiago, how can you feel that bad about a game?' I couldn't explain it. I'd been planning on going to Phoenix for the Super Bowl. I didn't have a ticket—I just wanted to be there. Even though the Packers lost, I still drove to Phoenix. Before the game, I went over to the stadium and walked around. The whole time I was thinking, The Packers should be here, the Packers should be here."

It was an agonizing loss. Even had it been a regular-season game, the way it ended—the suddenness and circumstances—formed bed-punching material. On this crisp fall day in mid-October, no 2008 game had yet ended quite so wrenchingly. Something to be thankful for, I guessed.

# CHAPTER 3:
## VISIT KANSAS, WATCH PACK

**THEY WEAR PACKER** T-shirts in Leonardville, Kansas. An 850-mile drive from Green Bay, this rural crossroads sits on a high wheat and cattle plain some twenty miles northwest of Manhattan, home to Kansas State University. Five blocks long and three blocks wide, Leonardville, named for Kansas Central Railway president Leonard Smith in 1882, boasts two dusty, frontier-feeling main streets, Barton Road and Erpelding Road, and one place to eat and drink, Nelson's Landing.

The eatery sits on Erpelding, adjoining a pair of century-old vacant brick buildings. A Packers flag hangs in the plate-glass front window. This is where I watched the Green Bay Packers play the undefeated Tennessee Titans halfway through the '08 season.

It was a glorious Indian summer day on the Great Plains, November 2. The 4–3 Packers were rested, coming off their bye. The Titans were already being called the best team in the NFL by some analysts, with speculation kicking up about whether they could run the table like the 2007 New England Patriots had. Thanks to a satellite dish and NFL Sunday Ticket, Tennessee's attempt to stay undefeated would be shown on a half dozen TVs and projected on one wall inside the two-room, plank-floored establishment. But the Kansans showing up were not there to watch Kerry Collins and the Titans. They were there to watch the Packers. In particular, they'd focus on a certain wide receiver. Just last week this Packer was in Nelson's Landing, helping bus tables while signing the occasional napkin. But on this day he'd be catching passes and returning kickoffs for the Pack in Nashville.

"Yeah, they'll definitely have the game on," said rookie Jordy Nelson in the Packers' football-shaped locker room three days earlier. He was speaking of his parents, Alan and Kim Nelson, owners of Nelson's Landing. Dressed in a charcoal-gray hoodie, their son was sitting on a low cushioned stool at one of the thigh-high snack tables, eating a post-practice salad with a plastic fork. Buzz-cut and blue-eyed, Nelson stands out for his low-maintenance look and style, especially against that species of receiver favoring flash and end zone stagecraft. Grouped with the Packers' own gifted wideouts—three-time Pro Bowler Donald Driver; Greg Jennings, who'd be named a Pro Bowl alternate at the end of the season; second-year man James Jones, who caught 47 balls in '07; and tall, durable possession receiver Ruvell Martin—Nelson is notable less for his peacock-free ways than for his skin tone, as his four receiving mates are all African American. There are no Ocho Cinco imitators or T.O. disciples in this corps. And fans of flamboyant deep threats may be waiting a while in Green Bay, as GM Ted Thompson by his own admission looks to sign "Packer people." He's never diagrammed exactly what a Packer person is, but it's safe to say he's a player promising few if any moments causing management to think to itself, *Well, if he keeps producing, we'll keep ignoring the theatrics, histrionics, and shirtless sit-up demonstrations.*

Yes, Donald Driver busts out a finger-pointing, *Thataway* first-down shimmy. And Jones, if he stays healthy, seems destined to mint a shimmy of his own—or at least enjoy many shimmy opportunities. Martin is master of the aerial shoulder-bump (harder than it looks; give it a try). Needless to say, all Packer receivers—indeed all Packer players—have *carte blanche* to execute a Lambeau Leap for the ages, but that's about as far as it goes. Jennings, a Western Michigan grad and the son of a Kalamazoo minister, comes from the low-glitz, Larry Fitzgerald school of receiving: catch ball, run for or land in end zone, surrender leather, repeat.

The Packers wide receivers are a close bunch. Nearly every time I entered the locker room, they were seated at the same snack table, playing cards. The media gets about 45 minutes each day after practice to conduct interviews, and players are always walking in and out, headed to the showers or rehab room or lounge or a meeting, sometimes not entering the room at all (no, they're not required to post up at their lockers or at one of four low snack tables waiting to be buttonholed by reporters). Often the receivers sat all but silent, eyeing their cards, inside a Texas hold 'em bubble, while reporters gaggled around quarterback Aaron Rodgers across the room or beelined for a new arrival like running back Ryan Grant, safety Nick Collins, or cornerback Al Harris.

It seemed almost a special occasion the day I walked in and saw Donald Driver with a putter in his hands, tapping a golf ball across the green and white oval G in the middle of the carpeted room while Jennings and former long-snapper turned director of player development Rob Davis looked merrily on. The ball was headed for a foam "cup" twenty feet away. "Double D," in long gold shorts and skintight green and white sleeveless Packers undershirt, dashed after the ball with a huge grin on his face, got down on his hands and knees, and scooted along, practically kissing the ball as it traveled, laughing and chanting, "Cup, cup, cup." He just missed.

For this pro-locker-room greenhorn, two things stood out. The first was how approachable the Packer players, none of whom knew me from Adam, were when I came up. I was on guard for, and half expecting, some fake affability, some attitude, a look. I did get a few semi-blank stares, but that was mainly because I was speed talking through a book spiel, and the cornered player might simply be wishing to put on a shirt.

"Some guys might say yes to an interview but sometimes it's hard getting it to happen," one of the Packer PR guys informed me, non-judgmentally; they know as well as anyone how little free time NFL players have during the season. Save for the bye week, the players are overscheduled in the purest sense of the twenty-first-century word. You have only to glance at the six overhead locker-room TVs, screens aglow with the day's breakdown, sometimes beginning with a 6:30 team breakfast and continuing through nine or ten at night, to know the score.

True, there's an element of waltz in the players' relationship with the media—a feint, a slide, a twirl. Giving writers what they need is part of their job, but I never left the Packers locker room feeling I'd mingled with sweat-clothed thespians. As for razzing—verbal towel-slapping—it got no rougher than this. After meeting Driver, I asked him about a kids' book he'd just published, *Quickie Makes the Team*. The illustrated thirty-pager draws on his memories of being a small but speedy little boy in Texas nicknamed "Quickie," one initially discouraged from playing football because of his size. Just then punt returner and nickel cornerback Will Blackmon crossed the room from the D-back lockers and handed Driver a thank-you card, expressing sincere gratitude as he did so. A study in contrasts, the Providence-raised Boston College standout Blackmon dresses with flair ("It's Cavi," he told the host of a local Packers TV show when asked, Oscars-pre-show-like, about the stylish jacket he was wearing), co-owns an edgy clothing line called Dirty Couture, dates a pretty pop singer named Ashley Danielle, jukes like nobody's business to make the gunner miss after fielding a punt, and takes hairstyle risks (he 'fro-hawked in 2007). On the other hand, he's one of the more philosophical Packers, a spiritual man with serious eyes and a broad, pensive brow. He's one of the least jokey.

"Hi, my name is Phil," I'd begun with Driver. "Hi, my name is Will," spoofed James Jones in imitation of my earnestness, and possibly Blackmon's, for the benefit of his fellow receivers, all of them sitting on their locker ledges. Or maybe the joke was 100 percent on me, I don't know. But that was it. That was my brush with getting twitted by an NFL player. I don't count the time when, in response to my asking if I could have fifteen minutes of his time, tattooed 300-pound Alaskan lineman Daryn Colledge said, "I'll give you twelve," then added "Nah, just bustin' your balls. Whatever you need." We got through every single question on a long list.

Not to extrapolate too much from those minutes with Driver at his locker, but they do seem kind of emblematic. Sitting beside him on the ledge of Jennings' locker (hinged, these seats lift up for storage beneath), I listened as the 33-year-old spoke fondly of his young son and daughter enjoying the book, the kids in the story partly modeled on them. Then he proudly added that Packers president Mark Murphy had given his niece the book and that she had loved it. "Uncle Mark, Uncle Mark, can we read the Quickie book again?" Driver piped like Murphy's niece had piped, the Blackmon thank-you card still in his hand.

Double D had done a Barnes & Noble book event two nights earlier. The line of people waiting to get a copy signed, mothers and fathers and kids, stretched the entire length of a long store, snaking between bookstands, and continued out the door onto the sidewalk on a 15-degree Monday night. Raising the handheld mike at exactly 7 P.M., the gregarious receiver, sparkles showing in his studded ear and in the tiny sequined swirls across the chest of his tight, black long-sleeve T-shirt, welcomed the crowd, then spoke a few more words in an unexpectedly heartfelt tone.

"I know Packer fans support their players a long, long time," said the Houston native, an Alcorn State grad whose early teen years saw his family homeless for a time, living out of a U-Haul trailer. "One of my best friends is gone now. Brett Favre. But he'll always be a Packer. And I know you all know that." A brief pause. Then a smile. "Okay, let's get started!"

I scanned the crowd for reaction, but there was none. Most of the waiting fathers and mothers knew Driver was close to Favre (he'd caught 500 of his passes since 1999, for one thing), but still, Driver wanted to assure them the friendship continued, and seemed to be implicitly encouraging them to keep strong their own affection for No. 4, despite all that had happened. His remarks felt unplanned, like they'd just bubbled up. They were tinged, too, with a hint of Driver's own future valediction. Some day—perhaps sooner than later—Double D would be a former Packer as well, but took comfort in knowing these fans, Packer fans, support their Green and Gold alumni for "a long, long time."

I watched Driver sign a few books, his million-dollar smile much in evidence, then took off, my plan to get a signed copy myself dissolving under the thought that I'd be at the back of a three-hour line. Thankfully for all, it went quicker. "Donald, how long were you at the bookstore?" I asked him that day in the locker room. "Two hours," he said. When I inquired if he got everyone in, every last mom, dad, and kid, he said warmly, "Oh yeah. Everybody."

This is a Packers story, a Green Bay story. Tales from the Lombardi years—the hijinks of Paul Hornung and his partner-in-crime Max McGee, rollicking curfew scofflaws—have a different, boozier flavor. As, frankly, do some tales from the Favre '90s, convivial Brett out on the town in this or that upstate hamlet with his two amigos, tight end Mark Chmura and center Frankie Winters. Spend any time in Green Bay and you'll hear tales of the "Goodtime Charlie Packers." It's different now. Should these new Packers, the twenty-first century Packers, win championships, it's unlikely some scribe will one day write the Green Bay equivalent of Jeff Pearlman's 2008 tell-all *Boys Will Be Boys: The Glory Days and Party Nights of the Dallas Dynasty*, detailing philandering, cocaine use, and locker-room exhibitionism among 1990s Cowboys.

No roster boasts 53 angels, and the Packers' doesn't, but team culture, the fishbowl that is Green Bay, the area's low temptation quotient, and, yes, the type of players current management targets, combine to keep scandals few and small. (Now watch some player unleash his inner Pacman Jones just as this book comes out.) That the organization may care *too much* about character actually became a bone of contention among Packer fans in 2008, with radio callers and message-board posters suggesting that the team needed to up its nasty factor, which could mean bringing on board players with a little devil in 'em. Rebutters pointed out this same team culture and nearly the same group of players had the Packers knocking on the door of the Super Bowl nine months earlier.

It seems a question one could debate till the end of time, there in the Great Packer Bar in the Sky, since for every Super Bowl champion led by "McNasties," as former Packers safety turned Green Bay radio host Johnnie Gray calls them, there's a ready counter example. Though the debate is irresolvable, it doesn't make it any less worthwhile; indeed, this matter of the team's non-nastiness would be raised by some expert Packers observers, including Gray.

The other thing that struck me about the Packers locker room was the minimal machismo on display. I had arrived with movie-fueled preconceptions of strutting, growling, sassing, testosterone-infused, overt bad asses. I know Hollywood exaggerates but still I expected some macho projecting. There really wasn't any. About the closest thing I saw to a strut was the room-crossing walk of rock-jawed linebacker Brady Poppinga, but his is really more the regal and contented gait of a flab-free athlete comfortable without his shirt on. Not to mention Poppinga's the wackiest guy on the Packers, a 250-pound quotable, caffeinated goofball who grins easily and wears a small, private smile whenever he's in his strut or stroll or whatever it is, as if perpetually tuned into a monologue of amusing quips. Poppinga is naturally caffeinated, I might add, since he's a practicing Mormon. Raised in Wyoming, he starred at Brigham Young after a two-year mission in Uruguay. He's also a husband, father of two, supporter of multiple charities, former Sunday school teacher, and one-time Eagle Scout who's taped public service ads for the Boy Scouts of America. Yes, the team eccentric is a Mormon with the heart of a Boy Scout. What a wonderful world, as the irrepressible Lombardi-era great Fuzzy Thurston might observe, having used the Louis Armstrong line for the title of his 2005 memoir.

"Get the quarterback off the spot, make him feel uncomfortable, make him feel like he's not back there sipping on coffee and enjoying himself," counseled Poppinga after a Week 13 game in which he was moved from linebacker to defensive end to add pass-rush. "I didn't know it was blood pouring down my face. I thought it was sweat," he said, grinning after gashing his nose in Week 10. As for being selected by the Packers in the fourth round of the 2005 draft, the future father of two-year-old Julius Maximus Poppinga (he got the name from *Gladiator*) was moved to say, "My wife's excited. She loves cheese."

Even allowing for the fact that media availabilities are restricted to after practice (the Packers don't allow writers in the pregame locker room) when players aren't operating at maximum vitality, still I was surprised by the civility, the lack of ambient aggression. Then again, my own team experiences are limited to rec-league basketball and softball, in which former male athletes and non-athletes alike have one chance a week to uncage their competitive id and show how tough they are. In rec-leagues, the top-dog stuff starts in the locker room or during warm-ups. The guys in this locker room, the Packers locker room, know how tough they are. They don't have to remind you of it. To this day, the guy with the most defined strut I've ever seen worked as a marketing manager for a New York publishing house. His job was to expand readership for classic novels like *The Vicar of Bullhampton* by Anthony Trollope and *Little Dorrit* by Charles Dickens.

"Will your parents be there?" I asked Jordy Nelson as he ate his salad.

"They should be," he said. "Unless my dad's out cutting."

You wouldn't call Nelson a man of many words, at least not in these settings, but his conversation's touched with a quiet, sneak-up-on-you sense of humor, and his eyes crinkle quickly in appreciation of levity. When he laughs, these eyes narrow down to slits, his grin growing broad. "Jordy," says a chuckling Daryn Colledge, one of the more garrulous Packers, "Jordy sits there looking at you with that squinty smile. When he's really amused, you can hardly see his eyes."

In card games with his fellow receivers, Nelson sometimes wore his yellow knit Packers ski hat (officially known as a Reebok Green Bay Packers 2008 Player Winter Skully Cap) high up his buzz-cut head to humorous effect. Other Packers pulled their skullies down over their eyebrows. No one held a candle to ninth-year offensive tackle Mark Tauscher when it came to toque comedy, however. The witty, farm-raised Wisconsinite and former Badger perched his cuffed yellow Packers ski cap flat on the top of his head during practices, even under the hot August sun, and purely for comedy, it seemed. Or maybe partly for the challenge—like in those waiter Olympics where servers have to speed walk with a loaded tray while balancing something on their heads. Tauscher's plopped hat never fell off, even during blocking drills.

Farm-raised like Tauscher, Jordy Nelson got tagged "The Hick from the Sticks" by some columnist while starring at Kansas State. The '40s-feeling nickname might be partly why he told the *Appleton Post-Crescent* in late October that the athletes he most admires are "Any of them that go out there and do their job and stay out of the media."

I asked Nelson what he'd meant by "cutting."

"Corn," he said. "Or milo wheat. We got both."

With help from Jordy's 26-year-old brother Mike, Alan Nelson works a 3,000-acre cattle-and-crops farm a few miles from Leonardville. Jordy grew up on this farm, and pitches in every time he comes home. Just four days earlier he was back home helping his dad and brother tend to their herd of two hundred Angus cattle. Nelson's Landing is a recent addition to their lives. After purchasing the trio of vacant buildings on Erpelding Road, Alan and Kim opened Leonardville's lone eatery in the most readily renovated of the three in autumn 2007, a few weeks before Jordy's stellar K-State career came to a close. They serve burgers made from Nelson steers, the butchering done in nearby Riley, home to the Fort Riley Army Base. (Paul Hornung fans might remember he was stationed there with the National Guard during the second half of the '61 season, furloughed just in time to play the Giants in the NFL title game thanks to a timely phone call from President Kennedy.) The restaurant's delicious pies—blueberry, apple, cherry, Snickers, banana cream, gooseberry—are made at home by Jordy's grandmother, Betty Wohler. Kim runs the place during the day. Alan drops by in the evenings after farming.

I asked Nelson if he'd made the drive from Green Bay to Leonardville.

"Takes twelve hours," he said. "If you go fast."

He was right. It took twelve hours, Titletown to Nelson's Landing, not including my visit to the *Field of Dreams* farm and ball field in Dyersville, Iowa, where they shot the 1989 Kevin Costner movie, and a stop ninety miles west in tiny Kesley (population 80), hometown of two-time Pro Bowl Packers defensive end Aaron Kampman. Had the forecast been bad, I might have thought twice about driving 1,700 round-trip miles to watch the Packers on TV in a bar in rural Kansas, but with predictions of sunny skies and T-shirt weather, I hit the road in my '02 Subaru.

You pass through Parkersburg on the way to Kesley. On May 25, 2008, this town of two thousand was half destroyed by a force 5 tornado, as 200-mph winds leveled 220 houses, 22 businesses, and Aplington-Parkersburg High School, where Aaron Kampman played his prep football. Six people were killed and many were injured, including Kampman's 71-year-old grandfather, Claas Kampman, who was thrown from his house as he climbed stairs. Legendary A-P Falcons football coach Ed Thomas sheltered safely but lost his home. Along with Aaron Kampman, Thomas previously coached three other current NFL players: Lions defensive end Jared DeVries, Broncos center Casey Wiegmann, and Jaguars center Brad Meester. All four were back in

Parkersburg within hours of the tornado strike to help the relief effort. A month later, they returned bearing boxes of autographed NFL gear for a relief fundraiser. By then Coach Thomas had vowed that his Falcons, a perennial farm-town powerhouse from a school of just 260 students, would have a 2008 football season, no matter what. He, the players, and the community made good.

In a place like Parkersburg, the high school field is hallowed ground. For proof, look no further than the town's nickname for what is officially the Ed Thomas Field. They call it the "Sacred Acre." Each year the Falcons bury beneath the grass of the Sacred Acre a football signed by the seniors, along with their notes expressing what the team and game of football has meant to them. Not long after the tornado hit, townspeople found themselves drifting toward the Sacred Acre, needing to see what happened to this place that gives them so much pride. The goal posts were twisted, the scoreboard bent, the grass Ed Thomas weeded and watered himself was spiked with boards, ankle-deep in debris. For days people picked shards of glass out of the turf.

The day of the disaster, Aaron Kampman was in Kansas City visiting friends with his wife, Linde, who was raised in Parkersburg. They were on-site the following morning. Kampman visited his grandfather Claas in the hospital, bear-hugged Ed Thomas, then set about hauling debris, chain-sawing trees, and helping patch the roof of Linde's parents' home. On June 5 he returned from Green Bay after three days of Packer OTAs (Organized Team Activities) with former Iowa Hawkeye teammate Colin Cole, Will Blackmon, long-snapper Thomas Gafford, and longtime Packers athletic trainer Pepper Burruss. The five were in Parkersburg for two days, mainly removing rubble from home sites where owners were going to have to rebuild from scratch.

Joining Colin Cole were his wife, Kaye, and 16-year-old stepson, Andrez. The Toronto-born, Fort Lauderdale–raised defensive lineman met the future Dr. Kaye Cole while at Iowa. He was a football player majoring in African American studies. She was a former prep basketball player and cross-county runner getting a PhD in counselor education with a cognate in sports psychology. As it happened, Kaye and Andrez were back in Iowa City that week. Cole picked them up there and the three headed north on Interstate 380 to devastated Parkersburg.

Spend a minute talking with Cole about one of his favorite subjects (African American history; movie acting; vintage cars; or the Cole Group, a company he co-founded with Kaye to help high-school student-athletes pursue college careers) and it quickly becomes unsurprising that this former Florida state heavyweight wrestling champ and first-team All-Big Ten defensive tackle fell for a social science doctoral candidate six years his senior. Reflective and gentle-voiced, the 335-pound Cole, who took acting classes at Iowa to help with his shyness, speaks in full, well-framed sentences that build into full, well-framed paragraphs. Seated at his locker five months after his two days in Parkersburg, the fourth-year Packer spoke of the experience:

"Prior to getting there I had read newspaper accounts and seen pictures on TV but seeing it in-person is something I'll never forget. I could describe it all day long but I still don't know if that would get across the feeling you get when you're actually there. Utter, utter destruction. We spent most of our time going in and out of wrecked houses, hauling out debris, helping tear down parts of ruined houses that needed to come down. I remember thinking it was good my stepson was there. I think it was important for him, at his age, to see something like this, up-close, the effects of a natural disaster. To see what can happen. To see all these people helping each other, pulling together to do everything they can to start over. I think it opened his eyes."

Rebuilding was much in evidence as I drove through Parkersburg on November 1. It was like a Tyvek village, that white house-wrap sealing newly framed and walled homes, its pink or yellow name-stamp visible everywhere, a colored insignia of hope. But here and there were also the open maws of basements stripped of houses, denuded lots where once stood stores and gas stations, tree stumps but barely any trees. There was a concrete grayness, under a gray sky.

Kesley, twelve miles on, had been spared. As I arrived, sun slanting in between breaking clouds to the west lit three white grain silos just past Kesley Lumber, a building-supply store run by Aaron Kampman's father, Bob. It and nearby Kesley Diner had closed a couple hours earlier but the hands of a paper clock hanging on the diner door signaled a 5 P.M. re-opening. Warmth was finally pushing in from the west. A thermometer fixed to a wooden stop-sign post read 60 degrees.

"Blink and you miss it," said Colin Cole of this no-stoplight town. "Surprised you actually found the place," Kampman chuckled on hearing of his town's visitor. There was a tang of burning leaves in the air. Sheep grazed in a field a stone's throw from Kesley Lumber. Tractors were parked in house driveways. Main Street signs advertised KELLY TIRES and KESLEY ELECTRIC MOTOR SERVICE. A lanky man in sand-colored overalls drove a tractor pulling a leaf-green Balzer vacuum tank. Turning off Main, it rumbled along a no-sidewalk lane ending in a T one block down, opposite the neatly kept ranch home where Aaron Kampman grew up. Farm fields stretched to the horizon just beyond the light brown house.

Steve was the guy on the tractor. I caught up with him and two friends, Tammie and Randy, after touring the six-block town. They were taking in the mellow sun on a patio bench beside Tammie's house, kitty-corner from the Kampman's. Steve had been helping someone drain a septic tank—that's what he does for a living. "I'm the poop man," he said cheerfully, his blue eyes bright behind steel-frame glasses. Randy worked twelve years at Kesley Lumber but switched to farming after encountering back problems. "It's easier sitting on a tractor than lifting lumber and going up and down ladders," he said. "And falling off ladders," joked Steve. Both men praised Bob Kampman as an employer and vendor. "Bob's real good to his people," Randy said. Steve nodded agreement, adding, "He follows through. You know Bob Kampman would never give you the shaft."

Tammie, a custodian at the Iowa State Bank down the street, is the football fan in this group. When I mentioned that Iowa was playing Illinois that very minute, Steve and Randy kind of shrugged. "We're not that big into football," Steve explained. "There's lots of other stuff to do," added Randy. Tammie stepped inside her house a moment and returned with a *Denver Post* clipping sent by her dad showing Kampman tackling a Viking in the Packers home opener.

"I'm a Broncos fan," Tammie said. "But I like the Packers, too. Because of Aaron."

"Aaron's pastor is a Bears fan!" Steve said with a laugh.

Tammie recalled a teenage Kampman always working out in his dad's lumber yard. "You'd stop by and he'd be lifting railroad ties overhead," she said. Steve quoted a babysitter claiming young Aaron was "strong as an ox even as a one-year-old. Strong as an ox. Like he'd squeeze your hand and you'd remember it." Kampman's neighborliness was also memorable. "If Aaron saw you doing anything outside, he'd always come over to help," Tammie said. Randy nodded, adding, "All the Kampman boys were like that. Aaron, Andy, and Curt. Always helping out." Steve still retains a vivid memory of 14-year-old Aaron helping him rake sand and rock salt from the edge of his lawn after a sudden spring thaw melted heaps of banked snow back in 1994.

43

When I mentioned Parkersburg, faces grew serious. "Not everyone can afford to rebuild," Steve said softly. "Bob's probably over there right now," Randy suggested. "With his dad." But in the wake of this unprecedented disaster, there was inspiration, too. Tammie proudly cited the Aplington-Parkersburg football team. "Despite everything, they had their home opener on schedule," she said. "Aaron came down and addressed the team before the game. And they won. And kept on winning. Right now they're 10–0. They haven't lost a single game!"

"It's pretty much a miracle," Randy said. "Considering."

From atop his rumbling tractor beside the diner fifteen minutes later, Steve had a last thing to tell me about Aaron Kampman. Steve was headed home. I was getting into my car to head to Kansas. He waved me over, a thoughtful expression on his face. Choosing his words with care, enunciating over the idling engine, Steve said, "The reason Aaron has done so well in his chosen profession is because of three things: his integrity, character, and Christian faith."

He noticed I didn't have my notebook out. "You might want to write that down," he said. I got out my notebook. Once again he spoke of his former neighbor, the 28-year-old Kesley product who's done missionary work in rural India and Africa, who takes seminary classes in the offseason, and who was named one of the NFL's "Good Guys" by the *Sporting News* in 2006 for his community contributions. This time Steve gave his observation a small confirmatory nod. "Integrity, character, and Christian faith," he said. "That's Aaron Kampman." I wrote it down.

Leonardville is bigger than Kesley, but not by much. Three tenths of a square mile, says the U.S. Census Bureau, but who's counting? Grain elevators rise from the edge of this town as well, the edge of town just one block from town center. The day I visited, nine red tractors sat outside L & S Service, a farm-machinery repair shop, three of them neatly slant-parked on Erpelding Road. With its turn-of-the-century former bank, half dozen ramshackle storefronts (derelict Jim's Books; Carol's Secondhand Store, closed on Sundays; Dr. Newman's Wonderful Emporium, door wide open, used furniture out on the sidewalk), and faded, homey signs, Leonardville feels like a cross between a quirky mining town and prairie outpost of the type John Dillinger or Bonnie and Clyde so loved to discover.

Sharing a block with Auntie Em's Hair Shack, a gray shingled saltbox where the proprietor lives and snips, Nelson's Landing Restaurant & Sports Bar seems to concentrate all of this little town's friendliness and do-it-yourself charm into one welcoming, cheerful place. A single-story block-and-siding structure occupying a site where B. L. Bredberg's Wallpaper, Books, and Paint store stood a century ago, the eatery draws people from all over this part of Riley County. It's a smoke-free establishment, so parents feel free to bring their little ones inside.

They served 350 meals Halloween night, a new record. Alan and Kim Nelson hosted a party that included karaoke, a country-western band, and a costume contest. Decorations were still on display Sunday afternoon, with cornstalks and a hay bale trimming a low-rise corner stage in one of the plank-floored dining rooms. Burlap seed bags and vintage agricultural signs (INTERNATIONAL HARVESTER, KEY WORK CLOTHES) adorn the walls while the front dining room features a display case containing Jordy Nelson trophies, clippings, and photos going all the way back to when he captured the national AAU 400-meters championship as a ten-year-old. Eight years later at Riley County High School he was named first-team all-state in basketball and won the long jump, the 100-, the 200-, and the 400-meters at the state meet, setting division records in the shorter sprints. Among the

45

newest framed photos is a newspaper shot of Nelson in his Packers uniform grinning broadly as he rides a kid's bike during training camp.

Burgers made from never-frozen beef are served by staff wearing forest green tees bearing Nelson's signature and Packers No. 87 on the front. On the backs, big gold letters urge Go, Pack, Go! Nelson's Packers jersey is framed on one wall. Also proudly displayed is a Kansas City Chiefs jersey signed by safety John McGraw, the other Riley County High product playing in the NFL. Cheeseheads Only Permitted Behind This Counter proclaims a cheddar-yellow sign on the countertop. Nearby sits a Packers Pro Shop catalog.

It was here, in his parents' restaurant, where the 6-foot-3, 218-pound receiver got his call from the Green Bay Packers on Draft Day 2008. He'd given up his idea of working cattle that April Saturday, so a barnyard soundtrack wasn't in store for whatever GM or team rep called (if one called). Instead well-wishers surrounded him: parents, siblings, grandparents, friends, neighbors, restaurant staff, and his wife, Emily, whom he'd known since kindergarten and to whom he'd proposed by writing "Will you marry me?" in the sand on a Cancún beach.

Early in round two, his cell phone rang. He didn't recognize the 920 area code. He said hello and listened. He didn't mouth "Packers" so for a time his ready-to-explode support team didn't know who'd called. "But his free hand started really pumping," Kim Nelson remembered six months later on this wonderfully warm autumn Sunday. "So we knew it was good."

"His eyes got huge," recalled Tom Fosha, Jordy's former Little League baseball coach, a Nelson's Landing bartender on Saturdays, and a builder who helped renovate the place. "Then he started jumping up and down. 'It's the Packers, the Packers!'"

Tom was my host for the Packers–Titans telecast. I caught up with Kim Nelson after the game, as she and Alan spent the afternoon in Manhattan watching their daughter Kelsey, a 5-foot-9 sharpshooting senior guard for K-State, play in the lady Wildcats' 2008 season opener. Their son Jordy might have had the greatest season by a wide receiver in K-State's history, but just a few months later Kelsey made some noise of her own by scoring 20 points in 27 minutes in her first Division I start as a junior-college transfer—in the NCAA tournament, no less.

"We watched the first quarter of Jordy's game in a sports bar next to campus," said Kim, a dynamic, quick-witted woman with short blonde hair, blue eyes, and smart wire-rim glasses. Not quite as tall as her daughter, she wore a purple K-State sweatshirt and blue jeans. "Then we raced over to Kelsey's game. A friend kept texting me updates on the Packers score."

I should probably mention that a purple K-State banner hangs beside the Packers flag in the restaurant's window. There's Wildcat purple on the walls, too, and when Kim's mom, Betty, stopped by with her husband, Fred, to drop off the day's pies, she was dressed in a purple K-State sweater with Kelsey's name and No. 2 on the back. "With both kids doing so well," Betty said before hustling off for Kelsey's game, "we do a lot of running around!"

Described as "sporty" and "a stitch" by longtime friend Tom Fosha, Kim has a decidedly down-to-earth manner, her humor the pretension-popping kind. With her around, there's not a chance in heck her son will ever get a big head, no matter how many passes he catches or touchdowns he scores. "I told Jordy he's probably the only pro football player to spend his bye week getting cowshit on his shoes," Kim said with a laugh while checking the day's receipts. "Care to donate?" she quipped a few minutes later, holding out a countertop jar after I'd praised the beautiful but unrenovated 1908 corner building she and her husband now owned, a stone-built former department store with stunning farmland views. The mother of the Packers' first pick in the 2008 draft even passed up a chance to rhapsodize about Lambeau Field. "It's great," she said, "but honestly I didn't have that much to compare it to."

She did hail the Packer cheerleaders, however, two G-rated squads drawn from a local high school and college. "That was refreshing," she said. "I hope they keep that."

Her son was the third receiver chosen, the 36th player selected overall. In keeping with the twin pillars of his draft philosophy—multiply picks and look for the best available talent rather than necessarily selecting for need—Packers general manager Ted Thompson traded a late first-round slot to the New York Jets for a pair of picks, an early second-rounder and a fourth-rounder. The Jets used the 30th pick to grab Purdue tight end Justin Keller. Six picks later the Packers secured Nelson. "The more you watch him, the more you like him," Thompson said. "He's fast, big, tall, and knows how to play contested balls."

That the selection of her son—on no draft guru's radar prior to his senior year—was not universally celebrated by citizens of Packer Nation is another thing Kim is up front about.

"I know there was some booing when they announced Jordy's name at the Lambeau Draft Party," she said matter-of-factly from behind the restaurant counter. "And Ted Thompson got some boos when he came out to explain the pick. I guess they were thinking, 'We already have all these receivers. Why do we need another one?' Well, Jordy's always had to overcome obstacles. Nothing's come easy. Hopefully he'll surprise some people."

Nelson didn't receive a single offer to play Division I college football despite his size, speed, and athleticism (as a high-school option quarterback, he ran for 1,500 yards and threw for a thousand in his senior year; in basketball, he set school career records for blocks, steals and assists). After walking on as a defensive back at K-State under living-legend coach Bill Snyder (they named a highway after him, the route from I-70 into Manhattan), Nelson was redshirted in his first year. Then Snyder had a brainstorm: convert this fleet, sturdy athlete to wide receiver. *Boom!* Forty-five catches sophomore year, second-team All-Big 12. Hobbled by injuries his junior year, Nelson went supernova as a senior, becoming a one-man "Miracle in Manhattan." Even with defenses geared to stop him first, second, and third, he snagged 122 passes at a 13.2 yard clip, the total crushing—make that *vaporizing*—K-State's previous season mark of 75 receptions, and setting a new Big 12 record for receptions by a senior.

"Everything kept rolling," Nelson told the *Green Bay Press-Gazette* the day after getting drafted, "and as the year went on, I was thinking more and more that I'd be making the NFL."

"This is not a slow receiver," emphasized Packers receivers coach Jimmy Robinson post-draft, aware of concerns regarding Nelson's so-so 4.51 40-yard-dash time at the NFL Scouting Combine. Such is the almighty sway of the annual Circus in Indianapolis 40—king of the "measurables"—that people had concerns about a guy whose 10.63 Division III high-school 100 meters time would have placed him second in the 2008 *collegiate* Division III race, just .04 seconds behind the NCAA champion. As for "football speed," feel free to download the YouTube clip of Nelson dusting All-American Kansas cornerback (and future first-round pick of the Tampa Bay Buccaneers) Aqib Talib on a 60-yard go route that begins with a burst and ends with Nelson scoring 10 yards in the clear. For his ability to catch the ball in traffic and run with it afterward, the Packers had Nelson ranked near the top of their draft board. And Packers scout Lenny McGill, their evaluator in the Central Plains, also gave Nelson "A-pluses" for character.

Immediately after being selected, Nelson naturally wanted to rustle up some Packers gear. But in a town like Leonardville, Kansas, that was no easy trick.

"We did have one Packer fan in the group who had a foam cheesehead at home," Kim Nelson explained. "So he jumped in his car to go get it. He would have brought it if he'd known Jordy was going to the Packers but we were thinking it might be the Redskins—they'd had Jordy out for a visit. But the Redskins went with another receiver, Devin Thomas. I remember being a little worried but just two picks later, the Packers called. Kelsey and some of the other K-State girls jumped in two more cars and drove down to Manhattan. They ran into a sporting-goods store and managed to find three Packer baseball hats. But there weren't any shirts. So they bought a bunch of white T-shirts and some markers and drove back here and made Packer T-shirts for everyone by drawing a big Packers G in black and coloring it yellow. And Jordy put on the cheesehead."

Stop by the Nelson's Landing display case and there it is, a photo of Jordy with one arm around his mom, the other around his wife, his sister Kelsey and friends left and right, everyone wearing white T-shirts with the yellow Packers G outlined in black. Jordy took off the cheesehead for this shot, but he is wearing it in a picture Tom Fosha took with his cell phone camera.

I asked Kim if she'd met Packers management.

"Everyone was real nice," she said. "They had us out in July, families of the draft picks. We met the president, Mark Murphy, Coach McCarthy, Ted Thompson. It's interesting because you don't meet an owner. You're not meeting Daniel Snyder or Al Davis. I'm not sure it would have been the same if Jordy had been drafted by Oakland. Which could have happened."

Kim saw Green Bay as a good place for her son, citing the small size, family atmosphere, and affordability. She added, "I'm not sure New York would work for him." A smile crossed her face. "Then again, if he'd gone to the Jets he could have caught a pass from Brett Favre."

A cheer went up in Nelson's Landing when Nelson trotted onto LP Field in Nashville. Though no Riley County native myself, no former neighbor, teacher, coach, or summer softball teammate of the Packer rookie, I cheered as loudly as anyone because up until this moment I hadn't been sure Nelson was even active for the game. Friday morning the Packers said the receiver had sprained an ankle colliding with a referee during Thursday's practice and was listed as "questionable" for Sunday. Thursday was the day I spoke to him about coming out here. He seemed a bit subdued eating his garden salad but that was about it. All during my drive west I worried I might be watching the game in Nelson's Landing with Jordy Nelson sidelined.

The Packers were healthier than they'd been in weeks and during their non-contusing bye had time to savor the season's most impressive victory to date, a 34–14 whipping of the Indianapolis Colts at Lambeau on October 19. The Titans, though, were the NFL's only 7–0 team and had the league's stingiest defense, surrendering a measly 12.4 points per game. Between the smash of punishing 240-pound back LenDale White and the dash of quicksilver rookie halfback Chris Johnson (he of the 4.34 Combine 40), they also possessed the league's fourth-best running attack. And they would be facing in the Packers the league's fifth-worst rushing defense. On paper, it did not look like an encouraging matchup for the Green and Gold.

But Titans quarterback Kerry Collins was entering the game with just a 72.9 passer rating (Aaron Rodgers' mark stood at 98.8) and would be throwing to an undistinguished corps of receivers. Beyond that, Pro Bowl Titans defensive end Kyle Vanden Bosch was playing with a strained groin and the team had a short week of practice after rallying from a 14–6 halftime deficit to beat the Colts the previous Monday night. The Packers, on the other hand, were well rested.

The extra rest didn't seem to help. From a Packers perspective, the game began brutally. Actually, things got screwy in pregame. Pro Bowl offensive tackle Chad Clifton, who'd missed just one game in the past eighty-five, took an anti-inflammatory for his knees—a med he'd taken before without trouble—and suffered an allergic reaction two minutes prior to the 10:30 A.M. deadline to declare inactives. Here in his home state, the former Tennessee Vol was hit with dizziness and full-body swelling, a locker-room version of post-shellfish Will Smith in the movie *Hitch*, or hives-covered Chris Elliot in *There's Something About Mary* (a.k.a. "The Movie Where Brett Favre Plays Himself"). Coach Mike McCarthy ended up keeping Clifton active but he didn't see any action. Forty minutes before kickoff his O-line teammates were informed there'd be musical chairs: Daryn Colledge moved from left guard to left tackle, right guard Jason Spitz slid left, and rookie Josh Sitton got his first NFL start at right guard. The switcheroos just added to the fun of facing Vanden Bosch, Pro Bowl end Jevon Kearse, and very big and very good Pro Bowl tackle Albert Haynesworth, all 6-foot-6, 320 pounds of him. Clifton-less, right tackle Mark Tauscher, center Scott Wells, and the reassigned three didn't shed a tear when the gimpy groin of Vanden Bosch caused him to exit the game before halftime.

Aaron Rodgers didn't shed a tear either, though he ended up getting sacked three times by Vanden Bosch replacements Dave Ball and Jacob Ford. Ford's third-quarter takedown was the costliest, as

Rodgers fumbled at his own 17 then watched from beneath Ford as linebacker Stephen Tulloch recovered the ball. Four plays later, Rob Bironas kicked his third field goal. The giveaway marked back-to-back turnovers by Rodgers, who had thrown deep for Greg Jennings on second-and-2 at the Titans 35 on the previous possession, Driver going vertical as well, and fast-closing safety Chris Hope made a splendid full-extension pick diving straight back into the end zone. The interception was only Rodgers' fifth of the season, a non-scary number, especially in light of a figure like . . . to take one at random here . . . the seven interceptions thrown by Brett Favre in the previous three Jets games.

Like a Halloween hangover, the game opened in a way to put fear in the hearts of Packers fans. On the first play from scrimmage, Aaron Rodgers, who forty-eight hours earlier had signed a six-year contract extension worth $65 million ($20 million of it guaranteed) was pancaked by an unblocked Jevon Kearse a split second after his pass was batted down. The Sixty-Five Million Dollar Man, flat on his back, nine seconds in. On second down, Greg Jennings tore past cornerback Cortland Finnegan squatting on his route and was home free. But Rodgers threw an out to where Jennings had been, say, 1.2 seconds earlier. Incomplete. On third down, the former California Golden Bear failed to get the play off in time, resulting in a 5-yard delay of game penalty. After the re-boot, Driver found a crease up the middle but Rodgers' low throw bounced off the top of the receiver's foot. The Packers were forced to punt.

Jordy Nelson had been back with Will Blackmon to receive the opening kickoff (Blackmon took it), then lined up for the game's first and third plays in a four-receiver package, delighting the people in Nelson's Landing. "We're all real proud of him," said Harley "Hal" Prichard, Jordy's middle-school football and basketball coach, and high-school golf coach and chemistry teacher. Hal retired the previous spring after forty-five years of district coaching, including thirteen as the Riley County High School Falcons football coach. "Jordy was fast," Hal remembered with a smile, "but not like he is now. And even if he was the best player on the team, he always gave his teammates credit. He didn't have a lot of ego."

Approximately thirty people aged 8–80 gathered in the tin-ceilinged room, the game being shown on a couple of mounted flat-screen TVs and projected on a brick wall just past the cornstalks and hay bales. They cheered the loudest when, eight minutes into the second quarter, Nelson caught a slant at the line of scrimmage, stopped on a dime, spun out of the grasp of cornerback Nick Harper, and burned up the right sideline for a 23-yard gain. That tackle-shedding reverse of direction, the final slicing back into traffic to gain another six yards instead of angling out of bounds—this was the receiver the Packers hoped they'd drafted. Nelson's grab and gallop keyed a 12-play, 71-yard march capped by the game's first touchdown. On third-and-goal from the 5, Donald Driver ran a hitch, caught a bullet pass, executed a nifty spin of his own, then Superman-dove across the goal line with the ball outstretched.

It was Driver's first catch of the day, and it marked a milestone. With it, he tied Sterling Sharpe's Packers record of 103 consecutive games with at least one reception. Double D went on to have a huge second half against Tennessee, catching six more balls for 136 yards, his first 100-yard game of the season. He was the recipient of two sweet throws by Rodgers, one a soft-touch rainbow for 44 yards on a post-corner route and another for 29 yards on a flawless pump-and-go. The Green Bay signal-caller shook off his nightmare start (bat-down, miscue, penalty, underthrow) to rack up 314 yards, the first time in twenty-two games the Titans had surrendered more than 300 through the air (though 168 were yards after catch). Rodgers nearly threw for a bunch more. A minute before half, he rifled a pass 51 yards downfield that whistled to the turf three inches beyond the grasp of Jennings. And with the game tied at 16 inside of four minutes, he faked a handoff, set his feet, and javelin-chucked the ball 63 aerial yards. Jennings had a step on Finnegan but the defender reached out and gripped the receiver's right arm just as the ball arrived. It plunged through Jennings' hands. No flag was thrown.

"I'm not a what-if person," said Coach McCarthy after the game. But if he were, he might have thought back to this non-call, the four dropped passes, and the two tricky but catchable first-quarter balls that rookie tight end Jermichael Finley got a hand on but couldn't haul in, one a short pass from the Titans 44 on fourth-and-1, the other a jump-ball fade in the end zone. For the Packers secondary, it was close-but-no-cigar three times on interception chances. A pressured Kerry Collins floated a wounded duck that clunked to the ground between cornerback Al Harris and safety Nick Collins. Another ball headed for Nick Collins got deflected by Packers end Michael Montgomery. And with four minutes to go, a too-high Kerry Collins pass bounced off strong safety Atari Bigby's shoulder pad. It was like this all day. In a game you knew would go down to the wire, a game in which points were at a premium, the Packers had both a first-and-goal at the 10 and first-and-goal at the 12 but couldn't score a touchdown either time. It was a contest Fox Sports sideline commentator Tony Siragusa twice labeled a brawl and which Titans tight end Bo Scaife compared to a boxing match, two combatants pounding, pounding, until only one was left standing.

Unfortunately for the Packers, it was Tennessee who was left standing. After Bironas doinked a 47-yarder off the right upright at the end of regulation, the Titans won the overtime coin toss. With frenzied fans waving the SMASH & DASH signs they were handed on the way in to the stadium, Smash and Dash delivered. Dash (Johnson) did the most damage, slipping into the right flat on a blown coverage on third-and-6 and taking a dump-off pass 16 yards to the Tennessee 42. Six straight running plays followed, the killer being a tackle-busting 7-yard gain by Smash (White) on a third-and-4 play from the Packers 38. Johnson gained 8 more on a pair of carries before Bironas split the uprights from 41 yards to keep the Titans' record unblemished.

Bironas' game-winner set off groans in Nelson's Landing. The only person who didn't groan was a Bears fan. But since he was the cook who prepared that tasty cheeseburger from Nelson farm beef I'd scarfed in the first half, he was forgiven. He'd come out of the kitchen and joined us for the overtime.

Here at least, there were ripples of what-if. What if that 12-yard cross intended for Jordy from the Titans 43 on second-and-10 with 2:30 to go in regulation hadn't been deflected by a linebacker then knocked down by Finnegan? Undeflected, it looked like it would have reached a diving Jordy for a Packers first down. If it had, the Packers might have won. It could have been the play of the game. Rodgers to the rookie Nelson. But the pass fell incomplete.

The Packers failed on the next down, too.

"We needed three more yards," McCarthy said in his post-game press conference. Had the Packers reached the 40, he would have sent in kicker Mason Crosby, who'd already nailed three field goals and set a Packers record with his eighteenth consecutive made kick on the road. The Titans rushed only three men. McCarthy called a shovel-screen for running back Brandon Jackson. But his blockers got jumbled and linebacker Stephen Tulloch, the guy who had just deflected the pass meant for Nelson, stormed in unblocked and tackled Jackson at the 41. McCarthy sent out the punting team.

An hour after the 19–16 loss, I stood on the field where Jordy Nelson played his high school football. A blue-surfaced, 400-meter track circled the grass. Farmland stretched beyond the wind-break pines bordering the far side of the field. Bleacher seating rose on the near side. The sun shone and the breeze was gentle and birds sang from the tops of the Musso light standards. It must have been 75 degrees. Beside birdsong, the only sound was the occasional pickup truck passing on neighboring Falcon Road. Across this asphalt farm road sat an old churchyard cemetery full of weathered stone markers bearing the names of pioneer farming families.

I was alone in the stadium. Upon entering, I'd turned around and scanned the bleachers and up by the press box I spotted a familiar name. HAL PRICHARD STADIUM read a big sign. I hadn't known they'd named the stadium after Hal. When I got back to Green Bay, I looked up an article about him. It said Hal Prichard takes care of this field, and has done so for decades. Despite battling a life-threatening illness the past couple of years, Hal still gets over to the field as often as he can. He cuts the grass on a riding mower, wearing shorts and his wife's sun bonnet on hot summer days. Hal Prichard, tending the field here. Coach Ed Thomas, tending the Sacred Acre. Two rural football fields where the dreams of six NFL players began.

Jordy Nelson caught just two passes against Tennessee, a pair of slants. It wasn't like a year ago this same weekend when Nelson broke the K-State single-game receiving mark by snagging fourteen balls for 214 yards in a 31–20 loss to Iowa State. But today's grabs both earned Packer first downs and gave the rookie eighteen catches against no drops through eight NFL games. Prior to gaining ten yards on his second catch, Nelson also returned a Tennessee kickoff 40 yards to an eruption of cheers in Nelson's Landing. People remembered the two punts he took back for K-State touchdowns in 2007, one a 92-yard thriller. But he hadn't returned kickoffs in college, and when he told his mom that he'd be doing that for the Packers, she said, in her matter-of-fact way, "You don't return kickoffs, Jordy." Her son replied, "I do now, Mom."

I left Hal Prichard Stadium. I got in my car for the drive home. 850 miles was plenty of time to stew this loss. It could have been a statement game for the Green and Gold. On Friday, *USA Today* had run a feature story headlined "NFL Season Packed With Parity, Drama." It mentioned the Packers as one of only four NFL teams that hadn't played a game decided by a score in the last two minutes or overtime. Well, they could take the Pack off the list.

With that kick by Rob Bironas, the Packers had already lost more games to date than they had in all of 2007. Right now, back in Green Bay, radio callers and message-board posters were already flogging this point, some kindly suggesting that Favre would have pulled the game out. Others were countering that Favre doesn't play run defense.

The last time the Packers were 4–4 at the midway point was in 2004. That year, they went on to win six of their last eight and take the NFC North with a 10–6 record.

But that was a different team. It had a different coach. It had a different quarterback. Could Aaron Rodgers lead a second-half charge? If he did not, would the doomsaying of Favre-backing cheeseheads revive and make the rest of the season a repeat of summer? It was not a pretty picture there for a time, up in Green Bay. It got pretty heated. Fans were bashing Packers management and predicting another slide into mediocrity or worse.

It was not the Summer of Love. It was the Summer of Favre.

# PART TWO:

# THE SUMMER
# OF FAVRE

# CHAPTER 4: WELCOME TO LAMBEAU, SHAREHOLDERS

B RETT FAVRE FOR PRESIDENT read the bumper sticker on a new-model hunter green Ford F-150 pickup merging onto the highway sixty miles south of Green Bay. It was a sunny Thursday morning four days before the start of the Packers 2008 training camp. ST. BRETT: PATRON SAINT OF CHEESEHEADS read a second sticker. IRON MAN 4 read a third.

Someone liked Favre.

A Packers jersey with Favre's name and number hung in the left corner of the Ford's cab window. A golden Packers sweatshirt hung in the right corner. The driver was alone and appeared to be wearing a Packers jersey with a green Packers ball cap. It's a tranquil drive coming up from Milwaukee, a stretch of farm fields and grazing cows, and I spaced on changing lanes as the pickup roared off the ramp and slid in just in front of me. Its side-view mirror briefly revealed a thirty-something guy with a set jaw and an unhappy expression. Lots of people trick out their rides like this in Wisconsin, but given the timing and highway, it was possible we were both headed to the same place. Today was the annual Packers shareholders meeting at Lambeau Field. Instinctively, I checked his cab for a gun rack. Nope.

"Fans to Demand Answers" headlined a story previewing this event, a normally sedate affair in which roughly 10 percent of the 112,005 owners of Packers stock gather in the stadium bleachers to hear team brass discuss player acquisitions and revenue streams. The majority of these fans bought their shares in the public company's last stock drive in 1997, when 106,000 people from every state and U.S. territory shelled out $200 per share for an ownership interest that confers voting rights but pays no dividends and can't be resold except back to the team for pennies on the dollar. The drive raised $24 million and helped fund the Lambeau upgrade.

That fourth stock sale in franchise history benefitted from timing and technology. It began ten months after the Packers won Super Bowl XXXI, and during its four-month run the team returned to football's ultimate game. In the sale's opening eleven days, 37,000 fans jumped at the chance to become citizen owners, calling a toll-free number or hitting the team Web site. Wisconsin residents bought roughly 55 percent of the mainly symbolic shares. Illinois, Minnesota, California, and Florida residents led the way after that. Twice as many Alaskans and Hawaiians purchased Packer shares as those living in Wyoming, West Virginia, and Vermont.

The team's three previous stock drives—held in 1923, 1935, and 1950—were small and local by comparison, though the one at midcentury, shortly after Curly Lambeau left for Chicago, did pull in some Green Bay natives living out of state. Lost to history is the name of the farm woman from Wrightstown, twenty miles south of

Green Bay, who arrived at the team's Crooks Street office bearing a matchbox full of quarters to buy her $25 share. That midcentury sale raised $118,000, funds much needed at a time when the cash-strapped franchise was being outbid for draft picks by teams in the new All-America Football Conference. But at least the team wasn't twelve grand in the hole as it was in 1935. That year a fan named Willard Bent had fallen out of the City Stadium bleachers and successfully sued the Packers. A town stock sale raised $15,000, funds used to move the team out of receivership.

It was in 1935 that the nonprofit Green Bay Packers Corp., formed in 1923 on the strength of $5,000 in share sales, reorganized into the Green Bay Packers Inc., our present company. Only from 1919–1923 could the Packers be said to have an "owner," namely the two meatpacking companies and Curly Lambeau. Acme Meatpacking walked away after the team was booted from the proto-NFL in 1922 for using an illegal college player. Securing a $1,500 loan from a lumberman's son who sold his cream-colored Marmon roadster for the sake of local football, Curly traveled to Canton, Ohio, to lobby league president Joe Carr for his team's reinstatement, entry fee in hand. When Curly returned to Green Bay, he honored the one condition attached to the loan: the lumberman's son got to play in a Packers game. Coach Curly put the guy out there at defensive tackle for minute one of game one, then promptly yanked him.

With Curly as owner, the team quickly fell into debt. Rainy weather nearly wiped out the company in 1922, one downpour proving big enough to kill a game's box office yet falling a hundredth of an inch short of activating Curly's insurance policy. The fiscal cavalry arrived in the form of four prominent local citizens: a doctor, a lawyer, a grocery merchant, and the publisher of the *Press-Gazette*. They took care of Curly's debts, arranged that first stock sale, and relaunched the

Packers as a community-owned nonprofit organization whose earnings would only flow back into the team, not shareholder pockets. To guard against franchise relocation, the original 1923 articles of incorporation stipulated that should the team ever be sold, all proceeds after meeting expenses would go to a local American Legion post to build a "proper soldier's memorial." In 1997, Packer shareholders voted to change the beneficiary to the Green Bay Packers Foundation, a trust created nine years earlier to aid charities and other worthy Wisconsin causes.

Today, the team's 112,000-plus citizen owners elect forty-five directors, who in turn select seven officers (president, vice-president, treasurer, secretary, and three members-at-large) for the executive committee. Officers meet monthly to review football operations and team finances. Only the Packers president gets paid a salary. Everyone else donates their time. Among current board members is ex-Packers linebacker and 1995 NFL Defensive Player of the Year Bryce Paup, who wore the green and gold from 1990 through 1994 before signing with the Buffalo Bills. An Iowa native who ended his career in Jacksonville and Minnesota, Paup returned to Green Bay after his retirement and was named head football coach at Green Bay Southwest High School in 2007. Former Washington Redskins receiver Pat Richter is also on the board. Raised in Madison, Richter was a star tight end for the University of Wisconsin before returning to the Badgers as athletic director in 1989.

When board members reach age 70, team bylaws move them to "director emeritus" status. Hall of Fame Packers defensive end Willie Davis, holder of a University of Chicago MBA who went on to equal success in the business world, is a director emeritus, as is Bud Selig, the commissioner of Major League Baseball. Joining them is Milwaukee attorney Bernie Kubale, corporate advisor to the team for many years. The son of a tavern owner from tiny Reedsville, south of Green Bay,

Bernie entered Wisconsin sports history in 1946 as the starting senior forward for the Reedsville Panthers. The smallest school ever to win the state's one-class prep basketball championship, Reedsville defeated Eau Claire before 14,000 spectators at the Field House in Madison. How small was Reedsville High? That year it enrolled 87 students, which made it almost half the size of the 161-student Milan, Indiana, school whose boys basketball team's one-class state championship run eight years later inspired the movie *Hoosiers*.

I met with Bernie Kubale (pronounced coo-BAH-lee) in mid-August in a small-town pub west of Milwaukee, a place not much different from the Kubale Tavern his father Joe ran from 1900 to 1950, and above which his family lived. A youthful eighty, Bernie still jogs three miles a day. Brett Favre had been traded to the New York Jets six days earlier. I asked Bernie if the trade had been discussed at the Packers board meeting he'd attended the previous day. "Indeed," Bernie said with a smile. Could he share some of what board members said? "I'm afraid it's pretty much a nothing-leaves-this-room kind of deal," Bernie said pleasantly. What about the general tenor? "Business-like," the Packers director emeritus replied. "No shouting but people had opinions." Then he offered some advice in terms of approaching the Packers during this delicate time. "Let them know you're not setting out to write some kind of muckraking book about the Favre situation," he said. "It's pretty tense up there right now."

Though Bernie wasn't free to discuss internal Packers business, he was happy to share Packer memories going all the way back to the 1930s, when Green Bay native Arnie Herber was the team's star quarterback. And he spoke glowingly of former Packers president and current chairman emeritus Bob Harlan (father of sports broadcaster Kevin Harlan), a gregarious Iowan and onetime Marquette University sports information director who oversaw the Packers renaissance during the 1990s. It was Harlan who hired Ron Wolf as general manager in '91. Wolf promptly signed free agent Reggie White, grabbed Brett Favre from the Falcons, and hired Mike Holmgren to coach. Quite a trifecta.

"Bob was the first Packers president who wasn't from Green Bay," Bernie said. "For some people, this was an issue. There'd been this long tradition of selecting prominent Green Bay citizens as Packer presidents, taking them from the executive committee. But Bob had been in the Packers front office since 1971. He knew everything about the operation. When he took over in '89, the franchise really got into gear. You know, there was a long stretch there when players didn't want to go to Green Bay. It was a threat—like going to Siberia. 'You better start producing or we'll ship you to Green Bay.' So Bob makes a great hire in Ron Wolf. He gets our indoor practice facility, the Hutson Center, going. And he has the insight to realize Lambeau Field should be the focus of everything, which meant no more games in Milwaukee. That caused quite a fuss down here, as you can imagine. It was Bob who engineered that terrific stock sale in '97, and who pushed so hard for the stadium upgrade. He went door-to-door making his case for that. He has a great ability to relate to people. How many company presidents do you think answer their own phones, or respond to a shareholder letter by giving that person a phone call?"

It was Bob Harlan's common touch that most impressed Bernie.

"I remember when we won the Super Bowl," said the former Reedsville Panther who contributed 14 points in that 1946 state championship game. "Bob wanted every employee in the company to get a ring, from people at the top to the guy who swept the locker room. And he made it happen. That's Bob Harlan."

Prior to selecting Harlan as the Packers president, the board's most far-reaching decision was approving Vincent T. Lombardi for the head coaching job in 1959. His selection came as a complete surprise to the people of Green Bay. Earlier, when his candidacy was brought before the Packers board, many members drew a blank at the name. One director, John Torinus, executive editor of the *Press-Gazette*, legendarily exclaimed, "Who the hell is Vince Lombardi?"

It was former Packers running back Tony Canadeo, serving on the executive committee, who brought the Giants offensive coach to the attention of then Packers president Dominic Olejniczak. "Ole," as he was known in Green Bay, was under enormous pressure to make a good hire. Just weeks earlier, fans disgusted with the team's hideous 1–10–1 1958 record (posted despite a roster studded with future Hall of Famers Paul Hornung, Bart Starr, Ray Nitschke, Jim Taylor, Jim Ringo, and Forrest Gregg) hung a dummy scrawled with Ole's name from a lamppost outside the team's Crooks Street office. The Packers had gone 37–93–2 since 1948. They hadn't had a winning season since 1947. *Hang 'em high!* was the general mood toward team management as 1959 began, and the quickest way for Ole to calm things down would be to hire a coach who met with fan approval, a man fans believed would end what some called "The Eleven-Year Famine."

And the people had their candidate. One Earl Louis Lambeau. Yes, the residents of Green Bay wanted a Curly sequel. By a 7–1 margin, according to one local poll. Never mind that the team went 3–9 and 2–10 in Curly's last two seasons before he left for Chicago. Popular radio broadcaster and sportswriter Fritz Van spearheaded a "Bring Back Curly" campaign. He pushed the notion on his radio show, peppered the media with press releases touting the strength of the pro-Lambeau movement, and organized rallies featuring former

Packers who'd played for Curly. Fritz Van and the players led crowds in rousing chants of *Bring back Curly! Bring back Curly!*

It didn't work. Though he was a former five-term Green Bay mayor used to heeding polls and pleasing constituents, Olejniczak agreed with the Gray Ghost that Vince Lombardi, and not Canadeo's onetime coach, was the man to turn the Packers around. "I don't believe it!" cried a shocked Lambeau supporter upon being informed by a newsman that Curly's candidacy was never even discussed when board members met in the Northland's Italian Room to vote on Lombardi.

Fritz Van couldn't believe it either. Looking back on the board's decision, he later wrote:

> *The Packers president, Executive Committee, and Board of Directors ruled the team's destiny with an iron fist. The highly criticized president and board [rode] out the storm our fervent forces had ignited. They alone would continue to run the show— public opinion be damned. To be sure, 1958 had been a terrible embarrassment to them, and for some there was a full decade of shame, but they were still in office and Curly Lambeau was still on the outside looking in. And that's the way they would keep it.*

## "BRING BACK BRETT! BRING BACK BRETT!"

Almost a half century after the Curly rallies, some two hundred Brett Favre fans chanted for his return inside the Lambeau Atrium at noon on Sunday, July 13. The event was organized by two Milwaukee-area brothers, mortgage bankers Erick and Adam Rolfson, ages 32 and 36. The rally's trigger—and for their new Web site

BringBackBrettFavre.com, which went live the night before and by midnight had received 7,000 hits, including some from soldiers abroad—was Friday's startling news that Favre's agent, James "Bus" Cook, had sent the Packers a letter asking for his client's release. The message was clear. And for Packer fans, it was mind-blowing. Brett Favre was telling his team of sixteen years that he'd play for someone else if they didn't want him back.

"Of course the Green Bay Packers will grant Brett Favre his release," deadpanned *Milwaukee Journal Sentinel* sports columnist Michael Hunt. "On the same day when swine take wing, that's when." Hunt's Saturday column ran beneath an alarmingly well-executed composite photo of Brett Favre playing quarterback in a Chicago Bears jersey and helmet. Seeing that image, cheeseheads across Wisconsin nearly choked on their Saturday breakfast.

Milwaukee TV news picked up the story on Friday afternoon. Stations interrupted regular programming and blitzed the development straight through the dinner hour, dispatching reporters to interview stunned Packer fans on the lakefront and elsewhere. Favre's March 6 retirement announcement had reduced some fans to tears on live TV. Reaction again was equally strong—it was another punch to the gut—but this time there were expressions of perplexity, anger, and betrayal to go with sadness. Some fans were upset with Favre, others with Packers management.

The *Green Bay Press-Gazette* spoke with a Packers fan visiting from Northern Michigan. Monica VanDrese had been dining at Curly's Pub inside the Lambeau Atrium when the "Favre wants release" news flashed onto the flat-screen TVs. The whole restaurant fell silent, said Monica VanDrese. People stared at the ESPN-tuned screens. "It was like a death in the family," she said.

While fans across the state messaged friends or watched the blanketing coverage, Erick and Adam Rolfson sprang into action. By 4 P.M. they'd purchased the BringBackBrettFavre domain name. That evening they set up a MySpace page and e-mail address to coordinate Favre fan outreach. And Saturday the brothers decided to stage a Sunday rally. They began randomly calling names in the Green Bay phonebook, inviting those who answered to gather at Lambeau to send a statement to Packers management. "Please call as many friends and relatives as you can to let them know about tomorrow," the Rolfson brothers kept repeating into their phones.

Meanwhile, down in Chicago, two other passionate Favre fans were also mobilizing. Marinette, Wisconsin-raised Tony Mars, a 32-year-old Internet entrepreneur, launched SaveBrett.net that same Friday, planning an online petition drive and contemplating a state bus tour to gather physical petitions. Across town, Milwaukee-raised political strategist, business communications expert, and crisis manager Thom Serafin, CEO of Serafin & Associates, 58, paid national polling firm We Ask America almost $10,000 to auto-call Green Bay residents on Sunday afternoon canvassing their opinions regarding the Favre dilemma. Setting out to phone everyone in the Green Bay white pages, the firm succeeded in generating 50,000 calls. Nearly 50 percent of those contacted took the survey. When residents picked up the phone, a robo-voice attributed the poll to "some Packer shareholders," then asked a series of questions including: Should Brett Favre stay retired? If Brett Favre comes back, should he be the Packers starter or a backup to Aaron Rodgers? Would you feel betrayed if Brett Favre won the Super Bowl with another team?

The (unscientific) results:
- 74% said no to trading Favre.

- 33% voted start him. 19% said backup. 17% chose "player-coach." 9% said release him.
- 54% said they would feel "betrayed" if Favre won the Super Bowl as a non-Packer.
- 18% identified themselves as Packer shareholders.

A couple days later, in an interview with the *Press-Gazette*, Thom Serafin said, "I thought I could do some good. I do a lot of these kinds of things in the world of public affairs and issues. So I thought, Why not find out just what people in Green Bay think? It's their team; it's their town."

Our twenty-first century Fritz Vans, the Rolfson brothers and Tony Mars, spoke clearly regarding their roles as fan tribunes, arguing that given the team's citizen ownership, the views of the people should not only be heard but weighed. "We want Ted Thompson to know what the people think," said Erick Rolfson at the July 13 Lambeau rally. "We want to show the Packers organization we want our quarterback back." That same day Erick told the Associated Press, "Last time we checked, Green Bay is a publicly owned franchise and is owned by the people in the community and by the stockholders." The Rolfsons called for an "emergency meeting" of Packer shareholders.

Tony Mars—who would come to deliver 6,000-plus signatures to Ted Thompson care of Lambeau Field, TV news cameras in tow; who did tour the state gathering signatures; and who even arranged for a Lambeau Field flyover during the August 3 "Family Night" Packers scrimmage, a prop plane towing a SAVEBRETT.NET banner overhead— had this to say to the *Press-Gazette* about his efforts. Note the hint of competitiveness with his Favre Web site counterparts:

"It's all about getting the fans a place to very responsibly and emphatically express their opinion. It's one thing to hold rallies and do that sort of stuff. But, really, from the political pressure perspective, what is going to put the most pressure on? I think it's systematic fan feedback, steady and consistent. From a business perspective, the fans are the customers. If we don't like the product you're putting together, we're not going to buy it enthusiastically."

Educated at Harvard and the University of Wisconsin-Madison, fluent in MBA-speak and media-savvy, the bespectacled Tony Mars, who delivered those petitions to Lambeau dressed in a Favre jersey over a blue button-down and striped power tie, a Packers ball cap completing his fashion first, could also drop the biz-school locutions for a regular-guy sports fan appeal.

"It's like making Babe Ruth sit on the bench," he said of turning Favre into a backup.

And to anyone put off by Favre's retirement back-and-forth ("They're gonna rename Brett Favre's Steakhouse *Brett's Waffle House*" was a Green Bay joke making the rounds), Tony Mars suggested that was just his hero being open and real, rather than plastic, PR-groomed, and calculated.

"Brett's a regular guy," Mars told the online magazine WisconsinNative.com. "He doesn't have ten people to comb his hair before his press conference. What we get is his honesty. When he's burnt out at the end of the season and says he doesn't want to play, we get that. We get his honesty. It's his greatest fault."

This strength of feeling is what made me mindlessly scan the cab of the Favre-stickered pickup for a gun rack. All the way up to Green Bay, local sports radio was buzzing with talk about the shareholders meeting—about how potentially unruly, even ugly, it could get.

# CHAPTER 4: WELCOME TO LAMBEAU, SHAREHOLDERS

Would Ted Thompson get booed off the stage? Would shareholders revolt?

MURPHY EXPECTS FAVRE TALK read one of the least surprising headlines in this headline-rich Summer of Favre. The July 23 *Press-Gazette* article asked new Packers president Mark Murphy to preview the meeting he would lead the following day. Just a week after his father died and two days after the funeral, the 53-year-old former Washington Redskins safety would take the stage before an expected 10,000 diehard Packer fans at arguably the most tumultuous time in the team's long history. Consider what Murphy was facing, just seven months into the job. A bitterly divided fan base. Public scorn for team management ("The Three Stooges," some fans had dubbed Murphy, Thompson, and McCarthy). And Brett Lorenzo Favre—one of the most popular figures in modern professional sports, a significant driver of team and town revenue, a future first-ballot Hall of Famer and indestructible signal-caller coming off a 4,155-yard, 28-touchdown regular season for a squad that just missed making the Super Bowl—wanted to return . . . *and the team was saying no*. What's more, the icon had started to talk to the national media and what he was saying was in no way intended to put smiles on the faces of Packers brass.

The worst of it? There was no clear way forward. No matter what, some percentage of Packer Nation would be alienated. Some damage would be done to reputations, to the Packers brand, perhaps even to the team. Murphy just had to hope the damage was limited, and more short-term than long. "Nightmare in Green Bay" was the headline of Peter King's mince-no-words piece in *Sports Illustrated* on July 7. "What began as a snit has become a barroom brawl, spilling into the street," observed *New York Times* sports columnist William Rhoden two days later. "Things only can get messier and weirder from here," predicted Tom Pelissero in the *Press-Gazette*.

"How did a situation that was once so beautiful turn out to be so ugly?" lamented Michael Hunt in a July 12 *Journal Sentinel* column, setting aside his trademark spiky humor. "That's one of the unfortunate byproducts of this royal mess. It's splitting along loyalty lines of Favre fans vs. Packers fans. . . . Why did it ever have to come to this, icon player against icon franchise? It was much simpler around here when Favre was the Packers and the Packers were Favre."

As Hunt tapped out these words, Mark Murphy was on a Packers team bus headed back to Green Bay from Marinette. He'd spent four days on a "Packer Tailgate Tour" with his predecessor Bob Harlan and three players: wide receiver James Jones, running back Brandon Jackson, and offensive lineman Jason Spitz. Wherever they went— Fond du Lac, Stevens Point, Janesville—the Favre questions kept coming. "We've had five-year-old kids ask about it," Murphy remarked during a stop at Fond du Lac High School. The tour was in Tony Mars' hometown of Marinette, fifty miles north of Green Bay, when the news came. It had reduced Curly's Pub to funereal silence but here just unleashed more fan and media queries. Sidestepping the Favre questions, Murphy paused for a quick comment before climbing back onto the Packers bus.

"Obviously, today there were developments in our situation with Brett Favre," he said, indicating that the team had just released a statement. "The only other thing I could add is that I've worked closely with Ted Thompson and Mike McCarthy on this, and they have my full support."

Here's the team statement, released just after 4 P.M. Friday:

*The Green Bay Packers are aware of the latest developments regarding Brett Favre. Brett earned and exercised the right to retire on his terms. We wanted him to return and welcomed him back on more than one occasion. Brett's press conference and subsequent conversations in the following weeks illustrated his commitment to retirement. The finality of his decision to retire was accepted by the organization. At that point, the Green Bay Packers made the commitment to move forward with our football team. As a retired player, Brett has the option to apply for reinstatement with Commissioner Goodell. If that were to occur, he would become an active member of the Green Bay Packers. As always, the Packers will do what's right and in the best interest of the team. As with all Packer greats, Brett's legacy will always be celebrated by our fans and the organization, regardless of any change in his personal intentions. Brett and Deanna will always be a part of the Packers family.*

A good team statement, as far as statements go. Which isn't very far.

"How do you not accept Brett Favre back?? He is f*****g Brett Favre!" posted one incredulous fan on the *Journal Sentinel* Packers blog moments after the statement went up. An asterisk-aided profanity cursing Ted Thompson followed.

"The Cheese can win it all with Brett," posted a fan on the *Press-Gazette* blog. "Without him they will sink into oblivion. You remember that place, don't you? It was the time between Bart and Brett. Strap in, folks, it is going to be several decades of continued Vikings dominance."

Clearly more than a statement was needed. The day after Favre signaled he was open to playing in another city, Ted Thompson, target of the F-bomb from the asterisk-wielding fan, ended a week of silence and met for one-on-one interviews with beat reporters, some sessions lasting more than thirty minutes. Opening up more than usual, the ex-Houston Oilers linebacker raised in small-town Texas acknowledged the depth of the Favre puzzle and its unprecedented challenges. "We're struggling to do the right thing. We don't have all the answers," the white-haired 55-year-old told Tom Silverstein of the *Journal Sentinel*. "This is a hot-button issue that surpasses anything I've ever gone through," he said to the Associated Press. "I think it's okay to let people know there is some vulnerability here," he told the *Press-Gazette*. "This is a gut-wrenching time."

Packer fans had never quite heard their GM speak this way before; "stoic" was the word Thompson had used in his interview with Silverstein to characterize how the public perceives him. "This Is A Gut-Wrenching Time" topped a *Press-Gazette* story. Other accounts highlighted the hard news Thompson made. And he definitely made some. In these July 12 Lambeau interviews, the GM presented a timeline of the team's communications with Favre since January. He confirmed that the Packers would not be granting Favre an unconditional release. And to Tom Silverstein, he said point-blank, "Aaron Rodgers is our starting quarterback."

When asked a follow-up question, the 2008 *Sporting News* NFL Executive of the Year refused to take the bait. With his best journalistic poker face Silverstein wrote, "Thompson declined to answer which quarterback gives the Packers the best chance to go to the Super Bowl."

The AP's Chris Jenkins asked Thompson to square *Rodgers is our starter* with *We're not releasing Favre*. Referring to the three-time league MVP and future Hall of Famer, Thompson replied, "We've never said that there couldn't be some role that he might play here."

Oh, the howls in Packer Land. The general manager didn't use the dreaded B-word—backup—but the media was happy to use it for him. Witness this surreal *Journal Sentinel* headline:

THOMPSON, MCCARTHY, SAY FAVRE CAN REJOIN TEAM AS BACKUP

This alone, posted online Saturday, may have been enough to provoke Deanna Favre to e-mail her friend Greta Van Susteren of Fox News that very evening. Van Susteren—an Appleton native, University of Wisconsin graduate, and Packers shareholder—happened to be in her office that night working on a story related to the death of former Fox News colleague and ex-White House press secretary Tony Snow. Then the e-mail from Brett Favre's wife arrived. It said, "Brett wants to tell his side of the story." By Monday morning Van Susteren was in Bus Cook's Hattiesburg, Mississippi, office interviewing the grizzled quarterback.

The outrage in Camp Favre (commonly understood to include Brett and his wife, his brothers Scott and Jeff, and his mother Bonita) stemmed not only from this face-slap notion of No. 4 returning as a backup mere months after posting a Pro Bowl (and near–Super Bowl) season spangled by a league third-best 95.7 passer rating, Favre's finest since 1995. It was also the Thompson timeline. Though the Favre contingent didn't accuse the Packers of out-and-out fabrication, they felt the GM's chronicle packaged and slanted things in a way meant to make Favre look bad and the team look better in the eyes of the public. And their concerns were understandable, as some of the timeline details were definitely far from image-enhancing.

Thompson's account suggested that just three weeks after Favre choked up during his March 6 retirement press conference while telling the world he didn't have "anything left to give," he changed his mind, spoke to Mike McCarthy, and was persuasive enough that McCarthy and Thompson secured a private jet from a Packers board member for an April 1 flight to Hattiesburg. There they'd meet with Favre and plan his return for a seventeenth Packers season.

Yes, the *I'm retiring—not* aspect would look a little goofy, but with some care, they could finesse it. Management figured most fans would give Favre a mulligan. In the end, all that would matter to Packers fans was they'd have their world-class QB back to lead the same group of guys who in early 2008 nearly met the Patriots for a Super Bowl sequel to their '97 clash. In a detail of almost comic specificity, the timeline had McCarthy "leaving for evening Mass" Saturday night, March 29, when Favre called to say, in essence, *Sorry, Coach, no need to come to Hattiesburg.* "We were all set for them," Thompson told Silverstein, "but Brett called back and said that he and Deanna had a long talk about it and they were going to stick with their original decision."

Favre had a different version of the story. And he told it to Greta Van Susteren that Monday morning in Hattiesburg. Some of what he said didn't make the televised clips, as show producers trimmed a few moments in which Favre worked through the chronology's nitty-gritty. But the full hello-to-goodbye transcript Fox News provided reporters has Favre confirming that he experienced "second thoughts" three weeks after he retired, and that he shared these thoughts with former teammate and current Packers offensive line coach James Campen. Favre told his interviewer that late in March he got a call from McCarthy, who, according to Favre, said, "*Hey, I heard you and James were talking . . . Do you want to come back?* And I said, 'Boy, that's tempting but I just—I don't know.' And [McCarthy] says, *Tell you what . . . Ted and I are going to be at the* [NFL] *owners meeting* [in Palm Beach]. *What do you think we stop there in Hattiesburg?* I said,

'Well, this is Friday, let me think about it, Mike, and I'll just call you back before you guys leave.'"

Favre told Van Susteren he called McCarthy the next day, reaching him just before church, shortly after the coach talked to his daughter in Austin, Texas, a background detail Favre retained. "She hurt her back playing basketball or something," Favre told Van Susteren. "That's something I remember. If they want to do timelines, I'll do it."

According to Favre, he then told McCarthy, "Mike, don't worry about coming by here, I'm still not 100 percent committed." Favre insisted to Van Susteren that the purpose of the Hattiesburg visit was not to put a handshake to an understanding he had earlier reached with McCarthy over the phone. Did Favre "renege" on a comeback deal, as the *Wisconsin State Journal* put it? No way, Favre said. "I never called them and said, 'Hey, I'm coming back, fly down here.'" Favre again insisted to Van Susteren, "I did not call them before they went to [the owners meeting] and say, 'I'm playing.'"

Packers management, for its part, never publicly discussed the timeline again, and when asked to respond to Favre's rebuttals, would only say they stood by their account.

Not surprisingly, Packer fans were less than thrilled by this "changing his mind about changing his mind" business. "The Packers are doing the right thing by exposing Favre for the Prima Donna he is," one fan posted to the *Journal Sentinel* Packers blog. But a second cheesehead felt uneasy. "Thompson shouldn't play this game," he wrote. "He's making it into a gossip game. Maybe Favre changed his mind depending on who talked to him last, but don't send the press a tally of the notes he kept in conversations. I think Thompson has done a great job bringing in new talent but he appears to be terrible with public relations."

As it happened, Favre used the same word—"tally"—to express to Van Susteren his displeasure with the Thompson/McCarthy approach, adding, "It's almost like they're keeping score."

Neither party disputed the fact that the GM visited Favre in Hattiesburg on May 6 while scouting down south shortly after the draft. They had lunch "on the veranda," Thompson said, and "had a long talk," one in which Favre "hinted" he might end up changing his mind, but went no further.

Favre's version? Thompson seemed to have stopped by principally to ask, *You think it would be okay if we dismantled your locker and sent it to you?* Which Favre naturally interpreted as Thompson encouraging him to stay retired. Not taking the hint, Favre claimed that as they walked to Thompson's car he told the GM, "Ted, I just want to give you a heads-up that, hey, you know, say July rolls around, I wake up and I say, Man, I made the wrong decision. I have to play. Or maybe it's June or whatever. [I] just want you to have a plan. And he said, 'Okay. Don't worry about that.'"

There is also no disagreement about the wording of a key Favre statement made in a June 20 phone call between Favre and McCarthy. At one point in the forty-five minute conversation, Favre said, "Give me my helmet or give me my release." This comes from McCarthy himself, who also spoke to the Associated Press on that explosive media Saturday at Lambeau. "Even so," the AP story related, "when McCarthy asked Favre if he was ready to make a 100 percent commitment to football—an issue Favre had brought up in his retirement news conference—the answer still was no." Now it wouldn't take a Favre loyalist to point out that "Give me my helmet" sounds a lot like the statement of a man who wants to play, and for the Packers. But the coach insisted he didn't hear the thing he needed to hear, which was full commitment.

# CHAPTER 4: WELCOME TO LAMBEAU, SHAREHOLDERS

According to Tom Silverstein, that was likely the crux of the matter, the answer to the question, "Why didn't the Packers take Favre back?" In a valuable July 16 *Journal Sentinel* blog post, Silverstein drew on the insights of "two long-time football gurus who will remain nameless" because he "wasn't interviewing them as much as picking their brain[s]." Both of his sources said the Packers must have made an internal decision that they were better off with Rodgers. And what would convince them of this? "Not physical skills," Silverstein wrote. "Rodgers doesn't have the arm Favre does, the body Favre does or the experience Favre does. The only conclusion is that they're concerned about [Favre's] commitment for the season . . . It has to be the reason the Packers are moving on. They can't predict Rodgers will be better than Favre this year, and they already showed they value Favre more than Rodgers when they agreed to take him back in April."

Silverstein went on to highlight part of Favre's exchange with Van Susteren where she asked him point-blank if he was "100 percent certain" that he wanted to play football. He seemed less than 100 percent, his replies halting as she pressed for a firm, unequivocal yes. The exchange ended with Van Susteren asking Favre whether he is physically up to the challenge of playing again. Still sounding unsure, he replied, "I think so, yes. I mean, I think I'm ready."

Of course Favre did go on to play. But the helmet he donned was not that of the Packers. And couldn't that be part of why he sounded so unsure in his exchange with Van Susteren? He is in the middle of processing a grim reality. If he does play, it likely won't be for the Packers. His verbatim answer to Van Susteren's "You're now 100 percent certain you want to play?" question was in fact, "Where is a different story. Yes." Favre was coming to grips with the fact that one of the great stories in modern sports—Favre and Green Bay; the kid from Kiln, Mississippi and the people of Titletown – seemed destined to include a chapter dominated by fracture and bad blood.

For Packers fans, Favre's interview with Greta Van Susteren made grim, gripping, dolorous viewing. Favre wore a light gray T-shirt and a large sports watch on his left wrist. His hair was cut short, he had his customary four-day stubble, he had been out in the sun a little. Behind him in Bus Cook's office signed footballs sat on display shelves. Viewers learned Favre had already been to the high school field that morning throwing passes to teenagers, his current workout regimen. Favre was personable, measured, understanding, upset, sarcastic, simmering, proud, humble, fair, unsure, sad, determined, hurt, and a little lost. He was angry but not volcanically so. He didn't seem to be vying, or angling for anything. Mostly he seemed concerned that his relationship with Packer fans, especially those in Green Bay, was suffering. He seemed worried that a situation "once so beautiful," as Michael Hunt put it, was in danger of being lost, if not lost already. When Van Susteren pointed out that Wisconsin fans were rallying on his behalf, Favre replied that he'd heard this, and you could see genuine gratitude in his eyes.

Fox News apportioned the interview over three nights of primetime cable on a hot July week in the midst of a heated presidential campaign. They promoted it heavily, knowing a coup when they saw one. "Can't envision being anywhere else . . . haven't envisioned playing with anyone else," Favre says early in the interview. Later he expresses concern that Packer fans will think he's a "traitor" if he ends up playing somewhere else. He insists to Van Susteren that Green Bay is the only place he wants to play, but claims McCarthy told him in their June 20 phone call that playing for the Packers "was not an option" because the team, owing to concerns about his level of commitment, had "moved on."

And though both coach and quarterback agree that at some point Favre demanded his helmet, Favre also tells Van Susteren that he began the call by saying, "Mike, I'm *thinking* about coming back" [emphasis mine]. As for McCarthy ruling out a Favre return, the coach would tell the media on July 26 in his pre-training-camp press conference, "My recollection of that conversation and his is a little different. It's not like Brett Favre called me up and I said, 'No way, you can't come back.' That wasn't the case."

\* \* \*

A huge billboard advertising Brett Favre's Steakhouse rises beside the highway just before the Fox River, greeting Lambeau-bound visitors driving up from the south. The Favre-stickered Ford F-150 drove past the sign, crossed over the river, and exited the highway. It shot across Holmgren Way just as the light turned red but I had to stop. I followed the Favre Mobile for sixty miles but lost it a mile from Lambeau. I'd look for it there.

Holmgren Way is a reminder of yet another famous Packers divorce. In 1999, just six weeks after the Green Bay suburb of Ashwaubenon, within whose boundaries Lambeau Field sits, renamed Gross Avenue in honor of the coach who took the Packers to two consecutive Super Bowls, Mike Holmgren resigned to become the head coach and general manager of the Seattle Seahawks. People up here have long memories. Nine years later, two local radio DJs asked the village board to temporarily change the street's name when Holmgren came back to town for the Packers–Seahawks playoff game in January 2008. The board declined. But Appleton's WAPL-FM came up with some temporary monikers anyway: Traitor's Trail, Defector Drive, Benedict

Arnold Boulevard, Holmgren Way Overrated, and last but not least, If I Can't Be GM, I'm Going to Take My Ball and Go Home Highway.

Now you see why Favre worried fans might call him a turncoat.

Oneida Street is the gateway to Lambeau from the south. It could be mistaken for a commercial strip anywhere in suburban America. There's an Arby's. An Ethan Allan. A FedEx/Kinko's. About the only edifice that'll put a song in cheesehead hearts is, of all things, a McDonald's, its trademark roof painted Packer green instead of its customary red.

After eight or nine blocks of franchised Americana come a couple blocks of small, neat ranch homes on your left with more service and retail joints opposite. Just when you're wondering if you're really approaching pro football's mecca, stadium towers rise on your left, green steel and red brick, faced with the Packers G, and gleaming light standards, and an enormous video scoreboard. Lambeau Field! Face-lifted and enlarged but still majestically retro. Pigskin's premier castle, Lambeau doesn't need a palatial approach. Palatial approaches are for kings and imperialists. This is Green Bay, Wisconsin. Here there is splendor in the ordinary. The backyards of small homes abut the stadium's Oneida Street parking lot, their low chain-link fences with latched gates the only barriers between Packers property and citizen lawns.

I pulled into the Oneida lot. Here and there Packers shareholders drank beer in the mellow sun. It was 9:30 A.M. The meeting would kick off at 10. Would the hops loosen any tongues? "Obviously, there's an issue that's foremost in most people's minds," Mark Murphy observed to the *Press-Gazette*, not needing to utter the name Favre. "Like anything else, you anticipate what may or may not happen. [But] at the end of the day, it's a business meeting."

Murphy wouldn't be banking on Packer shareholders complying with NFL owner etiquette rules prohibiting "criticizing" of one's team, behavior subject to fines and even league suspension. Asked about precisely this issue back in November 1997—Packer shareholders criticizing the Packers—NFL spokesman Greg Aiello told the *Business Journal of Milwaukee* that "in a theoretical sense, those rules apply to all owners. We would reserve the right to enforce the rules at any time." Aiello hastened to add, however, that the NFL had no plans to hunt down vociferous Packer citizen-owners, like, say, those who call a sports-radio show advocating the deep-frying of GM Ted Thompson. "Packer shareholders have always been subject to those rules," Aiello pointed out. "These people are just out to have fun and own a piece of their home team." Except back in 1997 the team still wanted Brett Favre under center.

The tailgating was modest this morning. People drank and grilled bratwurst behind and before every tenth or twelfth vehicle. Unlike on Packer game days, there was no rowdy filling of the aisles, no dancing, no people playing beanbag or plastic horseshoes, no speakers blasting music. Not a single raised voice could be heard, whether in anger or support. I headed for the Oneida Nation entrance gate, passing a huddle of guys in their forties and fifties gathered before a rented champagne-colored minibus with tinted windows. They held plastic bottles of Miller Genuine Draft. They were dressed in belted khaki shorts or chino pants, with white, green, or yellow golf shirts. Two wore penny loafers, one a pair of docksiders. One said, "We're playing hooky" into his cell phone while another took a sip of beer and opined, "I say you go with the guy who gives you the best chance to win. I don't understand this whole youth movement." None of the men were wearing Favre jerseys, but that was deceptive. On my way into Lambeau I counted twenty such jerseys out of roughly a hundred shareholders on the stadium walkway. It was a small sample size, but still, one out of five shareholders was sending a sartorial statement to management. Oh, and moments earlier I'd spotted another Favre jersey. It hung in the cab of a hunter green Ford F-150 with a FAVRE 4 PRESIDENT bumper sticker. So yeah, in case you had any doubt, the Sheboygan guy in the Favre Mobile was a shareholder, too.

Just outside the Atrium, I met an Elvis impersonator wearing a foam cheesehead bearing the motto FAVRE IS KING over his dyed black pompadour. His name was Tom Rakowski. He'd driven up from Wind Lake, thirty miles southwest of Milwaukee. I asked Tom how he thought the meeting would go. In a non-Elvis voice, he replied, "I think Ted's gonna get an earful." Then this fan of Favre and Elvis posed for some photos snapped by smiling fellow shareholders.

There was a solemn hush in the bright airy space of the Atrium. People were staring at a huge banner three floors up. It hung above a square yellow banner reading WELCOME SHAREHOLDERS. Beneath it were permanent banners honoring Don Hutson, Tony Canadeo, Ray Nitschke, Bart Starr, and Reggie White, the five Packers greats whose numbers the team had retired. THANKS 4 FOR THE MEMORIES! 1992-2007 read a white script message across a picture of Brett Favre, his arms raised in triumph, index fingers pointed skyward. That's what everyone was staring at. You didn't thank someone for the memories unless they were gone.

I entered the stadium bowl and joined a crowd later reported as numbering 9,500 people. "This is a business meeting. Proper decorum is required," intoned a voice coming from two large portable speakers. The business aspect of the gathering registered the instant you entered Lambeau this day. Red-vested greeters handed each shareholder a fancy financial report for "Green Bay Packers, Inc.," printed on cardstock. One page listed 2007 and 2008 income statements. The facing page conveyed balance sheet information via words like "unamortized," "accrued," and "payable." Sitting on a bleacher bench in warm sunlight, I squinted through sunglasses at the financials. After player salaries, administrative expenses, marketing costs, etc., the nonprofit company netted $23 million in the fiscal year ending March 31, 2008.

But few of the shareholders seated here in the east bleachers were studying the financial report. They were waiting for something, anything, to happen. It was almost eerily quiet. A black stage topped by a royal blue canopy sat on the unlined emerald grass at approximately midfield, near sideline. Atop the stage stood a wooden podium, backed by about twenty chairs. The air was muggy, already almost 80 degrees. "I hear you've had a little controversy up here," joked a shaven-headed out-of-town newspaper photographer in a black SAPP ATTACK T-shirt. He was shooting from up in the stands instead of down at field level with the other dozen photographers and video operators. Shareholders chuckled nervously. Yes, a little controversy. You could say that. Suddenly something did happen. From those portable speakers came Brett Favre's quavering voice, speaking words from his tearful March 6 retirement speech.

"I don't think I've got anything left to give, and that's it," Favre said. "I know I can play, but I don't think I want to." ("Then why are you coming back?" cracked one bleacher wag.) Once again we heard Favre say his career was over, as he felt he could no longer give 100 percent, and that was the only way he knew how to play. Once again we heard him salute the people of Green Bay. "When I laughed and when my family laughed, they laughed," Favre said. "When I cried, they cried. When I cheered, they cheered. . . . It was a perfect fit for me. . . . Southern boy from Hancock County who had big dreams, no different than any other kid, to play here, and there's no better place to play. . . . As they say, all good things must come to an end."

You could have heard a pin drop in the stadium. Shareholders stared into space. So it really was over. Favre really wasn't coming back to the Packers. The team's playing of his goodbye speech was the closing of a door. It worked like a collective reality check for 9,500 fans. Here in the stadium where he'd etched so many remarkable memories over sixteen years, the door had just closed on Brett Favre.

The stage was still empty. The hush ended when a 2007 NFL Films Packers highlight reel titled "The Young and the Fearless" filled the video screens. We watched Ryan Grant running. Greg Jennings catching. Tramon Williams returning. But of course the old fella had a pretty good year as well. So there was No. 4, both onfield and miked-up on the sidelines and in the locker room. "In a season where Brett Favre seemed to break records with every throw . . ." the narrator intoned as Favre tossed career touchdown No. 421 to Jennings, passing Dan Marino's mark. There was playful Brett, shaking hands with teammates on the sidelines, saying over and over, "Put 'er in the vice!" And there was reinvigorated Brett, encircled by fellow Packers, saying, "I love playing with this team so much. I do. Let's keep this going." Shareholders watched with thoughtful, melancholy faces. This film was opening a big ol' can of bittersweet.

Cheers briefly erupted as the review reached the "snow-globe" playoff game against Seattle. But the crowd hushed a moment later when the narrator said, "In a game for the ages, Brett turned in a play for the ages" over footage of No. 4 executing a stumbling, underhanded shovel pass to Donald Lee in swirling snow. No one had to say it. That guy improvising in a storm wanted to come back and make some more clutch sandlot magic, but his team was just thanking him for the memories.

Moments after the film ended, Murphy, Thompson, and McCarthy came out of the players' tunnel, all three in dark suits. With them were members of the Executive Committee and others in upper management. Many carried bottles of water. They filed in procession across the brilliant grass toward the canopied stage, a black mesh scrim rippling gently in the breeze at stage rear.

"Looks like a funeral," said a Packer-capped, tank-topped woman sitting behind me with three forty-something female friends. "I don't remember it being this somber before."

Modest applause greeted Murphy as he took the podium. Just that morning in the *Press-Gazette* a letter read: "Note to Mark Murphy. Saying you support Ted Thompson and Mike McCarthy is not enough. Your job as president is to make sure the corporation runs smoothly. That means settling differences. Bob Harlan would never have let this continue to be played out in the media. He would have gotten the parties together and got it settled. Please do your job."

All right then.

Mark Murphy was no stranger to professional challenges. A look at his résumé makes it clear why the Packers board found him so appealing, a candidate impressive enough to assume the mantle worn so well and so long by Bob Harlan. The 6-foot-4 redhead with a passing resemblance to Conan O'Brien boasts a mix of elite athletic, legal, business, and leadership experience. After eight years of playing safety for the Washington Redskins, for whom he won a Super Bowl, led the league in interceptions in 1983 and earned Pro Bowl and All-Pro selections, he took a job as assistant executive director of the NFL Players Association. Simultaneously he earned a law degree from Georgetown to go with his MBA in finance from American University. He later worked for four years as a trial attorney at the U.S. Department of Justice. A Buffalo-area native who received serious interest from Major League baseball scouts while in high-school, Murphy came to the Packers after four-plus years as athletic director at Northwestern.

Prior to that, he served as AD at his alma mater, Colgate, for eleven years.

"I'm Mark Murphy, your new Packers president," Murphy said cheerily into the podium mike. Exactly sixty-five seconds later, after welcoming the crowd and providing a quick meeting overview, he bolted to the topic on everyone's mind like an NFL safety racing to make a tackle. A head-on tackle. "I do want to comment on the current situation regarding Brett Favre," Murphy remarked, causing shareholders to look at each other and mouth, Wow.

His face magnified on the scoreboard's video screens, age lines and some weariness showing around his eyes, Murphy forged onward. "Obviously it's a very sensitive situation that will have long-term ramifications for the organization," he said. "It is a football decision, but because of the magnitude of the impact that the decision could have, I have been actively involved. Brett will always be remembered as one of the finest players to play this game. We want to be fair to Brett, but we also must act in the best interests of the Packers."

"Then bring back Brett!" one woman yelled, above a mix of cheers and boos.

If Murphy heard, he gave no sign.

"The next item on our agenda will be the national anthem," Murphy said seconds later. He introduced a local woman in a sun dress who sang in a trilling, old-timey way. Shareholders stood, a number of them white-haired, many with hands on hearts, all gazing toward a huge American flag flying atop the stadium. For at least a couple minutes, 9,500 Packer fans were all facing in the same direction, forming the same words, singing the same tune. Unison.

Brett Favre was never mentioned by name again, at least not by anyone on stage. The icon was consigned to the preliminaries, to the meeting's housekeeping, to the pregame before the anthem. And it worked. The subsequent proceedings were free of any real disruption.

Ted Thompson received more cheers than boos. Some shareholders rose to their feet and applauded. Like Murphy, he got one item out of the way quickly. "We are a family," Thompson said. "Families sometimes disagree. But we will always remain a family. This is a very difficult time. We ask God for the strength and wisdom to do the right thing." He then commenced his football report, a straight-ahead, position-by-position breakdown peppered here and there with dry humor. Referring to McCarthy, the GM told the crowd, "Mac promises no injuries during training camp." And he singled out veteran cornerbacks Charles Woodson and Al Harris for praise as level-headed professionals, his implication being that some of their positional league brethren were not as firmly grounded. "If you guys have ever been around defensive backs, they're not normal people," quipped the former NFL linebacker.

When he got to the signal-callers, the snowy-haired Texan with the steady gaze stated matter-of-factly, "We have three young quarterbacks on the roster." The remark drew scattered boos from the shareholders. "Easy," Thompson responded. As in, pipe down, folks.

By way of conclusion, Thompson spoke of Packers culture. "Our guys are good players and good people," he said. "They enjoy living here. This team does not talk trash. We don't try to make predictions. You don't see a lot of newspaper articles with us talking about how well we're gonna do. We go out and play. We're all proud to be Green Bay Packers. This concludes my football report and I thank you very much."

"Great report, Ted!" Murphy exclaimed as he returned to the podium, then joked, "I do have to take issue with your comment about defensive backs, but I can take this up with you later."

Coach McCarthy followed Thompson. The 44-year-old was addressing Packers shareholders for the first time. Gripping the podium with both hands, his husky frame clad in a navy coat and tie instead of his customary Packers sweatshirt or windbreaker, this Irish Catholic son of a firefighter, cop, and bar-owner in a steel mill Pittsburgh neighborhood (like Packers director emeritus Bernie Kubale, McCarthy used to help out in his dad Joe's tavern) appealed with his plainspokenness. "I'm not tryin' to throw around a bunch of positive B.S.," he said in a flat Steeltown accent, positive pronounced *paw*-sitive, "but we had a great offseason program."

"Defense is the starting point of the Green Bay Packers," the 2007 Motorola Coach of the Year continued, triggering a few raised eyebrows among shareholders. McCarthy was a former quarterbacks coach (Packers, 1999) and offensive coordinator (Saints, 2000–2004; 49ers, 2005) who in 2007 delighted offense-loving Packers fans by deploying five-receiver sets. Was he implying that Rodgers was no Favre and the defense would have to compensate? "Handling success," he told the crowd, would be the defending NFC North champion's biggest challenge. "I also told the team back on March 17 to prepare for obstacles and distractions," he added. That was the closest McCarthy came to touching on the Favre situation.

Report concluded, McCarthy strode to the stage stairs, descended to the field, and headed back across the grass for the tunnel, a thick black binder beneath his arm. His no-nonsense exit sent a clear message: With training camp three days away, he had work to do. The crowd rose, giving Mac a standing ovation.

From this point, the meeting became very . . . corporate. A succession of people in business attire spoke words like "proxy" and "bylaws" and "convened." It's not often you'll hear "Do we have a quorum?" uttered inside a football stadium. A Treasurer's report was delivered, and an audit committee report, and a community relations committee report. Revenue pie charts appeared on the scoreboard. And organizational trees. And flow charts. Mark Murphy read a mission statement. And a "True North" statement.

Ninety minutes after it began, the 2008 Packers shareholders meeting ended. Attendees streamed back into the Atrium. Murphy and Thompson were scheduled to mingle and take questions. But before much got underway, a guy started shouting at the top of his lungs, "Brett Favre is a Packer! Brett Favre needs to play for the Packers!"

Camera operators from local TV stations, ESPN and the NFL Network rushed over. Finally some action! The shouter was a fireplug in his twenties dressed in a Favre jersey, knee-length basketball shorts, black high tops, and a black ball cap over dark hair held back in a ponytail. "If Brett Favre can play, it must be in Green Bay!" he began chanting. Veins throbbed in his throat and temples. Spittle flew. A half dozen other guys in Favre shirts joined the chant, including Erick and Adam Rolfson, but that was it. The uproar died within a minute. The ponytailed fan then bellowed, "Green Bay and Brett Favre foreverrrrrrrr!" drawing out that last syllable dramatically, operatically, before stomping from the media scrum and marching for the doors.

Cameras came down. Shareholders went back to munching food. The brothers Rolfson collected pro-Favre signatures on clipboards, did some media interviews. A couple of security guards observed from a dozen feet away, arms folded, walkie-talkies jutting from the pockets of their crisp, dark blazers.

Ted Thompson never joined the Atrium crowd. But an hour later he did make himself available in a fourth-floor hallway outside the Packers offices. The majority of those who approached him were supportive, though one teary-eyed woman in a pink Favre jersey said she was "very distressed." A male fan predicted the Vikings would go after Aaron Rodgers in game one because he'd be "the weakest link in the chain." Tom "Cheesehead Elvis" Rakowski had a moment with Thompson. So did Erick Rolfson. Dressed in flip-flops, Packers shorts, and a Favre jersey, Rolfson told the GM he respected him, but added, "We just want the voice of the fans to be heard, Mr. Thompson." "I think they are," Thompson replied.

Down in the Atrium, Mark Murphy smiled easily during some exchanges with shareholders, a bit tightly during others. He shook hands, signed autographs, patiently answered questions. A number of fans expressed condolences for his father's passing. Many, though not all, affirmed support for the team's position on Favre. One tall, clean-cut forty-year-old in khakis and a blue button-down said, "Mark, if winning is one of your core objectives, as you stated during your presentation, do you really think Aaron Rogers gives the Packers a better chance than Brett?"

"We do think we will win with Aaron," said Murphy equably.

Standing beside Murphy and the skeptical shareholder was a fifty-something man a head shorter than both. He wore a small mustache, brown plastic glasses, running shoes with socks, and a white ball cap bearing the name of an Atrium eatery, BRETT FAVRE'S TWO MINUTE GRILL. When his turn came to meet the new Packers president, he nervously mumbled something. "Thank you," Murphy responded pleasantly. "We're aware of the problem."

As the man walked away, he related the exchange to a woman about his age and height dressed in a Favre ball cap and shirt. She socked him on the shoulder. "You waited all that time and asked him about parking?" she exclaimed. "Honey," the man answered, "he got enough Favre stuff."

# CHAPTER 5:
## THE MAN FROM CHICO

**A**ARON RODGERS ALMOST gave up football. Not a single Division I college program offered him a scholarship. He'd enjoyed two of the greatest seasons for a high school quarterback in the history of Northern California football, but it didn't seem to matter. At 2,200-student Pleasant Valley High School in Chico, a town of 80,000 people some ninety miles north of Sacramento, Rodgers threw for 4,421 yards in just two years, breaking multiple school records and notching the sixth-most passing yards in Northern Section annals—a stat even more impressive when you consider the first five quarterbacks all played three seasons to his two. He understood Chico was no recruiter's idea of a prep football hotbed, but still, the passing numbers, the game tape, his coach's energetic advocacy—wouldn't that give him a shot?

And if the Northern Section didn't turn out a yearly bumper crop of blue-chippers like down in Southern California, it remained a healthy state assemblage of 75-plus schools from eight leagues in an area stretching from just north of Sacramento all the way to Oregon, a broad inland swath more than two hundred miles top to bottom. Granted, some schools were small, from sleepy hamlets like Weed and Hayfork and Gridley, a few high up in the Sierras. But Chico was the largest of the Northern Section communities, a burgeoning university town twenty miles east of Interstate 5 and a few miles west of the Sierra foothills. Each autumn the Pleasant Valley Vikings played solid conference competition, most notably crosstown rival Chico High in the Almond Bowl. The Panthers always had some top players, including a quarterback to watch called Brett Ratliff.

The University of Illinois, then coached by Ron Turner, did invite Rodgers for a visit but in the end the best they could do was say he was welcome to walk on. They had concerns about his 6-foot-2, 180-pound frame, and wondered about his tendency to throw 50-yard passes on a line rather than loft them to receivers with touch. Maybe he still had too much baseball pitcher in him. As a kid and early teen Rodgers was a standout hurler in Oregon and Northern California, playing for teams in a half dozen towns as his family moved around, dominating up to the regional level on all-star squads. He returned to the mound his senior year at Pleasant Valley and lost just one game, his fastball routinely registering in the high 80s. Once he hit 91 mph on the gun. There was no doubt Rodgers had an arm.

When after weeks of waiting it became clear that no Division I scholarship was going to materialize, the disappointed 18-year-old thought about pursuing a legal career. Aaron Rodgers, attorney-at-law—it had a ring. He also thought about minor-league baseball. But football was his true passion. It always had been. To play quarterback in the NFL had been his dream for as long as he could remember. It began when he was just three years old. His mother Darla remembers him glued to the TV as a pre-schooler, watching his favorite team, the San Francisco 49ers. "He had an extraordinary interest in the game from the start," she told the *San Francisco Chronicle* in 2004. When the Rodgers family—Darla, husband Ed, boys Luke and Aaron; a third son, Jordan, came along a few years later—got home from church, Luke might run outside to play with neighborhood kids but Aaron would make a beeline to the TV and flip on the Niners game, his big blue eyes barely blinking for the next four quarters. His favorite player was Joe Montana. By age five, he could name every player on the 49ers roster. By seven, he could rattle off stats. Passes caught. Yards per carry. Sacks. Touchdowns-vs-interceptions.

Ed Rodgers, a 6-foot-4 former Chico State offensive lineman who later played three seasons of semi-pro football, built a miniature wooden football field for his young son. Aaron spent hours before the board moving around little toy football players, executing plays he'd designed himself. He kept his plays in a handwritten playbook complete with Xs and Os, movement arrows, and an emphasis on passing routes. Ed, who worked a variety of jobs in Aaron's youth before settling on chiropractic medicine, loved to bring his two sons outside to play a game they called "Pass Patterns." With Ed calling the signals, one son raced down the street as wide receiver while the other played cornerback. "It got real competitive," Ed told the *Chronicle*.

Only 5-foot-6, 123 pounds when he started high school, Aaron's physique didn't exactly scream top-flight quarterback material. But Pleasant Valley football coach Sterling Jackson couldn't help but notice the kid's arm. He could whip a ball—football, baseball, tennis ball, softball—like nobody's business, for speed, accuracy, distance, you name it. He just needed to grow a little, and Sterling Jackson was betting he would grow. Not only because the kid's dad was 6-foot-4 with a lineman's build. There was also the matter of Aaron's *feet*. At the end of those skinny legs were size 12 canoes. It was one of the first things you noticed when you saw him—and you tried not to chuckle. Coach Jackson said with those outsized dogs, the 14-year-old Rodgers would have made a great circus clown.

During high school, Aaron's feet would grow another two shoe sizes. He'd sprout eight inches, and add a solid sixty pounds. His hands grew, too, big enough to palm a basketball and put an iron grip on a football, something that a few years down the road helped him log the best time ever in a Packers quarterback ball drill. The drill required Rodgers to lean over and circle the football around a lower leg, switching hands, gripping, re-gripping, as fast as he could. In ten seconds, Rodgers whipped the ball around a lightning-quick thirty times. When Rodgers holds a football, reported Lori Nickels in the *Milwaukee Journal Sentinel*, his ring finger reaches the second-to-last lace, his pinky rests near the bottom with his pointer on top, and his thumb wraps around nearly half the ball. It's a good-sized paw—especially helpful in frigid temps when that iced pigskin gets as slippery, Nickels noted, as a frozen Butterball turkey.

Of course a cold-weather mitt would have come in handy had Rodgers joined the Fighting Illini and played in the Big Ten. But rather than going 2,000 miles east to Champaign for a walk-on chance, the quarterback came around to a notion pushed by Butte Community College football coach Craig Rigsbee that he stay close and play for Butte, the campus just twelve miles south of Chico. Rigsbee made frequent visits to the blue-painted Rodgers house at the end of a dead-end street lined with portable basketball hoops. He'd turn the corner to find the Rodgers boys chucking a football up and down the block, or launching three-pointers, or firing a baseball from glove to glove. The junior college coach and the three-sport Pleasant Valley star came to an agreement: Aaron would play for Butte in 2002, but had Rigsbee's blessing to move on after one year if he finally got an offer from a Division I school.

Granted, the Butte College Roadrunners weren't the Fighting Illini, 2001 Big Ten champions and Sugar Bowl participants, but as junior college football programs went, they were right up there. In his dozen years at the helm, Rigsbee's teams were 92–21, regularly competed in the NorCal Conference championship game, and, crucially for Rodgers, had a noteworthy record of pipelining players to Division I programs. Nearly a dozen Butte College alums were currently playing in the NFL or CFL, including Cowboys offensive lineman Larry Allen, a ten-time Pro Bowler. Coach Rigsbee had become something of a specialist in developing players who didn't get sufficient exposure in high school or needed more size or who needed to improve their mechanics.

So Rodgers shelved ideas of the law and minor-league baseball and joined Rigsbee at Butte. Ed, Darla, Luke, and Jordan had to drive just minutes to watch Aaron tear it up at Cowan Stadium. Behind an offense geared around his passing gifts, the Butte Roadrunners went 10–1 his first year, won the NorCal championship, and ended the season the second-ranked junior college team in the nation. Rodgers threw 28 touchdowns, just 4 interceptions, and rushed for 7 more scores, and at season's end collected both the conference and regional MVP awards. Ten of his touchdown tosses went to 6-foot-5 sophomore tight end Garrett Cross, a former Chico High standout (later signed as an undrafted free agent by the Packers). It was Cross who first drew the interest of California coach Jeff Tedford. In 2002, his first year at Berkeley, the former Oregon offensive coordinator transformed a woeful 1–10 team into a respectable 7–5 squad. Tedford didn't normally do much recruiting of junior college players, but having lost a bunch of starters to graduation, the Pac-10 Coach of the Year was hoping to sign a tight end as he looked ahead to the 2003 season. Rigsbee sent him tapes of Garrett Cross, and Tedford liked what he saw. He also liked the kid throwing passes to Cross. He'd never heard of Aaron Rodgers, but the freshman had good mechanics, good arm strength, and accuracy. In a game against Shasta, the poised 18-year-old threw a school-record six touchdown passes. Visiting Butte, Tedford worked out Garrett Cross by having Rodgers throw to him in Cowan Stadium. The upshot? Both Chico natives became Golden Bears in '03. Aaron Rodgers finally got his Division I offer, and Coach Rigsbee was as good as his word, telling his freshman star, "You were meant to do this. Go get 'em at Berkeley."

When Rodgers looks back on his year at Butte, he is grateful not only for the coaching and mentoring of Rigsbee (now the school's athletic director), but also for the experience of learning to mesh with and lead a diverse group of players, most of them older than himself (Rodgers wouldn't turn 19 until December), all keeping their dream of big-time football alive. Unlike many community college coaches, Rigsbee recruited players from all over the country. And he took pride in harmonizing an eclectic roster.

"I was exposed to a ton of guys with different backgrounds and cultures," Rodgers told *USA Today* just days before his first start as a Packer in September 2008. "Guys from Florida, Texas and Canada. Guys at 25 and 26 years old, still trying to make it. My center was 25. Our free safety, the team leader, was 22 and had been to jail. To be, at a young age, able to get guys to play with you and raise their game, that was a huge lesson. Probably the best year of football for me, as far as personal development. I learned a lot about myself as a leader."

This ability to blend with different teammates, to build relationships and bridge gaps within a locker room—a true asset for a quarterback—is something Rodgers believes grew out of his early experience in a family that frequently changed addresses in his first twelve years, finally putting down stakes in Chico for good in 1996. Before Pleasant Valley High, he attended eight different schools, so he got used to walking into a room as "the new guy," always having to make new friends. And the family of five didn't have much money in those days, teaching Rodgers another lesson, one he values today. "As an NFL player," Rodgers observed to *USA Today*, "you're given a lot of stuff for free and have big contracts. But I learned at a young age to be content with the stuff we had and to be content with who I am."

Who he was by game five of the Cal-Berkeley 2003 season was the new Golden Bears starting quarterback. For good luck that day—and for many a Cal start thereafter—Rodgers wore a Joe Montana T-shirt "borrowed" from his brother Luke beneath his jersey. As chance would have it, Cal's opponent as the Rodgers Era began in Berkeley was Ron Turner's Fighting Illini, the program that gave him a look but never a scholarship. Extra motivation? Sure. In Rodgers' return visit to Champaign he completed 20 of 37 passes for 263 yards, throwing one touchdown and no picks to lead Cal to a 31–24 victory. Pleasant Valley coach Sterling Jackson said he got a call from an Illinois coach after the game admitting they may have been a little off in their assessment of Rodgers' potential.

A week later, Rodgers took the field against third-ranked USC Trojans and converted 18 of 25 passes for 217 yards and two touchdowns, scoring a third with his legs. Just a year earlier, Rodgers had been leading Butte Community College against teams like Feather River and Diablo Valley. Now—just 19 years old—he was taking snaps on consecutive weekends as starting field general against Illinois and USC, whose 2003 roster included players like Matt Leinart and Reggie Bush, LenDale White and Lofa Tatupu. The QB's heady ride was not without some bumps, however. With the Cal–USC score tied at 21, Rodgers was pulled from the game for the quarterback he'd replaced, junior Reggie Robertson. With Rodgers watching from the sidelines, Robertson led the Bears to one of their all-time greatest victories, stunning USC 34–31 in triple overtime.

Rodgers didn't stay on the bench for long. A week later, Tedford sent the transfer out to start against Oregon State. Playing injured, Rodgers endured the worst game of his college career, going just 9 of 34 for 54 yards, including a pick and a fumble. "I'm embarrassed," he said after the game. "I embarrassed my family, myself, and my team." What he didn't emphasize were his injuries. In that start against Illinois, he'd fractured the index finger on his throwing hand. Against USC he winced beneath his helmet with every snap. By the time he came out of the game, his ankle, ribs, and left knee were also battered. "He was banged up," said Tedford when asked why he went with Reggie Robertson after Rodgers threw a "pick 6."

But following the debacle against the Beavers, Rodgers bounced back—and never looked back. By season's end, he'd posted one of the greatest years by a sophomore quarterback in Pac-10 history, amassing 2,903 passing yards, second-most ever by a Golden Bear. Five times he passed for more than 300 yards. He threw 19 touchdown passes against just 5 interceptions, and rushed for another 5 scores. He opened his Cal career with a streak of 98 consecutive passes without an interception; later he strung together another 105 throws without a pick. In games he started, Cal went 7–3, clinching their first bowl berth since 1996. Against archrival Stanford in the "Big Game," Rodgers broke Jim Plunkett's Big Game total-yardage record with 414 all-purpose yards, guiding the Bears to a 28–16 victory. He was even better in the Insight Bowl against Virginia Tech, going 27 of 35 for 394 yards and no picks, throwing for two touchdowns and rushing for two more. California won the shoot-out 52–49.

His Insight Bowl performance went into the record books as the third-highest offensive output by a single player in Cal history. What makes it even more impressive—what makes that whole first season at Cal more impressive—is that he played every game with a torn anterior cruciate ligament in his left knee. As reported for the first time in September 2008 by the dean of Packer beat reporters, Bob McGinn of the *Milwaukee Journal Sentinel*, Rodgers had been taking the field with a partially torn ACL for four consecutive football seasons, beginning his junior year of high school. As a sophomore at Pleasant Valley, he tore the ligament playing pickup basketball. Doctors said he'd either need reconstructive surgery or, at minimum, he'd have to wear a brace and strengthen all the surrounding support, including his hamstring, thigh and calf. Choosing the latter route, he "rehabbed like crazy," Rodgers told McGinn, and wore a stabilizing brace during his two record-setting seasons at Pleasant Valley. Might the knee have been a reason why he didn't get any Division I offers? Rodgers and his father say no. The ACL tear, Ed Rodgers told McGinn, was known to very few people. "Everyone kind of kept it under the table," said the elder Rodgers. "Aaron didn't want anyone to know about it."

When Aaron Rodgers got to Butte, he decided to lose the hardware, believing Division I schools wouldn't recruit a knee-braced quarterback. He played that season support-free—and excelled.

But he hurt the knee again early in preseason practice at Berkeley, likely tearing some scar tissue formed after the initial injury. Cal doctors gave him an MRI. "You have a torn ACL," they said afterward. "You need surgery." He told them he'd played three years without trouble. They said he needed to wear a brace. He told them he'd prefer to skip the brace. Only after the knee flared up in that start against USC did Rodgers resolve to have postseason reconstructive surgery. Just days after his monster bowl game against the Hokies, orthopedic surgeon George Thabit of Redwood, California, transplanted a cadaver's ligament into Rodgers' left knee, a procedure known as a ligament allograft.

Though Packers head coach Mike McCarthy and offensive coordinator Joe Philbin told Bob McGinn they didn't know Rodgers had played four full football seasons with a torn ACL, general manager Ted Thompson confirmed the QB's knee history became known to NFL teams at the 2005 combine. But Thompson said he didn't think it had much bearing on draft decisions.

This was the "injury report" available to teams at the combine:

*2003— Joined California in fall drills with a pre-existing left knee injury. Re-injured knee during fall camp, but did not miss any time. His knee was again injured in the Southern Mississippi game (8/30), but he played with the injury throughout the season. Underwent surgery to repair the ligament damage on 1/07/04, sitting out spring drills while recovering.*

At any rate, Rodgers says the knee has never been an issue after the allograft.

Back behind center with the repaired knee in 2004, Rodgers started every game for Cal, powering the Bears to a 10–2 season, their best in fifty years. He led the Pac-10 with a 154.35 passing efficiency rating, converting 66.1 percent of his throws for 2,566 yards and 24 touchdowns, third-most in school history. Looking ahead to the game against top-ranked USC, the defending national champion, Rodgers was determined to be on the field in crunch time instead of watching from the bench like he had in 2003. Playing before 90,000 fans in the L.A. Coliseum, Rodgers began the contest *en fuego* and stayed that way for a long while, tying an NCAA record by completing his first 23 passes. Factor in 3 completions from the previous week's Oregon State outing, and the California quarterback had connected on 26 straight passes, breaking the NCAA record of 24.

Boasting the nation's highest-scoring offense (48.7 points per game through early October), No. 7–ranked Cal outgained USC 424–205 in total yards. On the debit side, they gave up six sacks, botched a snap on a punt attempt, and lost two fumbles, one by Rodgers, one on a punt return. Still, the Bears were only down 24–17 when they took over on their 35 with 4:31 to go. Rodgers marched his team to the 9-yard line of USC, his last big completion going for 17 yards to prime target Geoff McArthur. But in the red zone things broke down. Pressured into an incompletion on first-and-goal, Rodgers was then sacked for a 5-yard loss. Hurried on third down, he missed McArthur in the end zone. After a Cal timeout, Rodgers threw incomplete on fourth-and-goal from the 14. Receiver Jonathan Makonnen stumbled on his cut (he'd been bumped or held, Rodgers said later), Rogers threw to a spot, and the ball just eluded a diving Makonnen.

USC ran out the clock to preserve victory.

Three months later, two weeks after Texas Tech upset Cal 45–31 in the Holiday Bowl (Rodgers' line: 24 of 42 for 246 yards and one TD pass—to former Butte teammate Garrett Cross), Rodgers decided to skip his senior year and declared for the 2005 NFL draft. There were at least two good reasons to do so. One was financial. Prognosticators were saying Rodgers might go No. 1. If so, an eight-figure contract would follow. The second reason goes back to that T-shirt Rodgers wore under his Cal jersey. The loaner Joe Montana tee. As luck would have it, the San Francisco 49ers owned the first pick in the draft and desperately needed a quarterback.

The makings of a storybook turn in the Californian's life were in place.

All he ever wanted for Christmas and birthdays as a kid, Rodgers told Matt Barrows of the *Sacramento Bee* days before the draft, were 49er-related items. A Jerry Rice jersey. A Joe Montana poster. "The 49ers bordered on obsession," wrote Barrows of young Aaron's fandom. Even his mom was a huge Niners fan. As a girl, Darla used to accompany her parents to games at old Kezar Stadium in Golden Gate Park to watch the Dick Nolan–coached 49ers of the late '60s.

And who was the new coach of the current Niners? Nolan's son Mike. The Rodgers family was desperately hoping that the circle would complete itself with Aaron going to San Francisco. Rodgers himself couldn't hide his excitement at the idea of being picked by the Niners. "Being from Northern California," he told Barrows, "I'd love to play for the 49ers. They were my childhood team."

It didn't happen. And it didn't happen in an excruciating way. One of six draft prospects invited to sit in the green room at the Jacob Javits Convention Center in New York City on April 23, Rodgers had to watch San Francisco select quarterback Alex Smith of Utah with the No. 1 overall pick. Rodgers politely smiled and applauded as the twenty-year-old Smith got up, walked to the podium and accepted a Niners cap and jersey from then NFL commissioner Paul Tagliabue.

And that was just the beginning.

With more than thirty family members and friends in the Javits audience, Rodgers was soon the only player left in the green room. Auburn's Ronnie Brown, Michigan's Braylon Edwards, Cedric Benson of Texas, and Miami's Antrel Rolle all had their podium moment by the eighth pick. The draft kicked off at 11 A.M. Rodgers didn't get his turn at the podium until 3:44 P.M., nearly five hours later.

With live look-ins provided via ESPN, Aaron Rodgers became the "21st-century sports world's poster child for enforced patience," wrote Michael Silver of Yahoo! Sports. If Samuel Beckett was a football fan, he might have written a play about Rodgers' experience in the green room. *Waiting for Tagliabue.* Toward the end, it was just ESPN and a convention center cleaning crew in the room, along with Rodgers, his agent Mike Sullivan, and his parents Ed and Darla. Wilma McNabb, Donovan's mother, ducked in to offer emotional support. "It's gonna happen," she told the family. "Yeah," said Darla, "but they're starting to clean up the tables in here."

Rodgers' final minutes in the room were evoked in an April 2009 column by Andrew Brandt, former Packers vice president in charge of contracts, for NationalFootballPost.com, a lively, insider-driven NFL Web site he helped found in August 2008. As Rodgers sought to stay positive in New York, 800 miles away in a war room above the Lambeau Atrium GM Ted Thompson told Brandt to get Mike Sullivan on the phone as they might be selecting his client with the 24th pick. Brandt dialed the number he had for Sullivan. In the Javits Center green room, Rodgers' cell phone went off. He grabbed it and said, "Hello?" A voice on the other end of the line said, "Mike?"

"No," said Rodgers, "this is Aaron. Who's this?"

After Brandt explained who he was, Rodgers passed the phone to Sullivan, a moment Brandt watched on ESPN. With Rodgers and his anxious parents looking on, the agent spoke softly through clenched teeth. "Andrew, you taking him?" he asked. Doing as Thompson instructed, Brandt told Sullivan, yes, they might be picking Aaron, but needed a few more minutes. As the agent would have guessed, Thompson was working the phones to see if a high-value trade could be had for the pick. When nothing materialized, Thompson gave Brandt a nod, adding that he should remind Sullivan they'd be negotiating a contract for a No. 24 pick, not one based on Rodgers' elevated pre-draft projections. Seconds later, the Packers vice president, a Stanford graduate, had the "privilege of putting an end to [the] misery" of a California quarterback Brandt had twice watched lead the Golden Bears to victories over his Cardinal in the Big Game.

When the selection was announced, the relieved Javits crowd gave Rodgers a standing ovation. Suzy Kolber of ESPN embraced Rodgers both before and after her interview. Another hug and words of encouragement came from former 49ers safety Merton Hanks, now an assistant director of operations for the NFL. And after a grinning Rodgers held up a Packers jersey at the podium, Commissioner Tagliabue leaned over and said, "Good things come to those who are patient." They were words Rodgers would return to more than once up in Green Bay.

Why did Rodgers slide? The short answer is that the 49ers preferred Alex Smith and none of the subsequent twenty-two teams on the clock felt an urgent enough need to draft a quarterback. Or perhaps *this* quarterback. Not even the Browns? No, Cleveland used the No. 3 on wide receiver Braylon Edwards. What about Tampa Bay? The Bucs went with a ball-carrier, taking Auburn's Cadillac Williams with the fifth pick. With the sixth pick, the Tennessee Titans selected cornerback Adam "Pacman" Jones. Aaron Rodgers had his own take on the process, one voiced in the Javits media room shortly after being chosen by Green Bay and mere moments before answering "provolone" when asked to name his favorite cheese.

"Things get a little screwy on draft day," said the quarterback.

Was there a Tedford factor—a concern that Jeff Tedford–coached quarterbacks such as Akili Smith, Kyle Boller, and Joey Harrington failed to deliver when they got to the pros? Certainly Bob McGinn of the *Journal Sentinel* encountered such concern while researching his pre-draft article "Reasonable Doubt: Former Pupils of Rodgers' Tutor Have Struggled." McGinn, who's made an art of consulting with NFL scouts to get candid player assessments before the draft, asked thirteen scouts to rank their top five college quarterbacks. The scoring system gave 5 points for first place, 4 for second, etc. Eleven scouts ranked Alex Smith No. 1 with 63 points. Only two gave Rodgers the nod, his score 53. The next five quarterbacks were Auburn's Jason Campbell (25), Akron's Charlie Frye (17), Georgia's David Greene (16), Arizona State's Andrew Walter (13), and Purdue's Kyle Orton (7). And McGinn noted that one of the scouts who picked Rodgers said he would not place the Cal QB in the same class as the 2004 draft group led by Eli Manning, Philip Rivers, and Ben Roethlisberger.

"They all throw the ball the same way," said another scout of Tedford-coached quarterbacks. "What have those guys done? Nothing." A second opined, "They're all so mechanical, so robotic. They're so well schooled. I think Rodgers is in that same mold." An unnamed NFC personnel director was just as blunt: "I think Rodgers has a good chance of being a bust just like every other Tedford-coached quarterback. . . . He gets sacked a lot. Brett Favre can change his release point and find different windows. This guy is very rigid mechanically."

Rodgers himself was asked to comment on this storyline at his March 17 pro day workout in Cal's Memorial Stadium. "I don't really believe in the Tedford Curse," he told the assembled reporters. "It's been mentioned by a few teams, the Packers in particular."

Ah, the irony.

Here's more irony: Mike McCarthy was the 49ers offensive coordinator in 2005, hired by Mike Nolan not long after Nolan got the head coaching job. McCarthy was at the Berkeley workout, and had lunch with Rodgers afterward (along with Nolan and 49ers quarterbacks coach Jim Hostler). Rodgers thought the lunch went well, telling NFL.com, "I really enjoyed my time with the two Mikes."

By all accounts, Rodgers had a terrific pro day. Calling it "an extraordinary air show," Michael Silver, then writing for SI.com, raved that "Rodgers put nearly every pass on the money, showcased his scarily quick release and displayed equal helpings of touch and arm strength. He delivered picturesque deep balls with a seeming flick of the wrist, gunned deep outs and skinny posts that landed in the perfect spot and showed off his flawless footwork and fundamentals."

Watched by seventy hawk-eyed NFL talent evaluators and another 150 reporters and teammates in the stands, Rodgers threw 92 balls to four Cal receivers, including tight end Garrett Cross, all but one on target. With millions of dollars on the line and, quite possibly, a chance to play for the 49ers hanging in the balance, the 21-year-old found a groove. Some observers said it even reminded them of the rhythm he had displayed that day against USC, when he completed 23 straight passes. It was a different kind of pressure at pro day, but it was pressure all the same.

That 11–2 pro-Smith vote reported by Bob McGinn notwithstanding, other NFL reps gave the edge to Rodgers. Twelve days before the draft, Ira Miller of the *San Francisco Chronicle* surveyed the head coach, offensive coordinator, quarterbacks coach, GM, or top scout from eighteen different NFL teams. His group favored Rodgers based on "arm strength and experience in a pro-style offense at Cal." While Rodgers, like most NFL quarterbacks, operated under center and threw mainly out of the pocket, Alex Smith played primarily in the shotgun formation at Utah. "On a scale of 1-to-10, if you rated Smith's arm as a 7, then you have to give Rodgers' arm a 9," one evaluator told Miller. "What Rodgers lacks in mobility and athleticism, he makes up with his arm." Another liked Rodgers for what the first guy found lacking. "[Rodgers] throws well on the run and has nice movement in the pocket against the rush," he said. "I loved his mobility. If things don't go right, he's going to create something with his feet." *"Rodgers threw the ball deep as well as anybody I've seen throw the deep ball in a workout,"* said a third scout in Miller's survey of NFL evaluators.

The italics are mine. I use them because Rodgers' ability to throw long was questioned by other football experts. "Rodgers doesn't have the long ball in his arsenal," ESPN's Merril Hoge said before the draft. Even the team that drafted Rodgers seemed to have concerns. "Packers quarterbacks coach Darrell Bevell acknowledged throwing the deep ball isn't one of Rodgers' strong suits," reported the *Green Bay News-Chronicle* after the draft. "I graded him below-average on his deep-ball accuracy," Bevell said, "but we'll be able to work on that."

What did the 49ers think?

"They [both] did a very good job with all the mechanics," said head coach Mike Nolan a week after watching Rodgers and Alex Smith work out on consecutive pro days, "but Aaron is certainly ahead of Alex because of the style of offense he ran. . . . There's a polish in Aaron." Nolan was quick to add there's more to NFL quarterbacking than good footwork and arm angle, however. "Mechanics are all fine," he said. "Jeff George was mechanically pretty damn good."

Snap. Jeff George was the Colts' golden-armed No. 1 pick in 1990, a sensational workout quarterback, a talent who could rifle a football a country mile through a hanging tire but who slipped a little in game situations and had what could best be described as a journeyman's career in the NFL. Mike Nolan went on to say—cagily, even a touch cryptically—that should the Niners opt to use their No. 1 pick on a quarterback, they would focus on "intangibles" and put considerable weight on the ability to "keep drives alive."

Were "intangibles" what ultimately led the Niners to pick Smith over Rodgers? They definitely were a factor. Certainly there was little difference in terms of the quarterbacks' physical "measurables." At the 2005 NFL Combine, both men blazed the 40-yard dash in 4.71 seconds, a time, to give it some context, faster than 18 of the 20 college quarterbacks clocked at the 2009 Combine. Smith beat Rodgers in the broad jump by three inches (leaping 9'5"), but Rodgers had a better vertical leap (34 ½ inches to Smith's 32 inches). Their hand size was identical at 9 ⅜ inches. Rodgers bench-pressed 340 pounds to Smith's 335. Edge to Smith in the three-cone drill, his circuit completed in 6.83 seconds to Rodgers' 7.39. To be fair, though, Rodgers had to haul those size 14 dogs around the cones.

But Smith, an economics major who graduated from Utah in just two years, was known for his brilliance. At the 2005 combine, he scored a 40 on the Wonderlic intelligence test, vaulting him over every current and recent NFL quarterback save Drew Henson, who tallied a 42. Not that Rodgers was far behind; his 35 was a superb showing, putting him behind Eli Manning (39) and Tony Romo (37) but ahead of Tom Brady (33), Philip Rivers (30), Peyton Manning (28), Drew Brees (28), and Jay Cutler (26). Curious what Brett Favre scored? A 22.

So Smith had brainpower. And there were other intangibles that Niners coach Mike Nolan prized. For a revealing *Sports Illustrated* column published on May 2, 2005, Peter King spoke to both Nolan and Mike McCarthy a week after the draft. Nolan hailed Smith's "work ethic," admiring Smith's habit of using Sunday, a college player's day off, to break down film with his coaches. "Then there was a bunch of little things," Nolan told King. "Like when Alex talks to his mother, he says *yes, ma'am.* And what we put him through in his workout at Utah."

Nolan sent McCarthy to Salt Lake City with instructions to put Smith through a tough, unscripted workout. On a windy day in early April, McCarthy handed jump ropes to Smith and two Niner wide receivers, Arnaz Battle and Brandon Lloyd, acting as aides-de-camp. "You want to see how he'll accept coaching and if he'll compete," McCarthy told King. "So I told them they'd jump rope for 30 seconds on the right foot, 30 on the left, and 30 on both." Smith's eyes "got a little wide" at the assignment, McCarthy said, but "he competed. He got right into it." Later McCarthy had Smith do a "crazy ball-handling drill," in King's phrase. Smith was game.

The rest is history. Smith signed a six-year, $49.5 million contract with $24 million guaranteed. Since then he's been injured often and underwhelming when healthy. After a dreadful rookie year—1 touchdown, 11 interceptions, 11 fumbles—Smith took every snap for the 7–9 Niners in 2006, tossing 16 touchdowns against 16 interceptions for 2,900 yards. In 2007, he and Coach Nolan fought over the seriousness of a shoulder injury. The spat went "nuclear," wrote a *San Jose Mercury News* columnist. In 2008, Smith lost his starting job to journeyman J. T. O'Sullivan. A broken bone in his throwing shoulder ended Smith's season. That October, Mike Nolan was fired as Niners coach and replaced by Mike Singletary. In March 2009, the last two years of Smith's contract were restructured.

In July 2005, Aaron Rodgers signed a five-year contract with the Packers worth $7.7 million. Escalator clauses would bump his salary up if he replaced Brett Favre and took more than 50 percent of the team's offensive snaps. He probably wasn't holding his breath. So yes, when Rodgers slid down that draft board, millions slid with him.

I asked Rodgers if that experience added any fuel to his NFL fire. Though he's been asked this question once or twice before, he answered with energy and dispatch.

"Yes, absolutely," Rodgers said. "It's one of the reasons I play with a chip on my shoulder. Honestly, all along I thought I had the talent. Coming out of high school no one in Division I would take a chance on me. But I always believed I could play at that level. When there's a perception that I can't do something, it does act as extra motivation. On April 23, 2005 Merton Hanks came up to me as I was leaving the green room and said, 'I played my whole career with a chip on my shoulder and you should do the same.'"

As a devoted fan of the George Seifert–era Niners, Rodgers would have instantly known what Hanks was talking about. An All-Big Ten cornerback out of Iowa, Hanks ran a dismal 4.74 40 at the 1991 combine, dooming him to a draft slide of his own. He didn't come off the board until round 5, and only then because Niners' defensive backs coach Ray Rhodes had clocked him running 4.58 during a private workout. The time still wasn't great for a cornerback, but it was good enough for a day-two selection. Converted to safety, Hanks went on play in four straight Pro Bowls and win a Super Bowl.

In the media room after being drafted, a reporter asked Rodgers whether he felt "angry" about his board tumble. "Obviously a little disappointed not to be number 1," the quarterback replied deftly, "but I mean I'm going to a situation which is going to be great for me to play behind the best quarterback in the league and be in a storied franchise. For me the biggest thing, as I was telling my family and my agent, is I want to go to a place that wants me and they definitely do."

Rodgers was a little less politic talking to ESPN Radio.

"A lot of teams passed on me," he said. "And when my time comes to play, I'm going to show those teams they made a mistake. And if we play the 49ers at their place, I'm going to make sure the entire city of Chico comes down there to watch us beat them."

Unfortunately for Rodgers, his time to play didn't come until 2008, after three years of patiently waiting. And even as the opportunity was at his fingertips, it suddenly seemed in danger of being snatched away—a *Groundhog Day* experience of waking up one summer morning once again backup to Brett Favre. For a few more weeks, patience, hope, and self-belief, were needed. When finally the chance to play arrived, it did so to a great extent courtesy of a coach who'd been part of the first team to pass on him in 2005. One of the "Mikes."

Was there any tension between McCarthy and Rodgers when they came together a year later in Green Bay? "We went through that probably in the first conversation I had with him after I got here," McCarthy told *USA Today* in September 2008. "It was important that I addressed that." McCarthy added he's since told Rodgers he possesses more athleticism than he'd gleaned watching game tape of the quarterback at Cal.

"The past is the past," Rodgers told the paper. "I'm in Green Bay and I love my situation."

Aaron Charles Rodgers has large, deep blue eyes—that's the first thing you notice about him, at least when he's in one of his clean-cut incarnations. The eyes and dark hair give him a resemblance to the actor Jake Gyllenhaal. When he wears his brown hair long, center-parted with a goatee, he could pass for an alt-rocker in the Dave Grohl of Foo Fighters mold.

The L.A. Dodgers–rooting Rodgers likes to change up his look—not out of vanity, mind you, but for fun, to keep things light, to get laughs from teammates. Call it anti-vanity. He's rocked a preseason lumberjack look, a Fu Manchu, and a big ol' '70s 'stache, which was, he told *USA Today*, "A tribute to all the great people in history who had mustaches . . . Tom Selleck and Chuck Norris and Jesus and Ron Burgundy," this last a reference to Will Ferrell's San Diego TV newsman in *Anchorman*. But the QB's crowning effort came in August 2008, a couple weeks before his first NFL start, when he unveiled what he called his "Civil War look," complete with mutton-chop sideburns. He went whole hog on the transformation, even buying a replica Union soldier uniform and cap at an Army-Navy surplus store before boarding a team plane bound for Denver. The spitting image of a whiskered Yank who might have fought in the Battle of Bull Run, he managed to keep a straight face. Up and down the plane, teammates cracked up.

"No way he gets that from me," said his training-camp roommate Aaron Kampman. "He needs to get a real hobby," cracked Coach McCarthy when *USA Today* asked for comment.

It's a change from backwoods prankster Brett Favre (hot sauce in teammates' cereal, fake rats in lockers, doe urine on Rodgers' jersey to provoke an olfactory version of a bitter-beer face), but no less playful. Rodgers' humor is more absurdist, though, less *Animal House*, zanier, and often pokes the most fun at himself. If John Madden, in his retirement, ever decides to pick an All-Monty Python Team or give a Peter Sellers Award, Rodgers can expect a nod.

To nobody's surprise, Rodgers has also carried on a goofball tradition started by former Packers backup quarterbacks Doug Pederson and Craig Nall. Prior to every game, the Packers photograph that week's team captains on the sidelines. Copies go to these players and another copy hangs outside the head coach's office. Pederson and Nall made a habit of wandering into frame so they could appear in the background. Like Forrest Gump or Woody Allen's Leonard Zelig, they were always in the shot. Rodgers loves this kind of nuttiness, so he decided to take it up a notch. In 2006, he mimed a different facial expression or gesture in each week's photo; in one of them, he stares skyward, pointing at something overhead. In 2007, he worked variations on a theme, appearing in each week's photo doing something with two fingers, like pretending to hold a cigarette or seeming to secure an earpiece as if he's a security guard. Once his teammates caught on, that was often their first question to him after a game: Dude, did you make the captains' photo?

"He's just different," said wide receiver Greg Jennings to *USA Today*. "Not in a bad way. He's very spontaneous . . . That's just his own little thing." A guy described by his old prep football coach Sterling Jackson as "borderline-nerdy" starting high school is the same individual Jackson saw on television Super Bowl weekend 2005 displaying silky communication skills with supermodel Marisa Miller, host of that year's "College Football All-Star Challenge." (Rodgers easily won the speed, strength, agility, and accuracy contest, defeating fellow quarterbacks Kyle Orton, David Greene, and Heisman Trophy–winner Jason White.) It's the same person who commits to memory the birthdays of friends and teammates like he's learning a new Packers play (or maybe the way he memorized 49er stats as a kid), always making a point of saying happy birthday. It's the same Rodgers whose favorite all-time song (the somberly beautiful "Lightning Crashes" by the band Live) is about the least playful tune ever written, and who when asked for "dating advice" by a celebrity interviewer at a sports awards show spoke of being raised in "a Christian family" and saluted the stable, 27-year marriage of his parents. He's a guy who cites the Bible as his favorite book while praising *The Shack*, a popular 2007 Christian-themed novel about a man whose faith has been tested by the murder of his four-year-old daughter and subsequent period of "Great Sadness," a parable of grace and redemption that asks and seeks to answer, "Where is God in a world so filled with unspeakable pain?"

Aaron Rodgers is someone who, when you ask what Kampman is like as a training-camp roommate, answers first with a joke ("He's great—he doesn't snore real loud"), then grows more serious. "He's got a lot of wisdom," the quarterback says of his friend, pausing for emphasis. Then he adds, referring to the summer of 2008, when it seemed his chance to play might vanish before it began, "Aaron was great when all that stuff that was going down. He's a wise man."

Cheery, humorous, and friendly in person, Rodgers switches easily into a more philosophical mode if a question deserves thought, a trait also showing respect for the questioner. When a topic threatens to bring up strong emotion, he answers with fewer words, letting his tone convey the feeling beneath. For example, some pro-Favre fans booed Rodgers during training camp in 2008. Did he hear the booing?

"Yes."

That was it. The word hung in the air.

"Are you looking forward to next year, a training camp without drama?"

"Yes. Definitely."

"Are there things you do to distract yourself, to get your mind off something?"

"There's not a lot I can distract myself with. Talk to friends, family. Music helps a little. Playing guitar."

Rodgers loves music. Three acoustic guitars and a Taylor electric populate his Green Bay house; he picks them up and plays "all the time." He sings often, too, around the house, and even plays some tunes in the Packers training-camp dormitory at St. Norbert College in De Pere, ten minutes south of Lambeau Field. Apparently he's decent enough that Packers teammates, including roomie and quarterback mauler Kampman, don't tell him to put a sock in it.

Rodgers has been playing guitar for five years now, and works on his chops with help from an instructor at a Green Bay music store. He also plays some piano, having taken a year of lessons in high school after a firm nudge from his mother Darla. Along with the guitar coaching, he wants next to learn more about music's foundations. "I'd like to take some music-theory courses," says the quarterback. "I want to go a little deeper—get into the theory of music, instead of just learning strum patterns on a guitar or chords on a piano or whatever."

One of his best friends from Chico, Jeff Schneeweis, also happens to be a talented indie-rock songwriter, guitarist, singer, and producer for a band called Number One Gun. When Rodgers gets back home, he likes to spend his evenings taking in one of the bands making up Chico's thriving music scene. During his days, he takes advantage of the California town's beautiful setting. Chico is a park-filled, bicycle-friendly place with nearby snow-capped mountains and foothill forests. On the outskirts of town, there are river gorges and swimming holes. The region is kissed by sun most days of the year, its climate Mediterranean. Rodgers hikes Bidwell Park with its creeks and rock formations, or heads up into the Sierras.

Whenever he can, whether at home or elsewhere, he hits the links. He loves golf, and hopes to soon knock a stroke or two off his best score of 74. He also loves sweets. Asked to name his holiday meal of choice, he says, "Desserts. Anything with vanilla in it. Or chocolate chips." Pizza and ice cream are his favorite foods. Now you know why McCarthy had to get on Rodgers to eat a bit better and lose some weight in 2006 after the coach arrived from San Francisco. They "butted heads" about this in the beginning, to use the quarterback's phrase, but before long Rodgers got with the program. In 2008, he was down to 217 pounds from 228, and his body fat had dropped from 15 percent to near 10.

I asked Rodgers what he would be doing if he wasn't playing football. "I'd probably be in the military," he said. Which branch? "Well, my grandfather was in the Air Force," the quarterback replied, "but I'm a little afraid of heights. So something on the ground. Army or Marines."

Rodgers accepts the word "studious" to describe his approach to pursuits like football and music. Another irony in the Rodgers/Smith saga is that Rodgers is as much of a playbook grind and scholar-of-defenses as the former No. 1 pick, and would have been just as happy to spend hours with 49ers coaches on his off day poring over plays and schemes. "I've always been a big note taker," he said, and credits his coaches at Berkeley for helping him elevate his football study. "I was fortunate to play for Coach Tedford and have George Cortez as my offensive coordinator. They're both all about attention to detail. They taught me how to study film, how to analyze and break things down, how to beat up every single aspect of a play."

When the 21-year-old got to the Packers, he became, in a sense, a scholar of Favre, realizing he could do a lot worse in his continuing quarterback education than to take a course in No. 4. "I'd stick my head in there when [Favre was] talking in the huddle and listen to what he's saying and listen to him in practice," he told Tom Silverstein of the *Journal Sentinel*. "I'd watch him like a hawk. . . . Anytime he'd open his mouth in meetings to a receiver, I listened. I wrote it down. I have journals from the first three years, notes and notes. Notes from computers I've printed out . . . stashed in my filing cabinet."

In 2007, the last year he and Favre were teammates, Rodgers was tasked with scouting cornerbacks the veteran QB would be facing in the next game, his findings compiled in a Wednesday report Rodgers delivered before coaches and fellow quarterbacks. He'd study game tape Monday and Tuesday and draft his analysis Tuesday night. Taking to the assignment, Rodgers soon expanded his weekly reports into detailed evaluations of defensive schemes and player tendencies. As Silverstein reported, the third-year quarterback's study paid off nicely in the November 29 game against Dallas when Rodgers was thrust into action in relief of an injured Favre. Driving the Packers to the Dallas 8-yard-line, Rodgers instantly recognized a Cowboys red-zone defense he'd diagrammed and presented during the week. The end result was a touchdown pass to Greg Jennings.

Does the analytic Rodgers ever worry about information overload?

"No, I don't think in my case there's a potential for that. Maybe a guy who's been in the league ten years and seen just about everything, that could be an issue. But a guy in my situation, I can't overprepare. To get that recognition from studying schemes, players—it only helps."

What about his thought process when it comes to scrambling versus throwing? Does he ever hesitate between the two functions, one voice saying take off, the other (maybe sounding a lot like Coach McCarthy) saying, *Pick your spots with the running; we don't need you injured.*

"I think when it comes to running quarterbacks, you either have it or you don't," responded Rodgers, who watched a ton of speedy Steve Young in his youth. "You either have that switch—that gear—or you don't. It's not something you can be thinking about in the middle of a play, obviously, and I'm not sure how much you can 'learn' to be a running quarterback. My overall view or philosophy when it comes to running versus throwing is that when I'm out of the pocket I want to be *pass-first.* That's how you really stretch the field. The defense has to respect both your scrambling ability and your arm. The most dangerous guys are pass-first when they're outside the pocket, rather than making a play with their feet. That said, I do want to do some running every game—it's another weapon. Back in April, Coach McCarthy and I discussed our quarterback goals for the 2008 season and we came up with a total of 200 rushing yards as one of my targets, roughly 12 or 13 yards per game." Rodgers would end the season with 207 rushing yards.

Aaron Rodgers picked the Rob Reiner-directed 1987 comedic fairy tale *The Princess Bride* as a favorite movie in his team's 2008 media guide. A mock medieval fantasy helmed by the auteur behind *This Is Spinal Tap*, the film is marked by gentle, goofy, absurd humor. "Filled with good-hearted fun and a certain innocence that survives all Reiner's satire," wrote Roger Ebert. Its framing device features a grandfather, Peter Falk, reading a storybook to his grandson, Fred Savage of *Wonder Years* fame, dressed in a Chicago Bears jersey. "Any sports in it?" the kid asks when his grandfather proposes to read the story of the Princess Bride. "Are you kidding?" the grandfather replies. "Fencing, fighting, torture, revenge, giants, monsters, chases, escapes, true love, miracles."

The movie's many fans praise the quotability of the script's clever dialogue. I ask Rodgers if he has a favorite line. "Oh wow," he says. "I can quote the whole movie."

"As you wish," he recites a moment later, quoting a line spoken by the hero Westley, played by Cary Elwes, to communicate his heart to the princess, played by Robin Wright.

Rodgers went with a different movie in the 2007 Packers media guide. He picked *The Prestige*, a dark, thought-provoking period thriller directed by Christopher Nolan. Its plot concerns two rival magicians battling for stage supremacy in turn-of-the-century London. The performers compete to be considered the best at what they do, their obsessive one-upmanship pushing their lives to the edge. Hugh Jackman against Christian Bale. Battling to be . . . No. 1.

A bit like Aaron Rodgers and Alex Smith.

Or Rodgers and Favre.

# CHAPTER 6:
# DORM LIVING

**S**T. NORBERT COLLEGE sits on the west bank of the Fox River, six miles south of Lambeau Field. The first summer the Packers bunked there was 1958, back when the stadium was just ten months old and not yet named after Curly. The team had spent the four previous training camps in Stevens Point, ninety miles west, and another four summers before that in Grand Rapids, Michigan. The return to Green Bay did not bring good luck. First-year head coach Scooter McLean established the St. Norbert tradition but that's about the only legacy seasoned Packers fans care to remember. After lodging at the scenic riverside college, the team posted that dreadful 1–10–1 record, a horror show given immortality by *New York Herald Tribune* sportswriter Red Smith, a Green Bay native. "The Packers underwhelmed ten opponents, overwhelmed one, and whelmed one," Smith famously wrote.

Scooter McLean was gone by Christmas. The new guy, Vince Lombardi, changed much but stuck with Norbert for training camp. It rang some familiar bells, this private Catholic college, when so much else about northeast Wisconsin was terra incognita to the Brooklyn,

New York native. A graduate of Jesuit-run Fordham in the Bronx, Lombardi took pleasure in a school whose leafy campus paths were walked by priests and nuns, and whose most august structure was a centrally located Catholic church, Old St. Joseph, built in 1890. Here, though, the priests were not Jesuits but Norbertines, an order founded in twelfth-century France. The coach liked being able to walk from an Xs and Os session with his players in a college classroom to a Catholic chapel a football's throw away. The presence of nuns in habits was a staple from his boyhood, comforting in a way to this man of routine and ritual during the grind of training camp, though their presence also meant that his players had to maintain a certain modesty of appearance. "Watch dress in halls and dining hall— NUNS," Lombardi underlined three times in a note to self prior to addressing his players at the start of one Packers camp. Other items to emphasize early in camp included his rule about taping ankles before all contact work, the 11 P.M. weekday lights-out curfew, and the ban on entering the Piccadilly Club, a rock-and-roll strip joint. "Good morning, sisters!" sings Lombardi to a pair of strolling young nuns at the start of the Howard Cosell–produced 1964 documentary *Run to Daylight!* an hour-long feature on Lombardi and Packers training camp which ran on ABC in primetime.

In Lombardi's day, players spent eight full weeks on campus, living two to a room in a dorm a few paces riverward from the dorm players spend just three weeks in today. "I went to jail today," Jerry Kramer memorably wrote in his 1967 season diary *Instant Replay*. "I started an eight-week sentence in Sensenbrenner Hall." After ten years of training camps totaling over a year and a half on campus, Kramer joked, "I deserve an honorary degree from St. Norbert."

"The beds are a little small, the rooms are a little small," wrote another diary-keeping Packers guard in summer 2006, 6-foot-4,

308-pound Alaskan Daryn Colledge. The Boise State alum roomed with fellow 300-pounder Jason Spitz, a center/guard out of Louisville. Colledge, filing camp entries for the Packers team Web site, had recently bought a nearby house with his wife, Megan, a place they shared with their two beloved boxers, Duke and Dash. When he and Spitz had a free hour—a rare free hour—they'd race to Colledge's house, say hi to Megan and the dogs, then Colledge would get some quick shut-eye in his own bed while Spitz would fall asleep in a living-room chair. Or they'd "sit around and hang out" with Megan and the dogs.

Though the beds in Victor McCormick Hall, a three-story 1960s-era red-brick dorm, were no bigger than in Sensenbrenner, the rooms themselves were bigger, a good thing because there were no 300-pound Packers in Kramer's day. Accommodations in VMH, as it's commonly called, feature suite-style living with a bedroom, living area, and bathroom with shower. The suites house four college kids when school's in session. When the Packers are here—late July through mid August—veterans get first-floor rooms, while rookies reside above. The ground-level rooms have doors that open out onto a small central courtyard with a couple of trees and shrubs. Over the years players like James Lofton, Sterling Sharpe, Reggie White, and yes, Brett Favre have been able to step outside for a little air or a little kibitzing when it's not too hot and humid without having to dodge autograph-seeking fans or nervous, awestruck rookies.

Nor did they have to worry about a patrolling stickler named Lombardi. That was really the thrust of Kramer's Sensenbrenner "jail" analogy. "Lombardi runs this place like a penal colony," the lineman wrote. He also tells a story from the coach's first Packers training camp. At precisely 11 P.M. one night, Lombardi entered the room Kramer shared with running back Jim Taylor. Taylor is sitting on the edge of his bed with shorts and socks on, seconds from hitting the hay. "Jimmy, what time you got?" asks Lombardi. Taylor whips out his watch, says, "I've got eleven o'clock, sir." Boom. Lombardi fines Taylor $25 for not having his head on the pillow at the stroke of eleven.

In the first sixteen years of the Packers' existence, preseason didn't mean training camp but rather a daily gathering of players in town for practice. Then, in 1935, Curly Lambeau tried something different and bused twenty-four players to Rhinelander, 130 miles northwest of Green Bay. They spent a week at Pine Lodge on Thompson Lake in the middle of deep woods outside town, heading by bus to the high school field for a pair of weekend practices and two-a-days during the week. No players had cars, so no one was going anywhere during breaks or at night. Lambeau was nowhere near the taskmaster Lombardi was when it came to putting players through their training-camp paces, however. "He never worked anybody hard," fullback Chester "Swede" Johnson recalled. "Some of these coaches make you run, run, run. Curly never did that."

Midway through that North Woods week, daytime temps dropped to the 40s, and players practiced in wool shirts and hooded sweatshirts. One night it got cold enough to snow.

Finding the controlled environment of a getaway training location beneficial, Lambeau made more pro football history twelve years later by purchasing a 55-acre estate on the bay fifteen miles northwest of Green Bay. Its centerpiece was a 40-room stone chateau called Rockwood Lodge. Lambeau marked off a football field on acreage before the lodge and had contractors erect six prefab cottages to house players with wives, the small houses named for former Packer greats. Unmarried players lived six to eight in a room, sleeping in army-style barracks. Following Lambeau's dietary strictures, the team ate ketchup-free, non-fried food in a grand dining room, gathered for

A pair of junior Packer quarterbacks confer while waiting for players on bikes.
*(Courtesy of Mary June Hanrahan)*

Packers founder Curly Lambeau in bronze on the Lambeau Atrium plaza. *(Courtesy of Mary June Hanrahan)*

Vince Lombardi looks out toward Lombardi Avenue. *(Courtesy of Mary June Hanrahan)*

Aaron Rodgers watches the end of a pass play. Behind him, head coach Mike McCarthy looks on. *(Courtesy of Mary June Hanrahan)*

Packers president Mark Murphy signs an autograph. *(Courtesy of Mary June Hanrahan)*

Packers management and executive committee members make a solemn procession to the Lambeau stage for the annual Packers shareholders meeting, July 24, 2008.

My "leatherhead" bench neighbors for the September 20 Dallas game at Lambeau: (*left to right*) Chuck Watson, Steve Stoffel, Dan Cotey, and Trent Graham.

Jon Neuhaus and his father Lee visit Lambeau during the renovation in July 2001.

Thanks to a pregame field pass, Kathy Neuhaus shares a moment with hip-hop superstar Jay-Z before the Sunday night game against the Cowboys at Lambeau on September 21.

Packers general manager Ted Thompson appears on a video screen inside the Lambeau Atrium during the 2009 Packers Draft Party on April 23.

Packer fans inside the Atrium await the team's first 2009 selection.

Wide receiver Jordy Nelson heads to practice in style.

Strong safety Atari Bigby, proud father of baby boy Atari Kente Bigby (born February 10, 2009), rides a three-wheeled bike as a fan carries his pads and jersey. *(Courtesy of Mary June Hanrahan)*

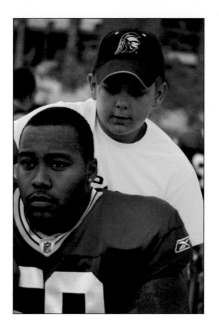

Linebacker Danny Lansanah, ex–UConn Husky, transports a future USC Trojan. *(Courtesy of Mary June Hanrahan)*

Cornerback Tramon Williams rides one-handed while greeting some fans. *(Courtesy of Mary June Hanrahan)*

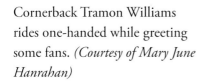

Meet fourth-year wide receiver Ruvell "Gumby/Rooster" Martin. *(Courtesy of Mary June Hanrahan)*

Wide receiver Greg Jennings rides past a young fan in a Donald Driver jersey. *(Courtesy of Mary June Hanrahan)*

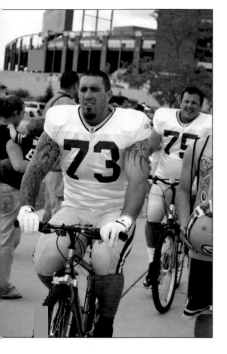

Alaska-born left guard Daryn Colledge without his scholarly glasses. Keeping pace just behind is fellow offensive lineman Tony Moll, a fourth-year player out of Nevada. *(Courtesy of Mary June Hanrahan)*

Linebacker Brady Poppinga sports a classic Poppinga expression. *(Courtesy of Mary June Hanrahan)*

Packers running backs and receivers gather for some coaching. *(Courtesy of Mary June Hanrahan)*

Standing upright on defense *(left to right)*, are linebacker Brady Poppinga; corner Tramon Williams; and rookie outside linebacker Clay Matthews, a 2009 first-round pick. *(Courtesy of Mary June Hanrahan)*

Outside linebacker Jeremy Thompson and left tackle Chad Clifton do battle. Outside linebackers coach Kevin Greene looks on from the sideline *(green shirt, left)*. *(Courtesy of Mary June Hanrahan)*

Lineman turned linebacker Aaron Kampman does his solo sideline footwork drill.

Packers punter Jeremy Kapinos, who was sent out to punt eight times during his Lambeau debut in 3-degree weather on December 7 against the Houston Texans. *(Courtesy of Mary June Hanrahan)*

Jordy Nelson was here, inside his parents' restaurant and sports bar Nelson's Landing in Leonardville, Kansas, when he got a call from the Packers on Draft Day 2008.

Jordy Nelson celebrates with family and friends in Nelson's Landing not long after being drafted by the Packers. His mother Kim stands to his immediate left, his wife Emily to his right. *(Courtesy of Laura Rothlisberger)*

One of the finest Packer bars in all the land: the Broke Spoke in Kiln, Mississippi.

Your author visits Brett Favre Field at Hancock High School in Kiln, MS.
*(Courtesy of Jim Bloomfield)*

Rick "Ray Nitschke" Roystan and son Brett in Mabel Murphy's in Scottsdale, Arizona.

A wall in Mabel Murphy's, the unofficial home of the Arizona Pack fan club.

Snowbanks ringed the Lambeau lots on December 7, the day of the Houston game.

Tailgaters in the Oneida Lot brave the cold on December 7, flanked by Castle Lambeau.

Paul Radloff of Rice Lake enjoys a final moment in "Schwartzville" at the portable bar of Scott Schwartz in the Oneida lot's "Tailgate Row" on the December 28 morning of game 16.

Al's Hamburgers on Washington Street. Vince Lombardi used to walk to Al's from his Crooks Street office. In the 1990s, nose-tackle Gilbert Brown paid Al's a visit or two.

chalk talks in a classroom area, and had use of a large living room with comfy chairs, coffee tables, and an enormous stone fireplace. The hearth came in handy in the winter. Winter? Yes, a number of players lived at "The Rock" year-round, something Curly liked because he could keep an eye on them and keep them eating healthily. During training camp—a concept Curly had pioneered, via The Rock—the coach and his third wife, Grace, stayed in a lavishly styled cottage, the decorating tab courtesy of Marshall Field's in Chicago, so irritating the Packers financial committee that some members threatened to resign. Rockwood Lodge—especially the expense of it—became a thorn in the side of the Packers board, many members considering the whole facility an unnecessary extravagance, especially with the Packers losing and team finances suffering. Owing to faulty wiring in the attic, The Rock burned to the ground five days before Lambeau resigned in late January 1950.

During those three Packer training camps north of town, routines remained little-changed, but one aspect presented early problems and eventually underwent fine-tuning. It was just a small matter of the practice field itself. Beneath the grass of the Rockwood Lodge football field sat a thin layer of topsoil atop rock, part of a stony bayside shelf. Players called it "Shinsplint Field." They developed sore shins, sore feet, sore knees, and basically beat the heck out of their legs with every practice. You didn't want to get tackled on that ground either.

Lambeau ended up busing his players back into town to practice on a softer field.

\* \* \*

The 2008 Packers practiced on Clark Hinkle Field between Oneida Street and the hangar-like Don Hutson Center indoor training facility, both the field and field house across the street from Lambeau. Hinkle, in case you're wondering, was a pile-driving Packers fullback and knock-you-out linebacker during the 1930s, veteran of epic battles with his Bears fullback/linebacker counterpart Bronko Nagurski. So though the name "Clark Hinkle" has about a fiftieth the sonic smack of "Bronko Nagurski," don't be fooled—Hinkle could lay the wood. Not to mention, when Hinkle retired in 1941, he was the NFL's leading career rusher.

Packers training camp 2008 was Hinkle Field's last hoorah. In 2009, the team relocated outdoor practice to the better-lit, better-surfaced, and tougher-sounding Ray Nitschke Field on the east side of the Hutson Center. And it was a goodbye for the books, too, if you consider that the first dozen practices generally featured a handful of fans chanting for Brett Favre, booing the new No. 1 quarterback when he took a snap, cheering when Rodgers threw a bad ball, and here and there yelling some nasty things about general manager Ted Thompson. The boobirds and chanters, the shouters and sign-holders formed a small percentage of spectators, but they were audible and visible, to fans, players, staff, and the media. Media from other cities. National media. Credential requests for the first day of practice, Monday, July 28, were made by ESPN's John Clayton, the NFL Network, ESPN.com, the *New York Times*, the *Washington Post, Sporting News,* CBS Sportsline, Yahoo! Sports, *USA Today*, the *Minneapolis Star Tribune*, and Bryan Burwell of the *St. Louis Post-Dispatch* (in-state for Rams training camp at a lakeshore college just north of Milwaukee). Before long, Wendi Nix of ESPN would put down stakes, even contributing to the local economy with some clothing purchases when her suitcase ran out of on-camera outfits. ESPN's Rachel Nichols would also come to know Green Bay like the back of her hand.

But in other ways, it was Packers training camp as usual, maybe better than usual. The weather cooperated, as there wasn't a single rained-out practice and temperatures stayed in the 70s and low 80s. The only season-ending injury to a projected starter occurred a month after camp opened when long-snapper J. J. Jansen, a rookie from Notre Dame, blew out a knee in an August 29 exhibition game against Tennessee. On day three, Coach McCarthy called his squad the healthiest he'd had in Green Bay. This was all relative of course. Indeed receiver Greg Jennings (knee) and starting defensive tackle Ryan Pickett (hamstring) weren't practicing, and by week's end cornerback Will Blackmon sat with a foot injury, end Kabeer Gbaja-Biamila and fullback Korey Hall sat with knee issues, and starting center Scott Wells aggravated a side trunk muscle which, in addition to a bad back, would dog him the rest of camp. But there were no instant jolts as there were in 2007 when running back Vernand Morency sprained a knee ligament on day one and missed the rest of camp, and tight end Tory Humphrey broke his leg, ending his season. McCarthy had only to look at the Washington Redskins to count his blessings. The first NFL team to open camp 2008, a week before the Pack, the Skins lost veteran end Phillip Daniels to a torn ACL on the first snap of 7-on-7 morning drills while end Alex Buzbee ripped his right Achilles that afternoon.

Two practices, two season-ending injuries.

As camp drew on in Green Bay, linebacker A. J. Hawk strained a chest muscle, missing practices for the first time in six seasons (two in the NFL, four at Ohio State). Starting strong safety Atari Bigby would go out with an ankle. Running back Ryan Grant pulled a hammy. Number 3 wide receiver James Jones injured a right knee. Promising rookie guard Josh Sitton strained a left knee. But all these injuries projected to heal. And Jennings was back. Late in camp, Ryan Pickett returned, as did speed-rusher Gbaja-Biamila. Things looked okay.

Most of the new injuries were sustained in one of the four exhibition games, not during practice workouts. McCarthy is extraordinarily careful about risking camp injuries through too much contact or overworking players' bodies. When he arrived in 2006, he eliminated 25 percent of training camp practices, alternating two-practice days with one-practice days. He also scheduled a day a week without practice. In 2008, Clark Hinkle Field was quiet on three out of the first four camp Thursdays. When players checked their first-week schedule, they saw:

Monday: 8:45 A.M. (shells) 6:30 P.M. (full pads)
Tuesday: 2 P.M. (full pads)
Wednesday: same as Monday
Thursday: no practice
Friday: same as Monday

"Shells" are smaller, softer shoulder pads. While reducing the amount of on-field practice, McCarthy has upped the players' film study, scheduling sessions in the evenings in addition to those practice-free days.

So there is some, um, daylight between the camp philosophies of McCarthy and Lombardi. Not that McCarthy's camp is a picnic. It's clear from the rookie diaries of Daryn Colledge, Korey Hall, and Jordy Nelson on the Packers Web site that plenty of exhausting physical training goes on, all three players writing most longingly of . . . sweet slumber. "I usually look over my playbook, the install for the next day, and go to sleep," Hall noted in 2007. "When you're at the dorm, you're either eating or sleeping." In today's NFL, players are expected to show up to camp in good shape, and most have already been officially training in some team capacity since March. Players in Lombardi's day were on their own for nearly six months, and the majority worked offseason jobs, sometimes paper-pushing office jobs.

"Fatigue makes cowards of us all!" Lombardi would boom in his introductory training camp speech on the St. Norbert campus, either before or after reminding players to dress modestly because of the nuns. His goal was to hammer his Packers into shape with eight weeks of grueling two-a-days so they'd be brave and unweary during the season. (With the season shorter than today's by four games, Lombardi was less worried about late-season burnout.) Helmets and full pads were mandatory for every practice. He ran endless conditioning drills, including the dreaded "up-downs" where players would run in place, knees pistoning as high as possible, for thirty seconds, in the heat, whereupon Lombardi would holler "Down!" and players would hit the turf, belly-flopping, before popping back up on his command of "Up!" their knees re-churning. Three to five minutes of up-downs if Coach was "in a good mood," Jerry Kramer records in his book, but if "upset," Lombardi would have them drill like this until players could no longer move. "We've never had anybody die during grass drills," observed Kramer, but he did share a story of a rookie who began to hallucinate while drilling, telling Kramer he was seeing people "walking around in the air." The rookie was cut a few days later. Other rookies "cut" themselves, packing up and fleeing camp out of sheer exhaustion. The team even had a word for this—to escape Lombardi's helmeted hell by splitting town was to "domino."

McCarthy's Packers don't do up-downs. They don't furtively suck on ice chips smuggled in a towel under a jacket by an injured player, as happened when banged-up Fuzzy Thurston limped to the aid of parched teammates like Kramer with trainer's ice hidden from Lombardi's view. Though Korey Hall, like Kramer, grew up in Idaho, he didn't one day find himself at practice rhapsodizing deliriously about the "unbelievably cold and sweet water" that flows from mountain springs in the Idaho high country, his cotton-mouthed teammates wanting to "beat him to death" if he didn't shut up. No, McCarthy's Packers could hydrate when they wanted to, with $H_2O$ or Gatorade. And though the sight of some 75 football players running in place with maximum knee lift before hitting the deck as a gap-toothed coach bellowed orders in a New York accent was reportedly a highlight, spectacle-wise, of Lombardi-led training camps, the thought of the physical agony felt by these players—"It's impossible to put into words how horrible I feel," wrote Kramer on day three of camp after doing eighty up-downs in 90-degree heat—might take away from the pleasure of the spectacle, were one to think on it. Plus, twenty-first-century Packers practices have plenty of other winning sights and sounds. And upward of 120,000 people from across America and the world enjoyed them in late July and August of 2008, the Brett Favre Storm not nearly dark and sustained enough to take all the fun out of camp.

At least for spectators.

Though nowhere near the carnival of the game day tailgating scene, still, at any given practice, you had a couple thousand people enjoying themselves, watching the players run around, chatting in the bleachers, taking some sun, and munching snacks bought from one of the street vendors. Like it was a park or the beach, families picnicked with small coolers in the bleachers or in lawn chairs before the Hinkle fence. Kids with sippy cups, moms with babies in strollers, the occasional senior citizen in a motorized scooter or wheelchair. Kids say the darndest things, and a few did so in the Oneida Street bleachers. "Can anyone tell me how players blow their noses?" asked a boy of seven or eight as he took in the sight of lined-up, helmeted Packers. It was not a question a kid in the facemask-free Hinkle–Nagurski era would have asked. And for a reminder of the headgear difference between then and now, you had only to cast your eyes to the wall of the Hutson Center bordering the practice field, a big banner upon its wall bearing the cartoon of a toothless leatherhead muttering, "We wuh dere when facemath wuh waughed at."

We were there when facemasks were laughed at.

"Puh-PING-ga," intoned another young boy of seven or eight. He kept repeating the plosive-rich surname of linebacker Brady Poppinga. "Puh-PING-ga. I like his name, Mom. It's fun to say."

Sitting in the bleachers, I met a couple of Green Bay natives, Bob Fisher and Judith Murphy, who themselves had just met this fine August morning. Bob was a retired chiropractor who came back to his hometown from Flemington, New Jersey, where he'd had his clinic; Judith worked in the Post Office on Packerland Drive in northwest Green Bay. Both huge Packer fans, they shared stories of the Lombardi years. Judith recalled "Hornung and McGee always in the Spot Supper Club, and always with a drink in their hands. Back then players didn't mind being seen out drinking at all hours." Bob recalled driving past the Hotel Northland at 2 A.M. as a teen with friends, "all of us honking our horns to wake up visiting teams." Both Judith and Bob chuckled at the thought of the long-gone Piccadilly Club, the rock-and-roll strip joint that Lombardi had ruled off-limits to players yet Hornung and McGee managed to patronize.

\* \* \*

Punter Jon Ryan sends a ball spiraling 70 yards through the air against a blue sky. The tight ends—veterans Tory Humphrey and Donald

Lee, and rookies Jermichael Finley from Texas, Evan Moore from Stanford and 6-foot-8 Joey Haynos out of Maryland—catch balls shot at startling speed from short range by a Jugs machine, a contraption made of two spinning tires that sling the ball when dropped into the slot. *Boom! Boom! Boom!* Tight ends coach Ben McAdoo cranks up the Jugs until footballs start blasting off facemasks, through the hands and into the grill. *Whack! Whack!* Players laugh. TE after TE steps into the line of fire, sometimes with their backs turned for over-the-shoulder catches. "Right shoulder! Left shoulder! Left shoulder!" McAdoo commands, and the players twist their torsos accordingly. Footballs rocket through hands, hit the turf a dozen yards away, and skid a dozen more yards.

Another Jugs pointed skyward shoots balls end over end three-quarters of the field, the pigskin traveling magnificently high beneath the cerulean sky, the returners never muffing.

Mason Crosby boots 60-yard field goals with ease.

Players on defense wear bright red cotton caps on top of their yellow Packer helmets, these strawberry dots the brightest colors on a brilliant day on a bright green synthetic field. Wearing a beanie over a football helmet. Odd. Like pulling a sock over a boot. Or like an astronaut donning a scarf.

The red beanies never slip off. Nor does that yellow Packers tuque Mark Tauscher pancakes on his head, over his scraggly barbarian hair, a friendly, comical barbarian, with a slight jelly-belly. You half expect him to start calling teammates "hoser" in a McKenzie Brothers voice. Knowing Tausch, he probably does. Knowing him from the Packers TV show he co-hosts, *Tuesday Night Touchback*, and his weekly 540 ESPN Radio segment "Tuesdays With Tauscher," that is. It's no wonder Rodgers and Tausch get along. They're both smart, with a sense of the absurd.

Then there's Aaron Kampman. He's as "high motor" a guy as any on the team. Probably on any team. Always in motion, this lineman. Even in the heat, waiting for his spot to come up in the one-on-one rushing drill. While other linemen save their strength, Kampman does his own special footwork exercises, skipping backwards on an imagined tightrope, his foot placement nimble and precise for a guy 6-foot-4, 260 pounds.

The three quarterbacks all release balls at the exact same moment, aligned in a row, their three-step drops synchronized. Young guns wearing red practice jerseys, their jersey numbers in sequence: 10, 11, 12. Rookie Matt Flynn from Louisiana State. Rookie Brian Brohm from Louisville. Newly minted starter Aaron Rodgers from Cal.

Will Thompson and McCarthy really stay with such youth at QB all season long? Some fan bloggers have already labeled the possibility "insane." For if Rodgers goes down with an injury, it's Flynn or Brohm the rest of the way. Really?

Later Rodgers and Ruvell Martin do their goofy aerial shoulder-bump. For the hell of it. They get some good vertical. Rodgers calls Ruvell "Gumby." Martin's 6-foot-4, lean, flexible. Like Rodgers, Martin also takes guitar lessons at the Heid Music Company in Green Bay.

An air horn blasts to signal the end of a segment. From somewhere on the field a coach yells, "Quit fuckin' around!"

Kids in the bleachers: earmuffs!

Players jog off to different parts of Hinkle Field.

\* \* \*

"Jordy," I ask, "what was the most memorable part of your first training camp?"

"The bikes," he says instantly. In typical Nelson fashion, he doesn't generate more words to surround and amplify his reply but he does wear a small grin. Also typical.

The bikes. The tradition started with Lombardi in summer, 1961. His idea was to add to the player-fan bond, to build in even more closeness, and he could hardly have come up with a better way to do it. As players ride the bikes of neighborhood kids back and forth between Lambeau and the practice field, the kids hitch a ride on the seat, or stand on the rear-wheel pegs, or inline skate or simply jog alongside. For many visitors, the sight is a highlight of Packers training camp, a glory, impossible to forget. As spectacle, it's both touching and funny. The touching part is the kids' smiles, their pride, joy, and amazement. A child of seven or eight will stand on the pegs of a little BMX bike, arms around a player's shoulders, as a gigantic Packer lineman sits atop a seat he outgrew twenty years ago.

What's funny is the size mismatch. Watching 330-pound behemoths, their legs frogged to fit on the bike, doing all they can to pedal and stay upright. From a distance, the bikes beneath players look small enough to have training wheels on them. They remind you of Shriners sitting in miniature cars. Not every Packer player is gargantuan, of course, and many of the bikes the players ride come from kids nearing or in their teens, so the bikes don't appear as doll-sized. One cloudless day, the pairing that drew the most delight, even some applause, didn't involve a bike at all. But it did involve a size disparity. Towering rookie offensive tackle Breno Giacomini, a 6-foot-7, 311-pound former Fenway Park hotdog vendor from Malden, Massachusetts, walked back to Lambeau accompanied by a ceaselessly smiling six-year-old girl, the girl proudly carrying his helmet. Giacomini has a very upright walk and he was wearing cleats; next to his companion he looked eight-feet-tall and maybe 400 pounds.

Onlookers just cracked up. Others broke into applause. The rookie wore enormous yellow Packer shorts and a skintight Packers tank top, and when he wasn't swigging from a bottle of blue Gatorade, he was grinning too.

Spectators come from all over. Each day of practice an elderly woman in an electric wheelchair sets up a map board in the Lambeau parking lot, the United States on one side and the world on the other. Visitors sink pushpins to mark where they're from. By the middle of August, New Hampshire was the only state without a pin. On the international side of the board, visitors had pushed pins into Greenland, Iceland, Mexico, Costa Rica, Brazil, Peru, Sweden, Ireland, England, Holland, Belgium, Denmark, France, Italy, Germany, Poland, Russia, the Philippines, Israel, and Australia.

The kids and players talk while they ride or walk, and lasting friendships develop. Kurt Warner—yes, that Kurt Warner, signed by the Packers as an undrafted free agent out of Northern Iowa in '94—got to know Brennan Feldhausen during his short stay in Green Bay. Brennan, from nearby Biemeret Street, couldn't wait to get up each practice morning and ride over to Lambeau, looking for Kurt. Unfortunately for Brennan, the rookie got cut at the end of camp. But the two kept in touch via handwritten letters, this being a time before kids and quarterbacks were doing much e-mailing.

Another rookie QB, Aaron Rodgers, came to ride the bike of middle schooler John Gee in the summer of 2005. Rodgers and Gee are still in touch today, happy to talk music and sports. Rodgers once stopped by Gee's high school football game in 2007. "Aaron has been a wonderful role model for John," his mother, Lisa, told the *Press-Gazette* in 2008. "John strives for good grades in school because that's the first question Aaron always asks him!" Even Gilbert Brown, the 350-pound nose tackle nicknamed "The Gravedigger" for his habit of planting ball-carriers in the ground, joined the fun. I could find no evidence Brown ever broke a bike, though Mike Lovelace of Green Bay, whom Brown befriended one training camp, did tell the *Press-Gazette* that center Mike Flanagan was a little too much rider for his one-speed. You don't see every Packer on a bike; veterans entering their fourth season can instead opt for transport in a van. But the tradition is still going strong, and anyone who thinks this kind of thing takes away from football edge and focus should go back to the origins of the tradition and consider how the Packers did their first year on the bikes. The Pack went 11–3 in 1961 and won the NFL championship, demolishing the New York Giants 37–0.

Were it not for the approaching Brett Favre storm, Coach Mike McCarthy's biggest concern as camp opened would have been the contract holdout of running back Ryan Grant, his second biggest being the stoutness of the defensive line. Out with injuries were mainstay right tackle Ryan Pickett and defensive tackle Justin Harrell, the team's 2007 first-round pick. And a cloud now hung over third-year defensive tackle Johnny Jolly, arrested July 12 for possessing 200-plus grams of codeine. The February trade of fifth-year defensive end Corey Williams to Cleveland for a late second-round pick, though it made financial sense, took away depth at a formerly well-stocked position group.

What about Aaron Rodgers? Any concerns there?

No big ones. The Packers new starting QB had been poised and sharp in spring team activities, poised and sharp in June minicamp. ESPN's John Clayton visited the latter and came away impressed. His observations possessed considerable resonance given the doubters during Rodgers' draft year. "As it turns out, Rodgers has a very strong arm," Clayton wrote. "He's had the strong arm since he's been in Green

Bay. The ball explodes off his hand." Noting the passer's "smooth, polished retreat from center" in three- and five-step drops, Clayton continued, "The ball comes out unnaturally fast. [In] baseball terms, his 6-2 body throws the fastball of a 6-5 pitcher." And he shared some comments by receiver Greg Jennings that created a small stir in Packer circles, the wideout noting that on some throws, Rodgers guns the ball "a lot harder" than Favre. "He has a cannon," Jennings went on. "He throws it like a Jugs machine every time. And he can make every throw on the football field. Also, Aaron's deep ball is one of the prettiest. Brett had a great deep ball, but Aaron has a beautiful one."

Of course the 24-year-old Jennings wasn't catching Favre's finger-breaking passes in the '90s, as he acknowledged. Favre himself took note of the mustard Rodgers puts on nearly every throw, even in pregame. In 2007, the quarterbacks were warming up before a game against Minnesota. Ruvell Martin was catching Rodgers and handing the ball to Favre, and "Chuck," as some teammates call Rodgers, was really bringing the heat. Favre turned to "Gumby" Martin and said, "I used to be able to throw like that when I was younger. Can't do it all the time anymore."

So there were no worries on the arm front, especially now that Rodgers had lowered his release point from the high-carriage mechanics he had been taught at Cal. The more natural release point, closer to the way he threw in high school, promoted accuracy. "We dropped his ball carriage," McCarthy told John Clayton. "[Now] it's a little more fluid." But what about the game's mental aspect? Any quarterback stepping into an NFL starting role faces huge challenges in terms of leadership and media scrutiny. And for Rodgers, that was only the beginning. There was also the little matter of filling the shoes of one Brett Lorenzo Favre. When it came to grasping the offense, McCarthy was sanguine: Rodgers already grasped it. As for all that other stuff, the pressure and the taking command, so far, so good. "I've been waiting my whole life for this," Rodgers stated assuredly in a Lambeau press conference a few days after Favre announced his retirement. "I'm not Brett Favre. [I'm] not going to be him. I'm Aaron Rodgers. He did it his way, I'm gonna do it my way. And hopefully I'll be successful."

Rodgers went on to say he was aware the track-record of quarterbacks following legends was subpar at best, not needing, before this audience of football reporters, to cite the successors to Bart Starr, Joe Namath, Terry Bradshaw, Troy Aikman, and John Elway, among others. But Rodgers also pointed to a more cheering story, one he knew inside and out, that of Steve Young taking over from Joe Montana at Frisco. He said he and Young had talked about Young's experience, shortly before Rodgers got drafted in 2005. The young QB was nothing if not realistic, though. "I know I'm going to hear it my whole career," he said. "I'm going to be compared to Brett."

He'd hear it on the durability front for sure. And he did in this press conference, when a reporter asked for his reaction to the "injury-prone" label Rodgers had acquired after being out with a broken foot and torn hamstring during his three years with the Pack. Stiffening slightly, the northern Californian, hair reaching his shoulders, replied, "If you don't start every game for this team, you're gonna get labeled that. Because of what Brett did. I'm just going to get myself in great shape, and with a little luck, hopefully I can stay healthy all 16 weeks."

Rodgers had one slip-up in terms of ascension preparation. It became known as "The Comment." He uttered it to Chris Ballard of *Sports Illustrated* for a July 7 article on quarterbacks who'd joined the "We Followed Legends Club," a moniker supplied by the Packers' very own Scott Hunter, successor to Bart Starr. "I don't feel I need to sell myself to the fans," Rodgers said when asked if he felt pressure to connect with fans the way Favre did. "They need to get on board now or keep their mouths shut." The quarterback felt terrible about the gaffe, but didn't make excuses or blame the media like so many public figures do after they say things that don't look great in print. He simply pointed out that he has always had a good relationship with Packer fans, has been one of the more active participants in Packers fan events, loves Green Bay, and does a lot for the community. Though fans didn't deem the *SI* quote terrific public relations—it wasn't—many of those who posted to Packer blogs supplied context for the comment, taking it as an indication that Rodgers was just plain sick of being asked about Favre. And who wouldn't be?

The first fan to post to the *Milwaukee Journal Sentinel* Packers site wrote:

"Touche, Aaron Rogers. Touche. I'm on board."

Another posted, "I love the Rodgers quote. Just play the game and let that be your judge."

A third said, "I don't love the comment."

Whoops—sorry, Brett Favre said that. He went on to tell Greta Van Susteren in his July 14 interview that he made some "crazy comments" too when he was Rodgers' age, adding that he may have said something similar were he in the same circumstance. "I'm sure he's tired of answering questions about Brett Favre," said Brett Favre.

Favre's bitterness with Packers management bubbled up even here. He suggested to Van Susteren that the team may have strategically leaked information about him wanting to come back to get the "pot stirring" as a way of deflecting Packer fan attention from the Aaron Rodgers quote. News of "The Comment" broke on Tuesday, July 1. The next day, ESPN's Chris Mortensen reported that Favre was experiencing "the itch" to come back and was talking to the Packers. Later that afternoon, Jason Wilde of the *Wisconsin State Journal* went further, reporting that "a few weeks back" Favre had gone so far as to ask the Packers for his release if they did not want him to return. Ten days later, thanks to the infamous Ted Thompson timeline, we learned that June 20 was the date of that communication.

Wednesday, July 2, was also the day Favre text-messaged his friend Al Jones at the *Biloxi Sun Herald*, writing "It's all rumor" regarding a comeback and "No reason for it" regarding the media attention. Looking back, this week won't go down as a shining hour PR-wise in the biographies of either quarterback. As for Favre's specific charge that the Packers leaked information to rescue Aaron Rodgers, it's a little tough to see how stirring up Packer fans with news of a return by No. 4 necessarily accrues to the benefit of Rodgers and the team. With the two quarterbacks side by side in the media again, it just meant more icon-newbie comparison time. "Rodgers could really take a lesson from Favre here," one fan posted to the *Journal Sentinel* Packers blog on July 1, going on to suggest the veteran QB had mastered a winning blend of being "confident" and "aw, shucks" simultaneously.

"It's hard for me to trust, you know, this guy," Favre said to Van Susteren, referring to Ted Thompson. A moment later, he added, "And that's part of the reason for the release."

This comment was included in a page-one *Milwaukee Journal Sentinel* story that ran Tuesday, July 15, a day before the remarks aired in the third and final installment of Van Susteren's interview. Favre went on to cite three occasions where he felt Thompson was untruthful or two-faced. He said after the GM's first season with the Packers in 2005, Thompson said, "Okay, I'll do that" when Favre asked if he would sign one of two veteran guards, either Marco Rivera and Mike Wahle. Shortly after Favre decided to return for 2006, both signed with different teams. That was beef one. Beef two concerned Favre's friend Steve Mariucci. According to Favre, Thompson again said "Okay" when Favre asked if he would interview the recently fired Lions coach for the Packers head coaching job in early 2006. Thompson phoned Mariucci only after he hired Mike McCarthy. And Favre's third beef concerned Thompson's unwillingness to publicly acknowledge even when asked that Favre had lobbied energetically behind the scenes for the Packers to sign Randy Moss in 2007. Favre told Van Susteren he'd offered to give up part of his salary to seal the deal, information he'd also shared with the *Biloxi Sun Herald* during his annual golf tournament back in May of '07. In that same golf-tourney interview, he expressed disappointment with the Packers' failure to sign Moss and seemed alienated from the organization, saying he hadn't lost "faith" in management exactly but wondered how he fit into the team's plans. This was just a few weeks after a FoxSports.com story reported that Favre was so upset with Thompson for failing to snag Moss that he had Bus Cook call the Packers to ask for a trade. The story claimed Favre simmered for a time, ignoring Packer calls, before Mike McCarthy finally calmed him down in a phone call. Favre said there'd been no trade request.

Fan reaction toward the quarterback's take on Thompson was split. Some felt confirmed in their view that Ted Thompson was the problem. Newspaper blogs were filled with disparaging comments, the feelings of some fans toward the GM reaching a point of loathing. These were the fans spoofed by a canned teaser introducing the daily quick-hit "Green and Gold Report" on Milwaukee-based 540 ESPN Radio. "Is Ted Thompson Satan?" intoned a jacked-up sepulchral voice loaded with comical irony. The teaser ran for months.

Another, larger contingent of Packer fans sided with management. Who does Favre think he is, they asked. Where does he get off acting like the assistant GM? Let Thompson do his job.

The Packers had a high-profile beef of their own with Favre, and a more recent one. On the day Favre spoke poorly of Thompson on national TV, Jay Glazer of FoxSports.com broke news that the Packers had filed tampering charges against the Minnesota Vikings, alleging improper communication between Favre and Vikings offensive coordinator Darrell Bevell, Favre's friend and former quarterbacks coach from 2003 to 2005. The league was investigating, looking for evidence of "enticement." One report had Favre making calls to the Vikings on a Packer-issued cell phone, a report that turned out to be untrue since Favre didn't have a Packer-issued cell phone. Favre was furious. He accused the Packers of planting the story.

What followed during the first ten days of training camp was . . . well, remember Tom Pelissero's prediction that things would only get "messier and weirder"? They got messier and weirder. It's hard to isolate one moment as the peak of weirdness, but one candidate would be the hour Favre made his return to Green Bay, a stormy Sunday evening, August 3. That morning he'd been officially reinstated to the league by NFL commissioner Roger Goodell. Reporters and savvy fans tracked the progress of the private jet coming up from Hattiesburg via a Web site called FlightAware.com, not unlike TV weathercasters tracking Santa's sleigh on Christmas Eve.

If you watched Wisconsin TV news between 6–7 P.M. on August 3, 2008, you could get regular flight updates. About a hundred cheering, sign-holding fans greeted Brett and Deanna when they got off the plane. "We want Brett!" they chanted. Favre gave a wave, then slid behind the wheel of his waiting Cadillac Escalade. This was shown on live TV, as was the progress of the vehicle as it headed for Favre's home on Shady Lane, approximately a dozen blocks from Lambeau. The burgundy Escalade might as well have been a white Bronco. Shades of O. J. Simpson's chopper-tracked Los Angeles drive-around, a TV news helicopter followed the Favres all the way into their driveway, beaming images down into the Milwaukee viewing area.

Just a mile away a prop plane towed a SAVEBRETT.NET banner above Lambeau Field, the stadium full of kids and parents who'd snatched up the $8 "Family Night" scrimmage tickets back in June. With Shakespearian appropriateness, a thunderstorm delayed the game's start.

Lightning crashed.

And yes, there were some boos when Aaron Rodgers was introduced that evening and some more when he threw nine straight incompletions and an interception in the end zone.

Other weird and/or messy moments included the previous Thursday's team address by former Bush White House press secretary Ari Fleischer, now head of Ari Fleischer Sports Communications headquartered on Fifth Avenue in New York City. The visit had been booked "a long time ago," said Mike McCarthy, but news of Fleischer's appearance and subsequent hiring as a month-long PR consultant itself created bad PR, as bloggers had a field day with the notion of a "political spinmeister" helping the Packers. When to talk/when not to talk. How to prevent a crisis before it gets to the media. Image management. These were the specialties of Fleischer's firm. After his presentation, Fleischer spoke one-on-one with Rodgers.

Fleischer's visit was timely as just the day before news leaked out that team president Mark Murphy had flown to Hattiesburg and offered a $20 million marketing arrangement to Favre, one where he would become an ambassador for the Packers and engage in various promotional campaigns. The deal was partly modeled on one the Miami Dolphins worked out with Dan Marino upon his retirement. Left out of some media accounts was that the marketing offer hadn't been cooked up the night before—it had first been proposed to Favre shortly after his March retirement and in fact predated Murphy's tenure as president. The trip's purpose was to meet face to face with Favre and seek a solution to the impasse, Murphy said later; the marketing offer gained appeal as they talked. The catch? Favre had to stay retired, otherwise the payments would count against the team's salary cap.

"There isn't a perfect solution to this, but Mark Murphy is at least trying," Favre text-messaged ESPN's Ed Werder the same day Fleischer was in Green Bay. Five days later, with Favre and the Packers stalemated, his Green Bay career almost over, the quarterback expressed a different view of Murphy's offer in a conversation with ESPN's Chris Mortensen. "They tried to buy me off to stay retired," Favre said.

And that, of course, is how a good percentage of Packer fans saw it.

"Obviously, as I look back on it, I would do things differently," said Murphy in a press conference the following week.

Less than three days after Brett and Deanna Favre arrived in Green Bay to welcoming chants and signs, they got back in the Escalade for a trip to the airport and a flight home to Mississippi. It was Wednesday, August 6, about 10:30 A.M. Their departure was shown live on Green Bay television. A smattering of fans standing vigil on Shady Lane watched them go.

Brett Favre was gone. It was a colorless leave-taking, pedestrian. It was human. Favre got in his car and drove away. "No fanfare. No goodbyes," wrote biographer David Zimmerman of the frigid winter day hometown hero Curly Lambeau left for Chicago. "Ten years of brilliance gone in a flash," David Maraniss wrote of the day Lombardi left the Packers. The chapter covering Lombardi's departure is titled "The Empty Room." His account ends with longtime Packers photographer Vernon Biever snapping photos of the coach's empty office. "No one else could fill this room," Maraniss has Biever reflect. "There would never be another Lombardi."

The Packers had set aside a room for Favre in Victor McCormick Hall. It was not to be that he would enter it. It was not to be that he would spend part of a seventeenth straight summer in a dorm room on the campus of St. Norbert College. The last, best hope for Favre remaining a Packer had come and gone Monday night during an epic heart-to-heart between coach and quarterback in McCarthy's Lambeau office. It began at 6 P.M. and concluded well after eleven, interrupted only by pizza and when Favre walked down to Ted Thompson's office and spent an hour talking to the GM. "It's a situation that's extremely personal for him," McCarthy said the next day in a nearly as epic post-practice press conference. "The chain of events, the path that we have taken to get here, [has] done some damage."

McCarthy circled back to this point multiple times, working hard to give reporters an outline of what happened during one of the more momentous meetings in team history, while taking care not to betray confidences or do any more damage by going into too much detail. "Because of all the things that went on," he said, Favre "wasn't in the right mindset to play here." Play here or play anywhere? a reporter asked. "Here," McCarthy answered.

*Extremely emotional. Very personal.* Again and again the coach turned to these phrases to describe Favre's state of mind, avoiding words like angry or bitter or resentful. Upon using the phrase "negative mindset," he immediately corrected himself. McCarthy said he hadn't intended the meeting to turn into a marathon blow-by-blow, but that's what happened as Favre had a lot on his mind. "We were fine," McCarthy said when asked if things got heated. "We're adults. [We] agreed, we disagreed, we disagreed, we agreed. . . . Everything you wanted to say, everything you wanted to ask, went on in that conversation. [We] were brutally honest with each other."

147

"They're still meeting," was uttered or live-blogged by two dozen reporters that evening. Steve Mariucci took a shot at interpreting the meeting's protraction for the NFL Network, commenting that its continuing length indicated a "monkey wrench" had been thrown into the gears of a Favre return. Cheeky Packer fans wisecracked on Internet message-boards about all the media attention, one wag comparing Lambeau to the Vatican during papal selection. "Did anyone see what color smoke was coming from the Packers Headquarters chimney?" wrote the wag.

Favre finally exited Lambeau Field at 11:21 P.M. Seated behind the wheel of his Escalade, he drove down a ramp out of a stadium loading area, rolled past a crowd of reporters and cameras, and turned right on Oneida Street. Two nights later, he was traded to the New York Jets. At minimum, the Packers would get a fourth-round draft pick. They'd get a third-rounder if Favre took 50 percent of the Jets offensive snaps, a second-rounder for 70 percent and a Jets playoff berth, and a first-rounder for 80 percent of the snaps and a Jets Super Bowl berth. The deal also included a poison pill. Were the Jets to trade Favre to an NFC North team, they'd have to surrender three first-round picks. "I'll use their term," he said on Thursday, having already joined his new team in Cleveland for an exhibition game. "We're moving forward."

After the trade news broke, hundreds of Packer fans posted to message boards, needing to react, emote, articulate how they felt. Fans seemed divided into two camps, one of the *Commence the Favre Curse—the Packers are dead to me!* variety, the other of the *Good riddance—New York can have him* perspective. There'd been a similar split Monday night as the Favre/McCarthy marathon concluded. You had snark ("Did he throw an interception on his way out of the building?") and you had worries about more heartbreak.

Or maybe there were three camps. A third reacted with neither sarcasm nor anger. "It's a sad day today," posted one fan to the *Green Bay Press-Gazette* blog. Other posts were sad in themselves. One—a simple expression of hope, hope that Favre would remain a Packer, hope that he would occupy that room at Victor McCormick Hall—appeared on the *Journal Sentinel* blog shortly after Favre had left Lambeau Field late Monday night. "If Favre exited the Lambeau lot and took a right on Oneida," this fan wrote, "he'd be heading toward St. Norbert College."

But it was not to be. Turning right on Oneida Street was also the way to Shady Lane.

Brett Favre was headed home. And away from the Packers for good.

Rodgers was playing cribbage with Mark Tauscher, Korey Hall, and John Kuhn when he got the news that Favre had been traded to the Jets. A teammate heard the news on TV, came out into the courtyard of Victor McCormick Hall a little after 10:30 P.M., and spread the word.

Rodgers knew a trade was coming. Two nights earlier, Mike McCarthy had addressed the team and told them the "worst was over," according to Michael Silver of Yahoo! Sports, the quote supplied by McCarthy himself. He also apologized for Monday night, as five hours with Favre meant he had to cancel a team meeting and postpone a position meeting with Rodgers and the rookie quarterbacks. McCarthy—a planner, a details guy, a man who blocks out the training-camp schedule down to the minute all the way back in the spring—had not built into his schedule a full night of bone-picking with Favre followed by that delicate dance of a press conference.

The Wednesday Brett Favre left town, the team had two of its better practices, reported Packers beat writer Greg Bedard of the *Journal*

*Sentinel*. It was an encouraging rebound from Tuesday afternoon's practice, which Bedard deemed "sloppy." As Favre headed to the airport Wednesday, Rodgers himself looked sharper, his throws more accurate. He was poised and crisp in a no-huddle 11-on-11 drill with simulated crowd noise blasting from speakers. And by week's end, the pro-Brett signs in the bleachers were gone. No one was booing Rodgers. No one F-bombed him as he waited for the gate to open into "The Cage," the players' parking lot, as had happened one day the previous week. And though he was still getting plenty of questions from the media, it wasn't like day one of camp when he stood at his locker talking to both local and national reporters arrayed five deep around him for thirty straight minutes.

Thursday's press conference with Murphy, McCarthy, and Thompson was a dour session. The weight of what had unfolded showed on their faces, thickened their voices. "It wasn't Brett's fault and it wasn't our fault," said Murphy. "The relationship got to a point where it couldn't go forward." Asked for his take on what kept Favre at an unbridgeable distance from his old team, Thompson said, "There were some feelings that he felt were hard to let go." Was Thompson comfortable being forever known as the guy who traded Brett Favre? "No, I don't think anybody would be comfortable with that," the GM replied. "When the trade papers actually came and I was going to sign it, which would be my job, I almost wanted someone else to sign it."

For his part, Favre looked a little stunned (can you blame him?) as he held up his No. 4 Jets jersey at a press conference in Cleveland that same Thursday. "A lot of things happened this offseason, a lot of shocking things," Favre said when asked for his own version of what went down with the Packers. "I think we're probably both at fault. I'm not going to sit here and blame it all on one side or the other." Staying on the high road, the closest Favre came to referencing any bad blood was to cite "differences" between him and "a couple of other people." He'd taken the high road the day before, too, upon landing in Hattiesburg. "I know people say you need to put the personal issues aside," he told a reporter, "and I agree. But I couldn't do that."

"Probably only four or five people know what really happened, and some day probably four or five books will be written about it," said Mark Tauscher, Favre's lineman of eight years, in an interview nine months later with Steve "The Homer" True on Milwaukee's 540 ESPN Radio. Since that August 7 Packers press conference, the organization has divulged no further details concerning their interactions with Brett Favre. And unless there is some kind of ugly flare-up down the road, revelations provoking rebuttals, it will probably stay that way. What's to be gained, from a Packers franchise perspective, by saying more?

Brett Favre gave the Packers sixteen unforgettable years. In the franchise's big picture, that's what matters most. More detail from the Packers side regarding the Summer of Favre would only be a distraction to the team, an irritation to many fans, and catnip to the media. Long-term, the best thing is for time to work some healing, as it did in the cases of Lambeau and Lombardi, and for Brett Favre to some day once again enjoy a relationship with the Green Bay Packers.

As I write, it seems this day might be a ways off. Brett Favre nearly become a Viking in time for 2009 training camp. After serious discussions with Minnesota during the spring and early summer, and after having surgery on his injured throwing shoulder, Favre decided shortly before the start of camp to remain retired, citing concerns about his physical stamina at age 39 (with a 40th birthday in October). Had Favre actually joined the Vikings in late July, part of his motivation would have been to show the Packers they were wrong for not taking him back, and to get some revenge on the decision-makers (Thompson and McCarthy). Don't take my word for it, take Brett's.

"Part of me coming back last year, I have to admit now, was sticking it to Ted," Favre told Peter King of *Sports Illustrated* in February. "I was a little peeved," Favre told ESPN's Ed Werder that same month. "It was like someone was sitting on my shoulder, telling me I should stick it to them." Even back on August 7, 2008, in that first Jets press conference, Favre conceded, "My interest at first, as I'm sure we all know, was to stay within our division. Maybe that was a little bit of vindictive nature or whatever, competitive nature. I think in the end that was probably the wrong motive."

When Brett Favre talks this way, pointing to revenge as a motive potentially strong enough to pull him out of retirement, take him to a new city, and fuel him through a season's worth of bruising NFL games, he sounds not so much like a famous Shakespearean character ("Hamlet in a chinstrap," wrote Chris Erskine in the *Los Angeles Times*, Favre's drama being to play or not to play) but rather some warrior out of ancient Greek mythology. Classical Greek literature is full of tough, brave, emotional men—heroes—who fight a battle within themselves, with their passions, and sometimes lose. The ancient Greeks even had a word for this: *thymos*. Most simply, it means "spiritedness," a tendency to bristle, to push back when you feel disrespected or undervalued. "People believe they have a certain worth," wrote political scientist Francis Fukuyama of this ancient concept, "and when other people act as though they are worthless—do not recognize their worth or its correct value—they become angry."

According to the philosopher Plato, *thymos* joined reason and *eros* (desire) as one of three essential parts of the human *psyche* or soul. *Thymos* fuels pride, indignation, the need for recognition. It fuels warriors. The nearly indestructible Achilles was almost pure *thymos*, always battling his anger. *Thymos* motivates both good deeds and bad. It's the source of courage, self-sacrifice, and honor (*thymos* drives a person to race into a burning building to save a child, or charge a machine-gun nest to save fellow soldiers). But it can also overrule reason, causing a man to duel with pistols over an insult, or stop at nothing to achieve glory. The Greeks didn't judge *thymos* so much as acknowledge its importance and show it in action, capturing its workings in stories, in myths. To the Greeks, it was part of being human. It's oh-so-human.

Like a classical Greek hero, Brett Favre in 2008 came up against the power of *thymos*. In talking to Greta Van Susteren, the thing that seemed to most burn him is that the Packers didn't want him back. "I didn't want to go back there after that," he said point-blank, referring to the moment when the team conveyed to him that they were "moving on." That's why he was so lukewarm discussing this gambit of "forcing the Packers' hand" via a surge of pro-Favre public sentiment. That wouldn't address the central issue. It wouldn't change the fact that the Green Bay Packers, a team for whom he'd done so much for so long, didn't want him back. As Favre said several times in 2008, he gave everything to the Packers, he gave his all. And when he realized they wanted to move on without him? Well, maybe he'd move on, too. Maybe he'd even move on to Minnesota.

# PART THREE:

# THE RODGERS AUTUMN

# CHAPTER 7:
# LOOK BOTH WAYS

---

**T**HE STADIUM VIEW Bar and Grille sits at the corner of Holmgren Way and Brett Favre Pass. A refrigerator-sized replica of the Lombardi Trophy tops a head-high black marble base ten feet from its entrance. Husband and wife Jerry and Diane Watson opened the aptly named establishment in a former women's clothing store in 1992, just a few weeks after Brett Favre took over as the Packers starting quarterback. Block-walled and bunker-like from the outside, a green awning its only concession to color, the interior consists of one large TV- and table-filled main floor anchored by a four-sided central bar, and three banquet rooms. On game days, much of the action takes place outside its busy doors, the bar's parking lot becoming one giant Packer party.

Voted America's No. 1 sports bar by *Forbes* magazine two years running, the Stadium View has enjoyed years where it sold more Miller beer than any other drinking establishment in the state. It doesn't hurt that thousands of people drop by on good-weather game days to sample the tailgate carnival, boogie to live bands, pose for photographs with the kookiest-looking Packer fans, and get thrown by the mechanical bull. Nor does it hurt, beer-sales-wise, that one of the bar's signature sights is the "beer tower," a three-foot-high clear plastic cylinder that arrives at your table filled with 108 fluid ounces of the malt beverage of your choice.

If there were fewer beer towers (a.k.a. "beer giraffes") on tables than usual Saturday evening, August 16, it was because Packers fans wanted to keep at least some of their wits about them as they took in a striking preseason double bill. Game one featured Brett Favre in his Jets debut. Game two featured Aaron Rodgers in his first road start, against none other than the team that passed him up in 2005, the San Francisco 49ers. As on Draft Day 2005 in New York City, a contingent of some thirty family and friends would be on hand at Candlestick Park to watch the Chico native play the opening half against Mike Nolan's squad, with former No. 1 pick Alex Smith scheduled to see action for the Niners behind onetime Packers backup J. T. O'Sullivan.

The local TV news reporters trolling this Green Bay institution were gone by the time Rodgers threw his first pass, about 8:10 P.M. Central. Rodgers in Frisco wasn't the story. The story was Brett Favre wearing Jets kelly green, and how this crowd would react to the sight of something they'd never have imagined in their wildest dreams just a few weeks before.

"*Wooooo, woooooo,* that's my Brett!" shouted a woman from a rear table as No. 4 jogged onto the field to a rousing welcome from fans at half-full Giants Stadium. The cheer-to-boo ratio inside the bar was about 80–20, a strong majority clapping and yelling excitedly upon seeing Favre in his familiar trot, minutes from taking a snap. "It was weird seeing him in a Jets uniform," said 21-year-old Laura Luedtke when we spoke at halftime, "but I felt happy that he looked happy."

There was plenty of good will in the room. Here's a guy you've been pulling for, cheering for, giving over part of your Packer heart to for sixteen years—and now you get to see him do his thing again, after you thought you'd never see it again. The part of us that can't help but be stirred by the sight of someone getting to display an extraordinary talent—the part of us that knows there will never be another Brett Favre—that too came to the fore as No. 4 took the field against the Redskins.

More cheers rose—even shouts of triumph, pride—as Favre whipped a bullet to wide receiver Jerricho Cotchery on a quick slant for 11 yards on his very first play from scrimmage. You could almost see thought balloons above bar-patron heads. *Good ol' Brett! Still got it! Ten days removed from his riding mower, just a week of Jets practice under his belt. See, New York, we didn't sell you a bill of goods. He's the real deal. And we here in this little Wisconsin town whose whole population could practically fit inside your stadium got to enjoy him for a generation.*

In that spellbinding opening minute, there was no cursing of Ted Thompson. The moment was bigger than that. People felt confirmed in their view of Favre's gifts. With his second pass he hit tight end Chris Baker on a curl for another ten yards. Pass three was a deft dump-off to running back Leon Washington for a short gain. A sack and an incompletion ended the opening drive but Favre came right back on possession two and rifled a beautiful ball to Cotchery on a 19-yard crossing route, leading the receiver as he streaked across the field from right to left. Three plays later the newest Jet threw a 4-yard touchdown strike to rookie tight end Dustin Keller. The quarterback raised his arms skyward, hugged a couple of lineman, high-fived some other Jets. Oh, and during this same series he even executed one of his goofy trademark fake jump passes after a handoff. You could take No. 4 out of Green Bay, but . . .

"Whoa, Brett just threw a TD!" said a tan guy in a white long-sleeve "BRETT THE JET" shirt, narrating everything Favre did into a cell phone. "Now he's jumping around!" Not everyone was so delighted. One 40-something women in jeans and highlighted brown hair said, "You know, it's almost sickening watching this." It was sinking in. Favre had been uncannily good for a guy who'd more or less parachuted into the Meadowlands straight off his 400-acre Mississippi estate. He still had the magic but now he was wearing a different shade of green. With the excitement of seeing him throw spirals wearing off, there were frowns, some sour faces, in the bar. There were mutters along the lines of, *Um, remind me, how come he's not a Packer again?*

I headed over to the fan who'd yelled, "*Wooooo, woooooo,* that's my Brett!" Her name was Mariann Watson. Turns out she's the twin sister of Jerry, owner of the Stadium View. Indicating that Favre and her brother were longtime friends, she asked if I'd seen footage of Favre getting off the plane with Deanna here in Green Bay two weeks ago. I said I'd watched it live from down in Milwaukee. "Jerry was the first one to greet him off the plane," Mariann said.

I spent the next hour talking to Mariann and two of her friends, Terri Swiboda and Tom Van Calster. Tom and Mariann have known each other since first grade. Mariann sells "fasteners and fittings" for a trucking-supply company. Terri handles dispatch for her husband, a locksmith. Tom is a retired paper-mill worker. He lives on Oneida Street just three blocks north of Lombardi Avenue. People park in his driveway on game days. He told a story about offering supper and hospitality to some Canadians who'd driven down from Saskatchewan, parked at his place, and ended up getting snowed in. Tom's the guy who used to "peddle pop" on streets around Lambeau in his youth, the kid hailed by Paul Hornung sitting in his white Caddie Deville.

Mariann had been interviewed for an Associated Press video piece on the Favre controversy right here a month ago. That night I Googled the clip. "Favre Fan," read the caption as she delivered her defense of No. 4. "Hey, we all change our mind," said Mariann. "They always say it's a woman's prerogative to change her mind. Well, guess what, it can be a guy's prerogative, too. If he wants to come back, let him come back!"

Tonight she was reacting to a newer Favre development. "My heart is in New York now," said Mariann on this warm August evening. Out came a copy of a 15-year-old photograph showing Favre in his mid twenties standing with her brother Jerry and then Packers assistant coach Andy Reid at a golf outing. "There's my honey!" said grinning, quick-witted Terri Swiboda, pointing to the boyish Favre, his cheeks chubbier than they are now. "It's just a shame," Tom reflected a moment later, gazing toward the photo through steel-framed glasses, a black GRAND ISLAND RESORTS ball cap on his head. "It'd be one thing if Brett had a bad year. But he had one of his best. You saw him tonight—one day he's doing yard work, then he's throwing like that. I don't care how well the Packers do this year—they made a freakin' mistake. If they can trade Brett, they can trade anyone. This team is owned by the fans. But we didn't get any say so. They put the stadium upgrade to a referendum. Why not vote on whether or not to keep Brett Favre?"

The bar's multiple TVs switched to the Packers game in San Francisco. Rodgers had a tough act to follow, especially for this crowd. People's excitement at seeing Favre do so well in Giants Stadium (a crisp 5 of 6 before giving way to Kellen Clemens, who then gave way to Brett Ratliff, Rodgers' successor at Butte Community College) was all but gone after a couple hours of drinking, a drab Jets second half, and ample time to dwell on what the Packers no longer had.

Rodgers took the field boosted by a solid quarter of work against the Bengals at Lambeau Monday night. The crowd had given him a standing ovation as he jogged out for his first Packer start. He went 9 of 15 for 117 yards and a touchdown, numbers that would have been better had his receivers held onto a couple of passes, one for a first down on third-and-17, the other an on-target slant that bounced off a wideout's chest and was picked off. Sitting in the stands that night, I'd been struck by Rodgers' arm strength, his nimbleness on the roll-out, and his ability to throw on the run. Along with a quick release, he could set his feet with almost startling speed.

The highlight of the Cincinnati game was a 30-yard scoring strike to James Jones. A Bengal ripped Jones' helmet off at the 13-yard-line but the receiver kept going, dashing to the house without his hat.

And now, tonight, while one Chico native took snaps in Giants Stadium, another jogged out onto the turf of Candlestick for the first time, his parents and two brothers in the stands. Talking to Jason Wilde of the *Wisconsin State Journal* the day before, Rodgers again reflected on spring 2005 when what seemed then a "dream scenario"— Niner nut becomes a Niner—dissolved and he became a Packer. But it all worked out, and so Rodgers quoted from a Garth Brooks song: "Some of God's greatest gifts are unanswered prayers." While Rodgers seemed at peace, grateful for what fate had delivered, it was unclear whether Coach Mike Nolan felt the same equanimity. Asked by Wilde to revisit the team's decision to draft Alex Smith over Rodgers, Nolan replied, "You know, it was a long time ago. Let's not go there now, because it would be a lot of B.S."

As proof that the gods of football care nothing for poetic justice, Rodgers had an awful night in San Francisco. "Playing the entire first half, Rodgers was indecisive in the pocket, failed to make a play that counted, and paled in comparison to 49ers starter J. T. O'Sullivan, of all people," wrote Bob McGinn of the *Journal Sentinel*. Rodgers went 9 of 16 for just 58 yards. He was sacked four times for losses totaling 26 yards. He threw a couple of shoulda-been-picks. And speaking of drops, Donald Driver had a ball slip through his hands on a go route and Donald Lee did the same in the end zone. There were groans in the Stadium View. Expressions of disgust. A general vibe of deep unease. Was this a season preview? Anxiety turned to horror when Rodgers was demolished on a cornerback blitz by Shawntae Spencer, as bone-jarring a hit as you'll see on a QB. Would he even get up? He got up. But it was a spooky reminder that if Rodgers was knocked out of a game, his replacement would be a rookie, either second-round pick Brian Brohm of Louisville or seventh-rounder Matt Flynn from LSU. Brohm had been floundering in training camp. Flynn would likely get the ball.

"Remarkably putrid," was Tom Silverstein's overall verdict on the game, which the Packers lost 34–6. "We just stunk," said Mark Tauscher. "You can't color and put it in any other light."

Jordy Nelson was one of the lone bright spots. The K-State rookie who'd never returned a kickoff in college took one back for 56 yards, then topped that with a 58-yard return in the fourth quarter.

Still, Rodgers was the focus. "He looked lost," a fan commented on the *Journal Sentinel* blog. Another declared, "Our 25-year dry spell between great quarterbacks has begun. Anybody who thinks A-Rodge is the answer is kidding themselves. He's pathetic."

Denver was next, six days away. By the time Friday, August 22, rolled around, the Packers, if not quite in panic mode, were openly expressing a sense of urgency. McGinn reported that the team actually considered the game a "must-win." This, as much as anything else, spoke to the magnitude of the Rodgers over Favre decision. If the Pack lost to the Broncos, they'd drop to 0–3 in preseason (the Bengals beat them 23–21 in game one), and public bashing of the decision would escalate, while support for Rodgers would weaken. "We've got to win," said Driver. "We're back down in the dungeon now." A loss to Denver, McGinn pointed out, could very well mean going 0–4 in preseason for just the third time in history, since next up was Tennessee, a team that, unlike most NFL clubs (the Packers included), treated game four as a dress rehearsal for the regular season. They were in it to win it. For McCarthy's Packers, game three was the biggie.

And they won it. They beat the Broncos 27–24. Crisis averted. "Everything that Aaron Rodgers was not a week ago in San Francisco he was Friday night at Invesco Field," wrote McGinn. Efficient, accurate, decisive, Rodgers completed 18 of 22 passes for 193 yards, with a touchdown and no interceptions. And to the gargantuan delight (or was it relief?) of Packer Nation, his rhythm carried through to the Vikings game at Lambeau Field ten days later—a game that mattered worlds more than the Denver outing. It was the first contest of the 2008 regular season, against a division archrival. For extra motivation, this was the club the Packers accused of tampering with Favre (though Commissioner Goodell cleared Minnesota on August 4). And for extra pressure, the game was played before a national television audience on *Monday Night Football.*

In a quirk of statistical symmetry, Rodgers again went 18 of 22, this time for 173 yards. He passed for a TD, sneaked for another. He was neither picked nor sacked by the vaunted, Jared Allen–led Vikings defense. Rodgers also ran for 35 yards, notching three first downs with scrambles of 6, 8, and 21 yards. His 81.8 completion percentage, as an *MNF* graphic boasted during the telecast, marked the second-best in NFL history among quarterbacks with at least 20 passing attempts in their first start. In terms of Packers annals, it was the fourth-best completion percentage ever, surpassed only once by Favre in 275 games when he completed 82.1 percent of his passes against Cleveland in 1995. Rodgers took on what more than one sportswriter called "the toughest job in the NFL this year"—filling Favre's shoes—and nailed it, standing up to the pressure just as he had at age 19 when, as a junior college transfer, he started his first two Division I games against Illinois and USC.

Here the stage was land masses larger. And he put up better numbers.

And the Packers won, 24–19.

Favre didn't make it any easier on Rodgers by having a sharp outing the day before in Miami, completing 15 of 22 passes for 194 yards and a pair of touchdown passes worth 56 and 22 yards, the latter on a fourth-and-13 play attempted only because the Jets kicker was injured. Posting a superb quarterback rating of 125.9, Favre led the Jets to a 20–14 victory against the Dolphins and Chad Pennington, the quarterback he had displaced in New York.

Moreover, Rodgers took the field knowing Tom Brady had blown out his left knee following a first-quarter hit by Chiefs safety Bernard Pollard. Rodgers wouldn't want to spend much time dwelling on the fact that he would be facing both Pollard's former teammate Jared Allen and the "Williams Wall"—defensive tackles Pat and Kevin Williams, 630 pounds of ball-carrier-crushing purple—with a cadaver's ligament in his own left knee. Then again, Allen by his own words wouldn't be going for Rodgers' legs. "Hopefully, I can put my helmet square in the back of his spine," said last year's leading sacker (15.5 in 14 games). "If I can do that and knock the ball loose, it'll be a good day." As it happened, no small thanks to left tackle Chad Clifton, Allen posted a pair of donuts. No sacks. No tackles. "One of the least productive games I've ever had in my life," said Allen afterward. He even had some nice things to say about Rodgers. "I thought it was going to be easier playing against Rodgers than Favre," the sack artist continued. "But it was easier playing Favre because he was not as mobile. [Rodgers] froze the defensive linemen with the play-action and his movement."

Rodgers displayed his mobility on the third play of the season. After opening the game with a 3-yard pass to Donald Lee, he took a snap out of the shotgun on third-and-4, scanned the field, then brought the ball down and sprinted for 6 yards. At 71,004, the biggest crowd in Lambeau history erupted. A fan waved a sign declaring the stadium Mr. Rodgers' Neighborhood.

Cheers turned to boos in the next series when the Packers went backward. After a 1-yard pass to Lee, Clifton was flagged for holding. That was followed by a muffed exchange between Rodgers and center Jason Spitz, subbing for Scott Wells. On third-and-20, Rodgers threw incomplete to running back Brandon Jackson and the Vikings declined an illegal formation penalty on Clifton. But hey, at least the new guy Derrick Frost had a great punt. "His first kick as a Packer," said *MNF*'s Mike Tirico, "is a beauty." It sailed 48 yards, landing within inches of the right sideline. Frost had been with the team a week. In a move that dropped the jaws of Packers fans, the team released popular redheaded Canadian Jon Ryan on September 1 and brought in Frost, cut the last day of camp by the Redskins after three years as their punter. Special teams coach Mike Stock, who knew Frost from an NFL Europe camp, liked the Northern Iowa alum's directionality and "get-off" time. But gone was a guy whose 44.5 and 44.4 gross averages the past two years were the third- and fourth-best in Packers history. Ryan's 37.6 net average in '07 marked the best by a Packer since 1969. Were they trying to fix something that wasn't broken? (Hold that thought.)

After a penalty-filled first quarter, the score was tied at zero. From here, for the Pack, it was a game of big plays. Three huge gainers spurred their offense, one a pass, one a punt return, one a 57-yard gallop by running back Ryan Grant, seeing his first action since the January NFC championship game. Two practices after signing a four-year contract worth up to $30 million following his one-week camp holdout, Grant, acquired from the Giants for a sixth-round pick on September 1, 2007, pulled a hamstring and was out until the last exhibition game against Tennessee. But in that game he had time only to make a block and never touched the ball, as Rodgers threw a 68-yard scoring bomb to Greg Jennings on the first play from scrimmage and McCarthy pulled his starters right then and there.

Picking up where they left off, Rodgers and Jennings connected for 56 yards on the first play of the Packers' third possession against Minnesota. With Jennings racing up the middle covered one-on-one by nickel back Charles Gordon, Rodgers reared back and javelined a soaring ball that the leaping receiver reached back for and hauled in over Gordon. The pass traveled 65 aerial yards. Both Jennings and Gordon went down at the 6. Several tense game minutes later, on third-and-goal from the 1-yard line, Rodgers fired a bullet pass back across his body to his third read, cribbage partner Korey Hall. The fullback released from the right side of the line, traveled laterally across the middle of the end zone, and got a half step on linebacker Ben Leber. Rodgers danced out of the way of one rusher who hit the ground and started rolling, sidestepped a second rusher who tapped the QB's helmet, and throwing off his back foot hooked a tight spiral into a diving Hall's hands eight inches off the ground. It was a crazy, creative, eye-blink of a pass.

And it was Rodgers' favorite throw of the year. Yes, of all the passes he'd complete in '08, including multiple pinpoint deep balls, this

1-yard toss sang sweetest. "I kind of surprised myself with that one," he told me at season's end when I asked if one pass stood out. "I've thrown some crazy passes before, but that was a new one. In practice, I'd been hitting my number one and two reads. Korey was my third read in the progression. I've never thrown one where my stance was that contorted. Korey flashed across the middle. A guy was trying to wrap up my legs. The dynamic of the pass was, I threw across my body, torquing my shoulder around, and just squeezed it in there. I managed to put it in a good spot, right where I wanted it to go. And Korey made a great catch."

Tony Kornheiser of *MNF* took some grief from partners Tirico and Ron Jaworski for constantly referencing Favre during the telecast. "People in the stands are thinking of Favre getting 34 yards," said Tony K. when the Pack, after three consecutive first-quarter penalties, faced a first-and-33. "A Favre-like throw," he said of Rodgers' back-foot corkscrew zinger. His boothmates didn't want to hear it but I think Kornheiser was right. Packer fans were keeping "mental score." And he got it right when it came to the momentousness, the dramatic watershed aspect, of that pass to Hall. "You can sense how this place will explode if the Packers score," Kornheiser said. "If Rodgers completes a pass here, okay, now we can exhale, now we've got the guy. But if they're stopped . . ."

It looked like they might be stopped. Rodgers had overthrown Donald Lee in the end zone. Ryan Grant had been stuffed short of the goal line three times. Three Vikings penalties painfully elongated the moment. Third down on the 1-foot line, Minnesota up a field goal, it really did feel in Lambeau, rational or not, that the season might be hanging in the balance, with everything riding on what would happen next, all that had happened over the summer leading up to this juncture, this crossroads, this turning point. It was make or break for the Pack. Just like that milky low sky seemed like it could darken and pour rain, or lighten, thin, and let in some late sunrays. If they failed to score, darkness could follow. If they scored, the season—indeed the whole Aaron Rodgers era—could be bright.

The Packers scored. The place exploded.

Will "Fair-Catch is a Dirty Word" Blackmon's 76-yard punt return for a touchdown was the next big play. A weaving, highlight-reel dash, it put the Packers up 17–6 halfway through the third quarter. And it lessened the sting of having a 68-yard touchdown by Driver wiped out by an ineligible man downfield penalty called on right guard Tony Moll the previous possession. Feinting a slant, Driver got cornerback Antoine Winfield to bite, then blazed down the right sideline. After a pump, Rodgers arched a touch pass accurate down to the inch that Double D hauled in with extended hands in full stride.

On the punt return, Blackmon accelerated toward a 49-yarder by Chris Kluwe, caught the ball at speed, tight-roped the left sideline, then swerved right at midfield and cut almost all the way to the other sideline before racing to the house. Defensive end Jason Hunter leveled pursuing linebacker Chad Greenway at the 27. No one touched linebacker Leber who ended up on his backside—it was just the power of Blackmon's juke, an ankle-breaking move by a guy who likes to ride a skateboard and seems to take any opportunity to slalom as he runs.

After receiver Sydney Rice came free across the middle on fourth-and-1 from the 23, snagged a Tarvaris Jackson throw at the 13 and ran it in, the pair failed to connect on a two-point conversion, leaving the score at 17–12 early in the fourth quarter. Half a period later came big Packers play No. 3. Out of the I formation, Grant took a handoff and followed Hall through a massive hole courtesy of a zone-blocking triumph. Daryn Colledge sealed Pat Williams, Moll countered Kevin

Williams, and the 243-pound Hall thundered 9 free yards before pancaking former Packers safety Darren Sharper. Upright, one-cut Ryan Grant—a Notre Dame alum whose 929 yards in the last ten games of 2007 was second only to LaDainian Tomlinson's 947—stiff-armed Leber in a full sprint to help his cause and booked all the way to the Vikings 2-yard line.

One play later, Rodgers snuck it in from less than a yard, thanks in part to Colledge's bulldozing block on the 317-pound Pat Williams. After scoring, Rodgers jumped up, emphatically spiked the ball, then took off for his first Lambeau Leap, an effort he later rated a 3. Tired legs curtailed his hops. His hips didn't surmount the wall until some fans pulled him up the last couple inches to start the lovefest. Cue Todd Rundgren's 1983 rocker "Bang the Drum All Day" ("I don't want to play, I want to bang on the drum all day!"), a song that's been jazzing Lambeau touchdowns since 1995. The sky was now misting slightly—there were no glorious rays of late sun—but cameras were flashing and stadium lights were burning bright and yellow slickers glistened in the stands. And once safety Atari Bigby intercepted a Jackson misfire along the right sideline with fifty seconds to go, the Packers had their fifth straight victory over the frustrated Vikings.

"I've been dreaming about that for four years, to be honest," said Rodgers of his Lambeau Leap, standing on the field in the game's noisy aftermath. He then trotted towards the green-roofed tunnel, smiled and waved to the cheering crowd, and tossed a white wristband into the stands. Its whiteness caught stadium light, and with that last little throw he took a lightened heart into the tunnel, a smaller burden, things proven and accomplished and shed and put in place on this early September evening in Green Bay.

\* \* \*

Baumgartner's Cheese Store and Tavern sits on a Swiss-styled square in the small southern Wisconsin town of Monroe, about an hour's drive south of Madison near the Illinois border. Two days before I arrived to watch the Packers play the Lions on a pair of mounted TVs in Baumgartner's rear-room bar, the Monroe High Cheesemakers got destroyed 61–0 by the Milton Red Hawks. I didn't want to jinx it, but I figured the chances were pretty good that the Packers would do better in Detroit. Better than the Cheesemakers, that is.

They did. They won 48–25, though not without giving Packers fans a scare by actually falling behind 25–24 to the underpowered Lions with 7:41 to go. "This is too easy," said one of the patrons at the old wooden bar in the second quarter when the Packers went up 21–0. Aaron Rodgers had just thrown his third straight touchdown. This was the moment, related by ESPN Radio's Mike Greenberg on *Mike and Mike in the Morning* the next day, when radio partner Mike Golic sent him a text message. It read, "I am watching the best quarterback in the NFL." (I later asked Rodgers if he'd heard about this—indeed he had.) When Golic sent his text, it was after seeing Rodgers drill a 9-yard on-the-run touchdown strike to James Jones. And Rodgers toss a 62-yard bomb to Jennings on a stutter-and-go. And Rodgers loft a perfect ball to Jordy Nelson for a 29-yard back-of-the-end-zone catch—his first NFL catch a touchdown—on a post-corner route where he flat-out torched the defensive back. "Kind of an in-and-go," said offensive coordinator Joe Philbin after the game. "Bit of a double move, so to speak."

Rodgers was 16 of 20 at halftime. Since the Denver exhibition game, he'd completed 53 of his last 65 passes, with no interceptions. We'd seen him get in grooves like this at Cal. Now he was in one as a starter in the NFL.

They ring old Swiss bells at Baumgartner's when the Pack scores a touchdown. The bartender or youthful owner Chris Soukop or one of the sandwich-makers in their black I CUT THE CHEESE AT BAUMGARTNER'S T-shirts reaches up and yanks a rope. If you like bells, this was a great day to be at Baumgartner's, since the Pack scored six touchdowns. But after the bells had clanged thrice and it appeared a rout was on, many patrons shifted their attention to beer, lunch, and conversation. Pints of local brew go for $2.50. A Swiss cheese sandwich costs $2.75, a smoked brat $3.75. "In a time when things keep changing, it sure is nice to have one place that stays the same!" is Baumgartner's slogan, and it could apply to the prices as well as to the ambiance and décor.

Founded in 1931, Baumgartner's is Wisconsin's oldest cheese store. From the street it sports a Swiss chalet look, with black wood doors, red cross awnings, and Teutonic signage. Inside the rear-room tavern, wooden plaques name the cantons of Switzerland and a mural in a mock-medieval style depicts beer steins with Humpty Dumpty faces battling bottles of beer. I discovered this place thanks to a Packers fan Web site, PackerChatters.com, which boasts a searchable database of top places to watch the Pack statewide. Just as in the Lambeau parking lot during training camp, Baumgartner's displays maps of America and the world with push-pins marking visitor origins. Tourists come from all over. But on Packer game days, locals from 10,000-citizen Monroe and environs fill the small tavern with its mounted elk head, vintage menu signboard, and hundreds of dollar bills pinned to the high wooden ceiling.

After taking a seat at the bar, I met Nathan Phillips, who was overseas in the Navy during the last two Lombardi championships, then came home and, as he put it, "had to wait thirty years till we won another one." I met Paul Barrett, a wholesale dairy products rep, who offered advice should I order a Baumgartner's specialty, a sandwich made with locally produced Limburger. "Force it down with a cup of coffee," Paul counseled. And I met Andy Wilkie, who owns a heating and cooling business in town. "If the Jets start losing," said Andy, "the Favre thing should quiet down. Especially if Rodgers keeps playing like this."

A couple of guys to my right were discussing you know what. "Rodgers got lucky against the Vikings," said a fellow in a denim jacket with dark hair longish in back but bald up top. "I mean, Favre beat 'em 34–0 last year. Then Rodgers goes to do his Lambeau Leap and he can't even get his butt over the wall!" "He was tired!" said his friend. When I asked them how they felt about the Favre matter, the guy in the denim jacket replied, "Oh man, that's a touchy question." His friend said, "It feels about as good as being a kid in a divorce."

The one patron dressed in a Favre jersey turned out to be from Rockford, Illinois. Brian Barr and his brother Doug sat at one of Baumgartner's half dozen tables with their friends Mike Lauer, Scott Lauer, and Ed Lauer, their dad. Once a year they make the drive from Rockford to watch the Pack at Baumgartner's. "If they win," said Brian, "we celebrate with a Limburger cheese sandwich." Moments after the game ended, Ed got a text on his cell. It was from his wife, a Bears fan. Her message said, "Enjoy your Limburger sandwich."

The Packers led 24–9 heading into the fourth quarter. Then the Lions quit rushing the ball entirely and went at the middle of the field with their receivers, the biggest weapon being the long-legged speedster Calvin Johnson, the second-overall pick in the 2007 NFL Draft. Running a slant at the 13:20 mark, the phenomenally athletic Johnson reached back with one hand, popped the ball up, secured it, and loped untouched into the end zone. Two minutes later, a football sailed through the upraised hands of punter Derrick Frost on a catchable snap in the end zone. The freak safety narrowed the score to 24–18. Then, with 7:41 to go, Johnson released cleanly, stutter-stepped before cornerback Tramon Williams, snagged a 5-yard slant, and was tapped but not tackled by Williams, safety Aaron Rouse, and cornerback Al Harris. That made it 25–24 Lions. Better put a hold on those Limburger sandwiches.

It was Greg Jennings to the rescue. Playing before 85 family members at Ford Field, the Kalamazoo native caught a 5-yard slant of his own, tore across the middle, and sprinted up the right sideline for 60 yards. A Mason Crosby field goal quickly followed.

On the next series, former University of Michigan star Charles Woodson picked off an underthrown back-shoulder toss to Johnson on a pump-and-go. Three plays later, bells clanged at Baumgartner's when running back Brandon Jackson made up for a critical dropped pass on the previous possession by scampering 19 yards for a touchdown, a dandy cutback aided by an equally dandy block by center Jason Spitz. Twenty seconds later, Woodson, playing with a fractured toe, jumped a pass intended for receiver Mike Furrey on an out route and ran it back 41 yards to the house. Exactly a minute after that, free safety Nick Collins undercut a crossing route for Johnson and ran the Jon Kitna pass back 42 yards for his own "pick 6." Bells and more bells! After things had gotten a little hairy there, the Packers had scored 24 unanswered points in five and a half minutes. Finally it was Limburger time at Baumgartner's.

The following Sunday, I began my day in another southern Wisconsin town of 10,000 people, having driven down to Tony Romo's hometown of Burlington, thirty miles southwest of Milwaukee. It was my own way of adding buildup to the Packers-Cowboys matchup that evening in Lambeau, I suppose. Rodgers versus Romo. It would be Tony Romo's first start at Lambeau and only his third visit, the previous two as a Cowboys backup in 2004 and a teenaged Packers fan watching a preseason game in 1998. I ate breakfast at Sheila Mae's Town Fryer, where Romo had been enjoying pancakes and eggs since high school, and met friendly proprietor Sheila Renz, who told me Burlington's favorite son had last been by for breakfast six months earlier. I sat in a booth beneath a little Romo shrine, his No. 9 Cowboys jersey behind glass above two framed photos of the smiling quarterback taken during visits here in the past couple of years. Two photos of Brett Favre hung nearby on the same wall. In one, Favre rode a motorcycle wearing jeans and sporting sunglasses, a caption in gold letters reading LEADER OF THE PACK.

Romo jerseys were a common sight up in Green Bay that day. I counted eight of them along three blocks of Holmgren Way, including two worn by a father and son tossing a football back and forth in a warehouse parking lot. The September sky was hazy, the temperature about 70, the air humid. For blocks and blocks around Lambeau the scene was as festive as it had been for the Monday night game against the Vikings. Beer-bottle inflatables as big as Thanksgiving Day parade balloons swayed on a dozen corners. Two guys in Packers jerseys tossed a football with stogies planted in their mouths. A busker played a sax, another played a tuba. Adding to the Green Bay Mardi Gras feel, a blond kid of ten or eleven in a Donald Driver jersey tap-danced on a board across from the Hutson Center. On a stage set up in the backyard of a "Packer party house" overlooking Lambeau's Oneida Street parking lot, a Packer jersey-wearing lead singer and his band covered "Blister in the Sun" by Milwaukee's own Violent Femmes.

Al Michaels and John Madden were in town for NBC's *Sunday Night Football*. It was only the fifth time in Cowboys history that the team had come to Lambeau Field, and they'd never won there. There was a charge in the air. The Packers and Cowboys both stood at 2–0 and were looking good. Cheers rose from a hundred merrymakers at the Stadium View tailgate party when a buzz-cut, muscle-bound guy in jeans and a Terrell Owens Cowboys jersey got thrown by the mechanical bull. Even the Green Bay cop directing traffic at the corner of Lombardi Avenue and Oneida Street seemed to have matters cowboy on his mind. "Ma'am, this ain't my first rodeo," he said when an intoxicated Packer fan gave him grief for not letting her cross the street.

Kid Rock's infectious song "All Summer Long"—that hosanna to summertime and youth and love in northern Michigan—blasted from speakers set up in the beds of pickups and in the open cargo bays of former bread trucks and EMT vans painted Packer colors, most of them parked in formation in "Tailgate Row" centrally located in the Oneida Lot. It was while touring Tailgate Row that I saw my first Jessica Simpson mask (if a Xeroxed photo attached to a stick can be considered a mask) and ran into my first cheesehead wearing a T-shirt mocking both the Cowboys and Ms. Simpson (Romo's girlfriend at the time) in an off-color way. Game on!

Or maybe not. Things began poorly, from a Packers perspective. James Jones dropped a short pass from Rodgers to start the game. On the second play from scrimmage, Ryan Grant ran right, gained 9 yards, got slammed by cornerback Pacman Jones, and coughed up the ball. Pacman scooped it up and advanced it 21 yards to the Packers 14. Three plays later, Nick Folk kicked a 25-yard field goal to give the Cowboys an early 3–0 lead.

If the 71,113 fans (another record) waving their green and yellow G-Force souvenir flags weren't already battling despair it was because Ryan Grant has begun the previous January's playoff game against Seattle in just the same way, with an immediate fumble. He then proceeded, after a second fumble on the next possession, to play his best game ever, racking up 205 rushing yards.

Could a forced fumble be a good omen?

Not today.

Much like the Vikings contest, it was a game of three big plays, except this time it was the other team making them. The first was a 60-yard second-quarter run by the Arkansas rookie halfback Felix Jones, who looked like the fastest guy on the field. With help from a Jason Witten block, Jones hit a hole on the left edge in a heartbeat, then rocketed up the sideline, a Charles Woodson arm-tackle effort at midfield the closest anyone got to him. It was thunder-and-lightning, Cowboys style. They bashed, bashed, bashed with Marion "The Barbarian" Barber, then handed off to the lightning-bug, who made tacklers look like they were running in sand.

Big play No. 2 came courtesy of Miles Austin, an undrafted receiver out of Monmouth University in New Jersey and mainly a Cowboys special teams player to that point. With Dallas leading 13–9 nearing the end of the third quarter, it was still very much a game when Austin, running a play-action post, flew past a stumbling Nick Collins in zone coverage, caught the ball at the 32 and ran it down to the 2. Barber thundered in for a score two plays later.

It was only Austin's eighth career catch, good for 63 yards. There was more Miles Austin in quarter four. With the Packers trailing 20–9 at the nine-minute mark, Dallas faced a third-and-20 at midfield. It looked like Cullen Jenkins, who was having a monster game, was going to record his third sack, but no. Romo hit his elusiveness switch, dodged, stepped up in the pocket, and unloaded a perfect long ball to Austin, running a go route down the right sideline on Tramon Williams, in for an injured Al Harris. Like the craftiest of veterans, Austin gave Williams a slight push as the ball neared, creating just enough separation and adjusting well at full speed to haul in the ball and score a 52-yard touchdown.

Who needed T.O.? Woodson had shut Owens down, holding the star receiver to just two catches for 17 yards. Fleet linebacker Brandon Chillar held All-Pro tight end Jason Witten in check. His superior pass-coverage skills earning him the start over Poppinga, Chillar had a superb overall game, flying all over the place, breaking up passes, even forcing a Barber fumble, the ball flying up in the air only to be snagged by tight end Tony Curtis, who advanced it 14 yards. It was that kind of day for the Pack. At the end of the first half Jenkins stripped Romo while sacking him for a 17-yard loss, but the ball bounced the way of tackle Flozell Adams. Adams recovered it, preserving the Cowboys chance to attempt (and make) a field goal as time expired. And at the close of the third quarter, the Packers looked ready to enjoy some good field position when Cowboys punter Mat McBriar received a snap on his own goal line. But wouldn't you know, McBriar went all Ray Guy and smashed the ball 65 yards. After 10 more yards were tacked on (half the distance to the goal) for an unnecessary roughness penalty on rookie tight end Jermichael Finley, the Packers started the ensuing drive at their own 13.

It was pretty quiet in Lambeau Field in those final minutes. "A little air comes out of the balloon on a night like tonight," said Al Michaels at game's end, referring to the Packers posting their first loss after coming in with such high hopes. Big plays by Cowboy unknowns. A Dallas punt that gained them 75 yards in field position. And no less deflating, the way the Packers kept settling for field goals in the red zone. They didn't score a touchdown until Rodgers snuck one in with 2:11 remaining in the game. Jordy Nelson shone during the 11-play, 87-yard march, snagging four of eight Rodgers passes. But on three earlier Packer drives, two sacks and a dropped slant killed touchdown possibilities. The pair of third-down sacks both came with the Packers inside the Dallas 10. The Pack also wasted 44 receiving yards on two sweet Jennings catches in a first-quarter march and 50 yards on a beautiful curl-and-go by Driver in quarter three. Field goal, field goal, field goal. It wasn't enough.

Looking for grace notes in a losing cause? Right at the end, as Driver looked to lateral to Nelson on a failed gadget play, Aaron Rodgers knocked 6-foot-7, 304-pound defensive lineman Chris Canty on his can with a violent shoulder block. A quarterback who "relaxes" Saturday nights before games by watching Ultimate Fighting on TV in his hotel room continued to earn toughness points with his teammates, as he did the previous Sunday against the Lions by veering back into the action rather than out of bounds in a sideline tightrope scramble that gained extra yards and extra pounding. Speaking of toughness, cornerback Al Harris tore his spleen (let's put that in caps: TORE HIS SPLEEN) colliding with A. J. Hawk in quarter one, then came back into the game and had the tackle of the night, fighting off a Witten block before springing at Marion Barber in space and taking him down for a loss.

The Packers showed flashes on offense, and defensively kept the Cowboys off-rhythm for the first twenty minutes of action, though Barber was doing damage. He continued to do damage. Eventually so did other guys. Barber gained 142 yards on 28 carries. Romo completed 17 for 30 for 260 yards and a touchdown. Aaron Rodgers went 22 of 39 for 290 yards, with no touchdowns, no picks. With a passer rating of 80.1, he'd come down to earth a bit from the record heights of his first two starts. At the beginning of the NBC telecast, Al Michaels informed viewers that Rodgers was the "first quarterback in the history of the league to throw for 500-plus yards and complete at least 70 percent of his passes without an interception in his first two starts."

Ah, statistics.

Cowboys 27, Packers 16.

# CHAPTER 8: TRUE BELIEVERS & CLOSET CREEPERS

**B**LOOMER, WISCONSIN IS a town of 3,400 people located about a dozen miles north of Chippewa Falls in a west-central part of the state that I think of as "Fuzzy Thurston Country." The great Lombardi-era lineman grew up in Altoona, a short drive south from both towns. Bloomer is where I watched the Packers–Buccaneers telecast on September's last Sunday. I drove up from Milwaukee, a 250-mile journey on Interstate 94, a highway that continues on to Minneapolis just after the Chippewa Falls exit. I mention this because "Minny," ninety miles west, is twice as close to Bloomer as Green Bay. Because of the geographical proximity, there are actually Wisconsin Vikings fans afoot, as I experienced firsthand in a bar called Ruby's Roadhouse, where people at one end of the bar watched the Pack while people at the other end watched the Vikings.

I stayed in Chippewa Falls Saturday night, and as a movie-lover it was hard not to think of Woody Allen's *Annie Hall*. ("That's one of your Chippewa Falls expressions," says Allen's Alvy Singer to Diane Keaton's Annie after she uses the word "neat.") In one classic scene, Alvy visits Annie's hometown for a culture-shock Easter dinner. In another, Annie's brother Duane (Christopher Walken) drives Alvy to the airport. Which would be fine, except the night before Duane had confessed to Alvy that he often experiences a suicidal impulse to drive into oncoming traffic. Bloomer, for its part, earned its own place in entertainment history as the hometown of radio producer character Roz Doyle, Peri Gilpin's role on *Frasier*. In one episode, Frasier (Kelsey Grammer) even follows Roz home to Bloomer.

On the drive up, a kind of "deep diagonal" across the field of Wisconsin (to borrow John Madden's term for the route Miles Austin ran on his 63-yard touchdown the previous Sunday), I found myself comparing the Cowboys and Packers. "The Cowboys left no doubt which was the better team," wrote Bob McGinn in sentence two of his *Journal Sentinel* game story. "The Cowboys are farther ahead then we are right now," Mike McCarthy himself said, though hastened to add that it was only Week 3. Dallas dropped 453 yards of offense on the Packers, and that was with T.O. mostly in the holster. It was clear stopping the run could be an issue. Protection for Rodgers might be an issue as well. The Packers running game was still a work in progress. But things looked good at quarterback. Our wide receivers were superlative. And the secondary would be fine with some adjustments. There was a lot to like about these 2008 Packers. Absolutely.

Packers shareholder Jon Neuhaus agreed. He watched the Cowboys game with his mother, Kathy, sister Sarah, and nine friends who flew in from all over the country. Selected "Tailgater of the Game" by a Packers promotion crew roaming the Lambeau parking lots before the game, Jon and his gang were suddenly up there on the scoreboards in the third quarter. As a short video ran on the screens, a narrator announced that Jon had just earned "free brats for his entire row" courtesy of Johnsonville Sausage and Silver Spring Mustard. The video included footage of Jon's tailgate party. Dressed in a No. 12 Rodgers jersey, Jon tended to some brats smoking on a Weber grill while a few feet away a friend wearing a Favre jersey looked on.

"I know that guy!" I said to my dad, seated beside me on a bleacher in row 49, section 113. Chalk up another one to the small-world department. Of the thousands of people tailgating in the Lambeau lots that warm Sunday afternoon, the promo unit crowned "Jon Neuhaus from Los Angeles" as that week's king of the grill. I'd met Jon Neuhaus briefly two years before playing pickup softball on a field in scenic Topanga Canyon in the Santa Monica Mountains between Los Angeles and Malibu. We caught up by phone a few days after the Cowboys game, Jon back in L.A. by that point. Only then did I learn that he's a Packers fan of the highest order, a cheesehead *extraordinaire*. He's like that guy in the NFL Pro Shop commercial who literally bleeds green and gold. And he's not even from Wisconsin. He grew up in small-town Connecticut, the son of a Congregational minister. But the late Reverend Lee Neuhaus was a Milwaukee native, and like his own father before him, had an extraordinary passion for the Packers that he passed on to his son. Jon told me that in the days when his dad was still a Milwaukee minister, he used to bring a Packers mug into the pulpit with him on game days to remind his congregants that today's sermon might be a little short.

The future Reverend Lee Neuhaus played Division III football for the Lakeland Muskies of Lakeland College in Sheboygan. "Boy, did I hate it when anyone got a paw on my quarterback!" the former offensive lineman once said to his son. Later the white-bearded

Nitschke fan coached Pop Warner football, and was fond of hollering, "Wrap up and tackle!" at his young charges.

For Christmas 1997, Jon bought a share of Packers stock for everyone in his family: mom, dad, sis. His own stock certificate joined a chunk of Lambeau Field turf he'd purchased the previous January during the Packers' postseason run. That little boxed and iced Frozen Tundra keepsake will have pride of place in every freezer he ever owns until he moves on to that Great Lambeau in the Sky. Holder of an MBA from Northwestern's Kellogg School of Management, Jon devoted one of his central graduate research projects to the management style of—you guessed it—the Green Bay Packers. Traveling to Lambeau with three colleagues in the autumn of 2000, Jon and his project partners interviewed then president Bob Harlan and director of pro personnel Reggie McKenzie, today the Packers director of football operations. After the interview, Harlan took Jon and his colleagues on a personal tour of Lambeau. The tour included the Packers locker room, where, wouldn't you know, they ran into Brett Favre. Harlan introduced Favre to the grad students. Later, Favre's image would appear on the front cover of their case study.

Lee Neuhaus never got to a Packers game at Lambeau while he was growing up. After Jon graduated from Berkeley in 1995, he took his dad to a game as a gift. And so began a tradition, a yearly trip to Lambeau, one that quickly grew in numbers of participants. At Kellogg and in the work world, Jon kept meeting passionate Packer fans. During a job interview in Los Angeles, he noticed the interviewer had a Lambeau seating chart on his wall. As you can imagine, the interview took a sudden turn for the better. That guy became Jon's boss and one of the original Neuhaus Tailgate participants. The tailgaters came from all over, and pursued various occupations: a Deloitte Consulting partner in L.A., a Tampa dentist, a Kellogg professor, CFO of a San Francisco biotech firm, a Boston teacher, an Alabama management consultant, an Atlanta CPA. All huge Packers fans. And Jon was the garrulous ringmaster, his dad the bearded sage and storyteller.

Begun in 1997, the Neuhaus Tailgate tradition is still going strong. Each spring the instant the Packers schedule is released, Jon starts working the phones, e-mailing, locking things down. The booker at the hotel where his group always stays is ready for his call on Schedule Day. "How ya doin', Newey?" she asks each spring. "How many rooms do you need this year?"

Lee Neuhaus passed away in 2005. In his last days, he asked his son to continue the Lambeau tradition with Kathy and Sarah, and he has. Every year, Jon flies in from Los Angeles, his mother and sister from Sacramento. They carry on, too, a second, smaller family tradition. During non-holiday Packer games, Jon, Kathy, and Sarah conference call while they watch the action on TVs in their respective homes, commenting spiritedly on what unfolds.

But the biggie, the tradition nonpareil, is that yearly Lambeau visit. The group makes a whole weekend out of it. They usually get into town on Friday evening. That night they might assemble at the Stadium View. Since everyone comes from out of town, they spend part of Friday and Saturday morning buying stuff for the tailgate. They pick up two Weber grills (donated when they leave), utensils, a hundred bratwurst, rolls, green peppers, onions, butter, cases of Pabst Blue Ribbon, and more. "Butter is very key," Jon told me. In 2001, the *Press-Gazette* ran a story on the Neuhaus Tailgate. "Dunk brats in marinade and serve on fresh Kaiser roll with raw onions, brown mustard, and a slab of cheddar cheese," read a Neuhaus recipe sidebar. "Serve brats with mashed garlic potatoes, a dill pickle garnish and chips with Mom's favorite dip."

Saturday lunch is butter-burgers at Kroll's East, a Green Bay institution. "Begin the clogging of the arteries!" says Jon. Then they move on to Lambeau Field, visiting the Pro Shop and Packers Hall of Fame. While in the Hall, Jon, Kathy, and Sarah go over and touch a green commemorative brick on the Wall of Honor. The brick's golden letters read:

**NEUHAUS**
**ARTHUR, LEE & KURT**

Arthur was Lee's dad. Kurt was Lee and Kathy's oldest child. He passed away at age 19. Three dedicated Packer fans. The memorial brick sits inches away from a brick reading, "In Memory of Dominic Olejniczak." Yes, "Ole" himself, former Green Bay mayor and Packers president who had the wisdom to hire Vince Lombardi in '59. And out in the brilliant Lambeau Atrium, eight feet up on a wall lined with commemorative plaques, is a marker that Jon, Kathy, and Sarah always take a moment to stand before and take in each year. The plaque reads:

**THE NEUHAUS FAMILY**
**PROUD GENERATIONS**
**OF OWNERS**
**GO PACK FOREVER**

Respects paid, the Neuhaus trio rejoins their tailgate group of ten or twelve and it's on to Brett Favre's Steakhouse for dinner. They end their night with a bowling party at Dyckesville Bowl, prized for its beer-battered cheese curds. Come Sunday morning, if it's a noon game, Jon is up bright and shiny, determined to achieve one of his three weekend goals. Goal No. 1 is to be the first into the Lambeau lot. Goal No. 2 is to cheer a Packers victory. Goal No. 3 is to be the last to leave the Lambeau lot. He can't control the second goal, but he and his dad did open with a seven-game winning streak over their first seven tailgates.

The Lambeau parking lots open four hours before kickoff. Cars and trucks start lining up along Oneida Street at least an hour before that. By the time police start waving vehicles in, the queue might stretch for five or six blocks. For an early game, Jon will drive over between 6:30 and 7 A.M. For that 7:15 P.M. Sunday night Cowboys game, he got in line at 1 P.M.

I asked if he got bored, sitting in line.

"Oh, not at all!" Jon replied. "You'd have to have the personality of a doorknob to get bored. You meet all kinds of people waiting to get in. Everyone's rolling down their windows, getting out and walking up and down the line." What about that bulk bratwurst purchase? A hundred brats seems like a lot of sausage for a group of a dozen people.

"We hand out brats to anyone who wants one," Jon explained. "Everyone's welcome to eat. Plus, we come back after the game and cook up some more and hand them out to anyone who's hungry after the game." It was bratwurst largesse that led to making the 2008 Neuhaus Tailgate one of the most memorable ever, maybe *the* most. And no, I'm not referring to Jon's mug on the scoreboard video screens and coupons for free Johnsonville brats for everyone in row 50, section 112. I'm referring to school psychologist Kathy Neuhaus receiving a Lambeau pregame field pass, entitling her to stand down there on the sidelines with Brewers pitcher C. C. Sabathia, ESPN's Andrea Kremer, and last but not least, rap superstar Jay-Z. "Hey, mama," Jay-Z said to Kathy when they met. Moments later, he posed for a photo, his arm around Kathy's shoulder.

It all began with Jon saying, "Do you want a brat?" to a tailgate-aisle neighbor. The guy came over, had a beer and a brat, and ended up talking with the Neuhaus gang for an hour. "That's what always happens—you just start talking," Jon told me. The neighbor, Patrick Gillard, was Mark Murphy's football teammate and road roommate at Colgate. As in, Mark Murphy, president of the Packers. Patrick had an extra field pass. It went to Kathy after Jon and Sarah prevailed upon her to accept it rather than stepping aside for one of her children. As it happens, Jon had already been down to field level once with his dad. Remember his L.A. boss with the Lambeau seating chart? That guy knew a foreman in charge of the Lambeau renovation, and arranged a July 2001 stadium visit. There's a great photo of Jon and his dad down on the field, the Neuhaus men in white hardhats and safety glasses, Jon decked out in a Favre jersey.

That summer day in 2001, Jon and Lee bent down and touched the grass. They thought of two Packer fans who couldn't be there, Jon's grandfather and brother. And now, in 2008, it was Kathy's turn to be on the Lambeau grass. Her children knew she would think of her husband when she was down there. And she did. She thought of Lee, her husband of thirty-nine years.

Kathy also thought of her children in the stands. She called them on her cell and the first thing out of her mouth, she told me later, was, "I'm on the grass!" Jon still has the message saved. Moments later Kathy was meeting Jay-Z. The photo shows Kathy in a pink Packers-logo golf shirt, smiling hugely, while Jay-Z stands there in shades and a Yankees cap. "I met the singer," Kathy said when she reunited with her two kids in the stands. "I didn't know who he was, but he's really nice." Jon and Sarah both screamed, "Mom, that's Jay-Z! One of the biggest rap stars in the world! Husband of Beyoncé!"

"Oh, really?" said Kathy. "How about that?"

The 2009 Neuhaus Tailgate is scheduled for October 18, a noon game against the Lions. As it happens, Santiago Gardner of San Diego is flying out that weekend, too. I plan to be there as well. I'm hoping to bring them together, Santiago and the Neuhaus Tailgate gang.

I didn't run into anyone with the wattage of Jay-Z up in Bloomer, but I did meet Skeeter Stolt and his friend Hooter at Ruby's Roadhouse. They were great company during the Packers–Bucs game. Afterward, I ran over to the Badger Hole, a bustling Bloomer sports bar in the double-height space of an old middle-school basement cafeteria reached via a wooden ramp. The school's salvaged gym scoreboard hangs high on a wall, and still displays scores. It was here, standing at the bar with a couple of Bloomer sports fans in their twenties, both of whom had once eaten peanut butter and jelly sandwiches in this very space as 12-year-olds, where I watched C. C. Sabathia pitch the Brewers into the playoffs for the first time in twenty-six years. Working on three days rest and going the distance, Sabathia beat the Cubs 3–1 on the last day of the season. When the Mets lost 4–2 to the Marlins that same hour, the Brewers were wild-card champs! The Badger Hole went nuts. I toasted Theresa Hanson of Bloomer, an employee of Scheels sporting goods in Eau Claire. A huge Brett Favre fan, she told me she had something of a Favre Wall in her apartment. I asked her opinion of Aaron Rodgers. "I need to see more of him," she said. "He could be a hero or a zero."

That day in Bloomer was cloudy and cool (a little different from sweltering, 85-degree Tampa), the ashen sky autumnal, the foliage maybe a quarter turned to red and yellow. As I got out of my car in the Ruby's lot, a V of honking Canadian geese flew directly overhead.

It was coming—October chill, then snow.

Skeeter Stolt, 53, a trucker who hauls glass across northern Wisconsin, also serves as the sociable president of the Bloomer Rod and Gun Club. He was one of only six or seven patrons in the bar when I arrived, a lot of area residents at a parade in downtown Bloomer a mile away. Ruby's Roadhouse is a low, rambling, shingle-roofed pub and banquet hall just off a rural highway. Two cheery gray-haired women were playing video casino games in the rear of the bar, past the pool table. Florence, who called herself "a farmer's wife," wore a sky blue windbreaker; Charlene sported a yellow Packers sweatshirt. From where they were sitting, they couldn't hear Skeeter's R-rated joke about why Minnesota women don't date Wisconsin men. It has to do with gophers and badgers, their habits and habitats—if you've heard it, you know the one I'm talking about. Skeeter also shared a couple more Minnesota jokes, these two of a more PG-rated variety.

"What's the difference between a cheesehead and a dickhead?" Skeeter said.

"What?"

"The St. Croix River."

You don't even have to know that the St. Croix River forms a Minnesota–Wisconsin boundary eighty miles west of here beginning more or less at St. Paul to get that one.

Skeeter probably knows as many "Minny" jokes as there are bends in the St. Croix.

"How come Green Bay doesn't get swallowed up by Lake Michigan?" he asked.

"How come?"

"Cuz Minnesota keeps sucking."

Skeeter was the guy who broke it to me that there were actually Vikings fans in this part of Wisconsin. He said when the Packers played the Vikes, the green to purple ratio at Ruby's might be something like 60–40.

"I call 'em Closet Creepers," said Skeeter in his strong Wisconsin accent, referring to area Vikings fans. "Always hootin' and hollerin' when their team's winning, but as soon as the Vikings lose they go back in their closets and pout. I got a friend who's a Vikings fan—he's a good shit; I forgive him—and when he calls me up after the Vikings lose, I always say, 'You got the phone there in the closet, buddy?'"

On cue, a dozen Vikings fans entered Ruby's. No one was wearing Hagar horns or pigtails, but four guys wore Vikings ball caps. One of them, a forty-something man in jeans and a purple sweatshirt, asked the friendly bartender, Brianne Reischel, if she could put the Vikes game on the TV serving the far end of the long, L-shaped bar. Skeeter looked at me and shrugged. "Here we go," he said. Then he added, "On a day like today, it'll stay pretty civil. Let's just make sure we cheer louder than them."

Even if Skeeter had been tempted to tell some more off-color Minnesota jokes, he wouldn't have out of respect for the kids that came in with the two forty-something guys. They were brothers from Maplewood, Minnesota, a suburb of St. Paul, I learned when I went over and talked to them. Working construction in the area, they had their families in for the weekend, totaling three teenage girls, a teenage son, and another son about ten. One of the brother's wives wore a Packers sweatshirt. Turned out she grew up in Eau Claire, twenty miles south of Bloomer. I asked her and her husband if a Vikings fan being married to a Packer fan presented any problems. They looked at each other, then at me. "Yes!" they shouted simultaneously, and seemed pretty serious. They get points for marital candor. "We basically don't talk the weekends the Packers play the Vikings," the husband added.

Technically the brothers weren't Closet Creepers, I pointed out to Skeeter when I returned to his end of the bar, because they were just here working in 'Sconsin. But the two other Viking-capped guys in their early twenties who'd come into Ruby's at the same time as the families were actually from Bloomer. So by Skeeter's definition, they qualified as Closet Creepers. Quietly but intensely, they cheered on their Vikings in a game against the Titans in Nashville.

Speaking of brothers, Skeeter's own bro was the restaurant's cook. I met him moments after I'd been telling Skeeter about Roy Blount Jr.'s book on the '73 Steelers, *About Three Bricks Shy of a Load*. A lifelong hauler, Skeeter got a kick out of the titular expression, a variation on not playing with a full deck. I explained to Skeeter how Roy Blount got his title. He'd been standing next to reserve defensive end Craig Hanneman on the Steeler sidelines during the mother of all mud games in Oakland when Hanneman, looking out at all his rain-soaked Steeler comrades rolling around in the slop, facemasks full of turf, shouted merrily, "We're all about three bricks shy of a load!" Just then the kitchen doors swung open. A guy I didn't know was Skeeter's brother came out and took a spin around the bar. Skeeter hollered, "Hey, you're three bricks shy of a load, you know that?!" Not missing a beat, the younger Stolt replied, "Least it's only three bricks, Skeeter. Not ten like you!"

I don't mean to leave Hooter out of this. While I was talking to the Vikings fans, Hooter took off. "He had to go home to change the blades on his lawnmower," Skeeter explained.

\* \* \*

Six days later, in another victory for the small-world department, I was watching the Brewers play the Phillies in the Pizza Bowl in Algoma, Wisconsin, thirty miles east of Green Bay. Two guys at the bar next to me turned out to be from Tilden, ten miles south of Bloomer. Proprietors of the Shady Pine bar in their town of 1,400 people, they'd driven 230 miles east from Tilden for a weekend fishing on Lake Michigan. I asked them if they'd ever heard of Skeeter and Hooter.

"Skeeter and Hooter—are you kidding?" said either Larry or Randy. "We're good friends with Skeeter and Hooter!" And they were. They told me some stories.

This was four days after I relocated to Green Bay. It seemed like a good omen. I decided right then and there this was going to be a lucky book, about a lucky Packers season. It just hadn't quite kicked in yet. But it would. It was only Week 5. Good luck was on the way.

Down in Tampa that steamy Sunday, the Packers caught a small break as cloud cover kept temperatures in the mid 80s rather than the low 90s as forecast. While Skeeter and I watched from the Bloomer bar, offensive tackle Mark Tauscher, born and raised about eighty miles from Bloomer as the crow flies, appeared on the Fox telecast with a hose pumping cool air into his jersey. The game started off well. Mixing the pass and run, the Packers marched down the field on their opening drive, going for it on fourth-and-1 from the Bucs' 49. Rodgers snuck for the first. It was an aggressive call—good to see. A few plays later, Greg Jennings made a quick move off the line, cornerback Ronde Barber slipped, and Jennings waltzed down the left sideline into the end zone for a 25-yard touchdown reception. The first quarter ended with no further scoring, though the Pack did add a league-leading eleventh holding penalty of the season.

In quarter two, Rodgers made some history, throwing his first interception as a Packers starter. He'd thrown 108 passes without a pick. And dating back to last season, he'd recorded 158 interception-free attempts, an even better deadeye streak than ones he enjoyed at Cal. The pick wasn't his fault. Releasing into the flat, halfback Brandon Jackson turned his head to run before he caught the checkdown, the ball bouncing off his hands into the waiting arms of linebacker Derrick Brooks.

Following the interception, the Bucs needed to go just 32 yards to tie the score at 7. When tight end Alex Smith beat retreating defensive end Michael Montgomery, quarterback Brian Griese hit him for a 9-yard score. After that, things got uglier for the Pack. A penalty on Will Blackmon during Jordy Nelson's solid kickoff return put Green Bay back at their 11-yard line. Grant got tackled for a 6-yard loss. Rodgers gunned a short pass that bounced off the arm of a leaping Brooks. Then Rodgers overthrew Nelson on third-and-15, a possible route miscue. Fittingly, this ragged series ended with Derrick Frost taking a high snap in the end zone and punting the ball just 36 yards.

Penalty. Negative running play. Near-INT. Bad punt. A taste of things to come?

Fox Sports, providing little relief to Packer fans, cut away to Brett Favre zipping his third touchdown pass of the second quarter to Laveranues Coles in a game against Arizona.

Skeeter and I exchanged a look. We hadn't been doing much cheering.

Rodgers went on to throw two more interceptions. On the first, late in the second quarter, he was slapped on the arm as he threw, propelling a duck that overshot Driver on a seam route and was picked by middle linebacker Barrett Ruud. Then with 2:19 to go in the game and the Bucs clinging to a 23–21 lead, Rodgers was blind-sided by defensive end Greg White as he attempted to hit Driver across the middle on second-and-10. The ball popped up and fell neatly into the hands of White's agile DE counterpart Gaines Adams, who'd retreated quickly into coverage seven yards downfield.

The play had a Keystone Cops element to it. Tight ends Donald Lee and Jermichael Finley were paired on the left side of the line. At the snap, Lee drifted left, Finley downfield. Like Greg White had donned a cloak of invisibility, he charged untouched between the tight ends and continued straight to Rodgers, leveling him from behind, snapping the QB's head back.

On the very next play, Earnest Graham popped a 47-yard run down to the 1. Graham got the ball again and scored, putting the Bucs up 30–21 after the extra point. By then, the Packers defense was exhausted, having contended in the heat all afternoon against a team enjoying a field-position field day. Certainly, more time on the sidelines with those "spot coolers"—jury-rigged swimming pool hoses—would have been appreciated. And yet it was the defense—more precisely the secondary—that had gotten the Packers back into the game late in the third and early in the fourth. With the score 20–7, safety Nick Collins made a spectacular pick, leaping in front of tight end Jerramy Stevens on a corner route and running it back 17 yards to the Tampa 42. "I don't think Brian Griese in his career has seen a middle safety break like Collins did," said Bucs coach Jon Gruden after the game. Three plays later, Rodgers hit Jennings on a seam, an absolute laser through a tiny linebacker-safety window. The catch and run into the end zone covered 48 yards, narrowing Tampa's lead to 20–14. Three minutes later, Charles Woodson did as Charles Woodson does. Picking off a short pass intended for running back Warrick Dunn, he returned 62 yards the other way. Just like that, the Packers were up 21–20.

But former Super Bowl MVP Dexter Jackson returned a 38-yard, line-drive punt 19 yards to put Tampa at the Packers 36 with 8:45 to go. Nine straight running plays later, the Bucs kicked a 24-yard field goal to make the score 23–21 with 2:26 left.

The Packers got the ball at their own 40 when Tampa's kickoff sailed out of bounds. Rodgers' first pass went incomplete. Then on second down, Greg White leveled that blind-side hit. He arrived just as Rodgers released the ball. The pass to Driver never had a chance.

We didn't yet know it for a medical fact, but the QB White clobbered already had a separated throwing shoulder. Rodgers suffered the injury with five minutes left in the third quarter. On third-and-8 at midfield, he took a shotgun snap, scrambled up the middle, dove forward out of an ankle tackle, and reached out the ball with a fully extended right arm. Going down alarmingly hard, his whole body bouncing off the turf, he jammed his right elbow and wrenched his shoulder. To add insult to agony, Rodgers missed gaining the first down by inches. And yet it was on the Packers' very next series when he whistled that smoking seam pass to Jennings. He rifled one of his most breathtaking balls of 2008 with a separated shoulder.

After whipping that bullet, Rodgers walked to the sideline with his right arm close to his side, his right shoulder drooping a bit. He took a seat on the bench, tilted his head back, closed his eyes, puffed out his cheeks. It didn't look good. Taking over on the next Packers series, rookie Matt Flynn promptly went three-and-out, throwing two yards behind Jennings on a second-down slant. That led to Frost's low punt from the Packers 17, the one Dexter Jackson returned nearly 20 yards to the Packers 36, setting up Tampa's go-ahead field goal.

Flying back to Green Bay, Coach Mike McCarthy would have some serious concerns. First and foremost, the shoulder of Rodgers. Next the abysmal running game, which had managed just 28 yards on 18 carries. And Rodgers gained 8 of those. The feature back? Ryan Grant had 27 yards as the first quarter ended. Not bad. But he ended the game with 20 rushing yards. Explanation? He rushed for minus-7 the rest of the way. Six carries, 7 yards lost. Grant also fumbled after being hit by Derrick Brooks in the third quarter. Scooping up the ball, safety Jermaine Phillips ran it back 38 yards to extend Tampa's lead to 20–7. With a less-than-zero running game for three quarters, the burden of the Packers offense rested almost entirely on . . . the right shoulder of Rodgers.

The shoulder that might be separated.

Defensive end Cullen Jenkins, who'd enjoyed a monster September, had also suffered a possible season-ending pectoral tear. Reaching out to sack Griese early in the fourth quarter, Jenkins' right arm got levered as Griese sidestepped. The lineman dropped to the ground like he'd been shot. He'd been having another huge game, too, pressuring Griese, knocking him down, batting down a pass, tackling Earnest Graham for a loss. In the opinion of one Atlanta Falcons personnel man who spoke to Bob McGinn a few days later, Cullen Jenkins had been more valuable to the Packers this month than Pro Bowler Julius Peppers was to the Carolina Panthers. Injuries to Packer starters had been few and far between the previous few years, but it appeared the team's luck on this front had run out. Al Harris had a ruptured spleen. Hard-hitting strong safety Atari Bigby had missed both the Dallas game and this game with ankle and hamstring issues. And now Jenkins might have torn a pectoral muscle in a freak play where he simply stuck his arm out and the angle and timing of the minimal quarterback contact may have done catastrophic damage to one of the body's biggest muscles.

Not that McCarthy would pay it much attention, but a thousand miles east in the Meadowlands, Brett Favre had thrown a career-high six touchdowns passes to fuel a 56–35 Jets victory over the Arizona Cardinals, the most points the now 2–2 Jets had scored in a game since 1985. A performance like that would fire up the Favre backers in Green Bay, unleashing a chorus of *We Told You So*. At least the Vikings lost, 30–17 to Tennessee, their record falling to 1–3. The 1–2 Bears played a Sunday night game against the Eagles. But let someone else worry about Favre and other teams. McCarthy had his own team, not least his own quarterback, to worry about. They'd rolled the dice and gone into the season without a veteran backup QB. Would Rodgers prove to have a serious injury and have to sit?

Would Matt Flynn, the seventh-rounder, become the man?

"Tentative first-year men," Lombardi called rookies.

Tentative was not a good quality in a quarterback.

# CHAPTER 9:
# A VIKING FUNERAL

I SAW MY FIRST patches of snow driving back across Fuzzy Thurston Country en route to Minneapolis for the second Vikings game. It was Saturday, November 9. Just days before I'd been enjoying 75-degree weather standing on Jordy Nelson's high school field in Leonardville. What wasn't as enjoyable that day was the 19–16 overtime loss to the undefeated Titans, the Packers sliding back to .500 halfway through the season. A victory in Nashville would have made it three straight for the Pack, a stirring bounceback following a dismal three-game losing streak. After coming home from Tampa, they got run over by Michael Turner and Company, falling 27–24 to the Falcons at Lambeau. It was close, but they should have taken care of business. Three losses in five tilts was as many as they had dropped in all of 2007, a stat deployed as a verbal cudgel by any fan looking to pound away on Packers management.

Shouts of "With Brett we didn't lose three games until Week 16!" filled the airwaves of Wisconsin sports radio. The hue and cry began pretty much the instant Turner rumbled for his 120th and 121st rushing yards of the day, a late third-and-1 carry prompting a game-ending kneeldown by Falcons rookie quarterback Matt Ryan. Forgotten fairly quickly, especially by Favre fans, was that Rodgers had come out and played with a newly separated shoulder, and played well. He hadn't practiced all week. He woke not knowing if he could throw at all. He met McCarthy at the Hutson Center early Sunday morning and threw a variety of passes. McCarthy looked him in the eye. Rodgers said he wanted the ball, and they agreed he would give it a try, using a light shoulder brace that affected his flexibility but reduced the pain a little. He didn't take an injection. Early-arriving fans cheered as Rodgers came out of the tunnel for warm-ups. With Matt Flynn at the ready, No. 12 threw some warm-up tosses to Jordy Nelson, gave McCarthy a nod, then went out and performed, connecting on 25 of 37 passes for 313 yards and three touchdowns.

"It hurt the whole game," Rodgers said afterward. Teammates noticed some grimaces in the huddle. Fans noticed him grab his right arm after tough throws. Upon tossing his first touchdown, he pointed skyward with his left hand, his right arm drooping a little, then low-fived teammates with his left. There would be no leaping right-shoulder bumps with Ruvell "Gumby" Martin today. But this was football and the Packers lost—to a team supposedly in a rebuilding year, led by a rookie quarterback and first-year coaching staff. The Falcons had dropped eleven of their last twelve road games. They hadn't scored a road touchdown this year. "Ryan's had some slow starts on the road," TV viewers had heard as the game began. Looking back now, after the standout years enjoyed by Matt Ryan, Michael Turner, and Roddy White, the loss is less of a shocker. But back then, there was a general perception going in that this fifth contest was somewhere between a gimme and a trap game, one that was only the Packers' to lose, but which they surely wouldn't.

I sat as close to the field as I sat all season, row 11, section 111, 5-yard-line. It was a perfect day for football, sunny and 60 degrees. The tailgating jollity hit a high pitch by 10 A.M. and stayed high until kickoff. I was looking forward to the action moving down toward my end of the unfrozen tundra, but did it have to move that fast? On the very first play of the game, Woodson slipped when Roddy White stuttered and the Falcon caught a 37-yard out-and-up. The clock read 14:48. One play later, rookie cornerback Pat Lee slipped as White caught a 19-yard out. That was followed by another White reception, a couple of Turner runs, a few more drive-sustaining short plays, and suddenly the *can't score a touchdown on the road* Falcons were on the 1-foot line right in front of me, going for it on fourth-and-goal. In what seemed like a crazy call until it worked, Ryan bootlegged right and with Packers scrambling to respond, tight end Justin Peelle dashed all the way across the formation from left to right, did a swim move to get around linebacker A. J. Hawk, and caught a Ryan bullet while sliding on his knees like a guitar hero inches from the sideline. Hawk had actually done well to react and pursue given a groin pull suffered in the Tampa game, an injury McCarthy had deemed "a pretty good strain."

Welcome to The Roddy White Show. It ran for thirty minutes. White caught eight passes for 132 yards and a touchdown before intermission. The rugged, canny receiver from Alabama-Birmingham was the beneficiary of an iffy pass interference call on Auburn alum Pat Lee, who played great D on a third-and-9 breakup. Later, Lee had another impressive jam, cover, and ball slapdown. With six minutes left in quarter two, wanting White to exploit Will Blackmon in bump-and-run coverage, Ryan audibled out of a running play. The former Alabama state wrestling champ did a little juke to get clean off the line, tore around Blackmon, and raced down the right sideline for a 22-yard fade, his left hand giving Blackmon a slight nudge before receiving the ball.

Falcons 17, Packers 7.

White didn't catch another ball after that, thanks to Charles Woodson and help from the Packers safeties. But Turner continued to pound, Ryan continued to stand and roll with little pressure, and like it was down in Tampa, field position was a problem. Another short Frost punt, an Atlanta punt downed at the 2, a 54-yard tackle-busting fourth-quarter Jerius Norwood kickoff return (answering a Pack touchdown) helped tilt the field the Falcons' way. Nine Packer penalties for 97 yards (versus only 2 worth 15 yards for the Falcons) didn't help. One of the flags, a phantom hold called on rookie tight end Jermichael Finley, took a field goal off the board right before halftime. The infraction moved Crosby back 10 yards and this time he missed a 53-yarder.

The Falcons started fast, the Packers went three-and-out. The Falcons ran three straight times to seal it, Turner pounding for 1, 8, and 2 yards for a first down, despite the Packers stacking ten men in the box. The 8-yarder, beginning at the Green Bay 46 with the Falcons up 27–24 at the 1:49 mark, was a pile-driving, pile-dragging backbreaker, five Packers convening to bring him down. One play later, Ryan took his first of two kneeldowns.

For the Packers to even be that close was a testament to Rodgers' impressive showing, especially in light of his injury. Against the Falcons' potent, balanced attack and on a day when Ryan Grant couldn't match his Falcon counterpart's run dominance (Grant gained 83 yards on 18 carries), the Packers, as they were forced to do the week before against Tampa, had to ride the arm—and separated shoulder—of Rodgers. He made a valiant effort, though he wished he hadn't forced that 18-yarder to Gumby on a curl route on third-and-19 with 4:30 to go. Flushed right, he chucked the ball on the run and retreating linebacker Michael Boley picked it off. Boley returned the ball 16 yards to the Packers 19. Three Turner runs later, the Falcons were up 27–17.

When the Packers got the ball back, Rodgers led a gritty scoring drive with his bad wing. He said later his shoulder had tightened up as shadow replaced sunlight on the field. By now he'd fired a bunch of all-out throws, not the least his two touchdown passes. On third-and-1 in the second quarter with the Pack trailing 10–0, he play-faked to Grant out of a full-house backfield and launched another one of those javelin bombs, the ball spiraling 55 yards through the air before dropping into Driver's hands between two defenders practically on top of him in the end zone. A fabulous Tramon Williams interception set up the next Rodgers TD. After biting on a Ryan play fake, Williams recovered at lightning speed, raced back as tight end Ben Hartsock ran clear into the end zone, leaped high out of a full sprint and made a balletic, one-handed catch when a bootlegging Ryan underthrew the ball. A couple plays after whipping a 37-yard seam pass to tight end Tory Humphrey, Rodgers glided up in the pocket, spotted Greg Jennings, and flicked the ball on the run with perfect accuracy for a 25-yard touchdown to his receiver over another pair of blanketing defenders.

Had the Packers somehow pulled out a victory, the last, late drive led by Rodgers to make it a 3-point game would have been long remembered by Packer fans. It stretched 72 yards in eight plays. Working swiftly and efficiently out of the shotgun, Rodgers completed 5 of 6 passes for 69 yards on the drive. Jennings logged half the drive's yardage in one 36-yard reception, catching a pass near the left sideline and spinning out of a tackle to add 16 yards. Just as Rodgers threw that pass, he got hammered, defensive tackle Jonathan Babineaux's helmet smashing into the bent right arm of Rodgers then into his gut. The QB shook it off. Two plays later, he rifled a 16-yarder to tight end Tory Humphrey. Rodgers capped the drive with an underhanded toss to Donald Lee for a 4-yard touchdown at the two-minute mark. But Crosby's onside kick failed.

And the Packers lost.

For the third straight time.

This time at home.

"Our house is messy right now," said Mike McCarthy after the game.

They did some cleaning up in Seattle. Leading just 3–0 after one quarter, however, it wasn't clear early that the Pack would snap their three-game losing streak. Once again Rodgers wasn't able to practice all week because of the shoulder. Nor was it the most promising of signs when he one-hopped a pass to Driver on a medium-range attempt. But he was out there and with Matt Hasselbeck down with a knee and Seneca Wallace nursing a calf injury, the Packers were going against third-string quarterback Charlie Frye. After a 50-yard Olindo Mare field goal tied the score in the second quarter, Rodgers was sacked on third-and-3 by linebacker Julian Peterson and fumbled. Seattle recovered at the Green Bay 32. On third-and-2 from the 6, Frye flipped the ball to tight end John Carlson who caught it at the 5, burst for the end zone, and hurdled over two Packer defenders for the score. Down 10–3, would the Packers rally? They would, thanks to a wake-up hit by Pro Bowl defensive end Patrick Kerney on Rodgers midway through quarter two.

Drilling Rodgers with a leaning shoulder a split second after he released a pass, Kerney knocked Rodgers airborne for another hard landing. But the QB popped right back up and promptly hit Donald Driver for 19 yards against a zone on third-and-7. From there, the Packers offense found a rhythm, mixing the run and pass to march another 43 yards down to the Seattle 1. Apparently forgetting he had a separated shoulder, Rodgers evened the score at 10 with a sneak, his legs driving his upper half over players stacked like cordwood, right hand and arm extending the ball across the goal line, injured shoulder engaged and exposed.

"He's in, he's in!" yelled fans at the Stadium View, where I was watching the game. With a minute left in the half, the officials went to a booth review. "Hey, the refs don't need to check the video, they just need to call this place," joked Dan Nielsen, 39, who works for a Fond du Lac commercial sign company. He and his wife Cheryl had driven 75 miles northeast from "Fondy" on this glorious 80-degree autumn day for the express purpose of watching the Pack here at Jerry Watson's bar. And they weren't alone. I met a dozen other people who'd driven in from out of town, in one case all the way from Hurley, some two hundred miles north on the border with Michigan's Upper Peninsula, to watch the game here a stone's throw from Lambeau. It beats the living room, and beats the cost of buying a scalped or brokered ticket for a home game, too. Plus, what better place to watch the Packers play Mike Holmgren's Seahawks than right off Holmgren Way?

I met Bill Honey of Wausau and his girlfriend, Sue from Tomahawk. They were with a group of five or six, all employees of Tomahawk's PCA paper mill. Packer-cap-wearing Rick told me he'd been a PCA boiler operator for thirty years. This marked the fourth year in a row the festive group, outfitted in straw hats and Packer jerseys and green and gold beads, had driven in from Tomahawk, 140 miles west, to watch a Packers road game at the Stadium View. They make a weekend out of it, lodging at the nearby Days Inn, dining and making merry.

Beer giraffes rose from their two tables and from tables all over the bar. Back at the square central bar, Dan and Cheryl enjoyed a huge blue drink-for-two served in a goldfish bowl swimming with gummi bears, long straws poking up. It's called—what else—an "Ice Bowl," named after the fabled 1967 NFL championship game between Green Bay and Dallas played at Lambeau Field in cold officially measured at minus-13 degrees with a wind chill approaching minus-40. The Packers won 21–17 on Bart Starr's sneak with thirteen seconds left.

"We get it for the gummi bears," joked Cheryl. During halftime as bar employees came around with lime Jell-O shots, I told Dan and Cheryl the three Minnesota jokes I heard from Skeeter Stolt in Bloomer. Dan reciprocated with a Minny joke of his own.

"Why's Brett Favre moving to Minnesota when he retires?" he asked.

"Why?"

"Because he wants to get as far from professional football as possible."

The game's second half was prettier—cleaner, if you will—at least from a Packers perspective. It featured a quick-hit Packers TD pass as well as a clock-eating touchdown drive that kept the Seattle defense on the field for nearly eight minutes. On the third play of a Packers series midway through quarter three, Rodgers uncorked a 50-yard rainbow to Jennings. "He's never thrown me a ball that good," Jennings would say later of a pass (a mere 45 yards in the box score), that traveled half a football field before dropping neatly into his hands on a go route as he kept a step ahead of Pro Bowl corner Marcus Truffant. All told, the NFC leader in receiving yardage to that point (Jennings would finish the season sixth) caught five passes for 84 yards, all for first downs, four on third downs. During that subsequent 15-play, 84-yard, clock-munching drive, Jennings, Driver, and Nelson all caught third-down passes to keep the chains moving. Then fullback John Kuhn, a Shippensburg College alum, caught his first Packers TD on a 1-yarder matched against Seahawks linebacker Lofa Tatupu to put Green Bay up 24–10.

The defense did its part, too. After two games without registering a sack, Aaron Kampman had a pair of quarterback takedowns in addition to three pressures. Crediting laptop video study the night before, Woodson jumped a pass intended for John Carlson on an out. And for the third straight game, Tramon Williams notched an interception, grabbing an underthrown 40-yard fade to former Packer Koren Robinson at the 9. Like Woodson had done after his pick, Williams gave teammates a gentlemanly handshake and small Victorian head-bow, making the old new again. By now it was quiet enough at Qwest Field to hear chants of "Go, Pack, Go!" on the telecast audio. And Mike Holmgren, who'd thrown his gameplan to the ground in disgust after a pitiable third-down throw by Frye in the first quarter, now looked simply resigned, the heat gone from his cheeks. With Charlie Frye in the saddle and top receivers Nate Burleson and Deion Branch sidelined with injuries, the firepower just wasn't there.

As the Packers game ended, final score 27–17, the Stadium View TVs switched to the final minute of the Bears-Falcons contest. And as we watched, something amazing happened. After Kyle Orton threw a 17-yard touchdown pass with 11 seconds left, the Bears led 20–19. Assuming the game was over, Dan and Cheryl pulled out their cell to call their Fond du Lac friend Bob, a diehard Bears fan. Feeling expansive, they planned to offer Bob congratulations. But wait. Bears placekicker Robbie Gould's pooched kickoff was returned 10 yards to the Falcons 44. With six seconds on the clock, real-deal Matt Ryan lofted an exquisite 26-yard pass to Michael Jenkins at the left sideline. It was the only place to put it. Somehow Jenkins got both feet in bounds, then tumbled out with 1 second left. In came kicker Jason Elam, who atoned for an earlier 33-yard miss by splitting the uprights from 48.

The Stadium View exploded. Bears lose! And just like that the 3–3 Packers were tied with Chicago and Minnesota atop the NFC North. Dan and Cheryl called their friend Bob. He didn't answer.

* * *

"Not many games in the National Football League unfold just the way one of the teams drew them up," wrote Bob McGinn to open his account of the Packers' 34–14 thrashing of the Colts on October 19. Generally sparing of praise and often bluntly critical ("If the Packers don't find some answers fast on defense, their season will spiral out of control," the reporter warned in the aftermath of the Falcons game), McGinn went on to write, "When the team plays as the Packers did Sunday, the possibilities are limitless."

That had a nice ring.

Sure, the Colts were missing five injured starters, including All-Pro safety Bob Sanders and Pro Bowl running back Joseph Addai. And yes, Peyton Manning was coming off of two offseason knee surgeries. But then again, Indianapolis had lit up the Ravens just the previous week, dominating the NFL's No. 1–ranked defense in a 31–3 beatdown. On this day, aside from a meaningless late Dominic Rhodes rushing touchdown, the Colts scored only one other time, a 3-yard Rhodes run that gave Indianapolis its only lead, at 7–3 in quarter one. The Packers made Peyton Manning look human. A 21 of 42, two-interception performance earned him a 46.6 passer rating, his worst in 52 games and fourth-worst in his eleven-year career. Woodson held Pro Bowl receiver Reggie Wayne to just two catches. Williams shut down Anthony Gonzalez. Blackmon corralled Marvin Harrison. And the Packers D got back to their scoring ways. Early in the third quarter, Nick Collins ran back a deflected pass 62 yards to the house. Slipping Reggie Wayne's ankle tackle, the former prep running back scorched diving lineman Jamey Richard along the right sideline, Richard shaking the earth with a bellyflopping, arms-out whiff, then juked tackle Ryan Diem silly, another lineman grasping at air. Just as spectacular—and no less important—was Collins' pass breakup on the next Colts series. When Marvin Harrison got two steps on Blackmon down the right sideline, a 27-yard touchdown seemed certain. Collins—who'd studied the play during the week—raced over at a perfect angle, blasted off, soared with one hand extended, and tipped the pass away a split-second before Harrison would have easily caught the ball and converted. It was as well defensed a pass as you'll ever see.

Fellow safety Aaron Rouse joined the party with 4:27 remaining. As Gonzalez ran a square in from the 1-yard line, Rouse broke from the middle of the end zone, caught Manning's pass in stride and ran it back untouched 99 yards down the right sideline. Cue the Todd Rundgren!

For about the twentieth time that day, 71,000 people at Lambeau rose to their feet. That included A. J. Hawk's aunt and uncle, up from Ohio. By chance, seated in row 46, section 121, I was right next to Hawk's aunt Joan. Her husband was seated down behind the Packers bench, and at halftime they swapped seats. "A. J.'s the nicest, most down-to-earth person you'd ever want to meet," said Joan of her nephew. I can't disagree, based on a couple of locker room interactions with him. Another thing I can say about A. J. Hawk, while we're on the subject, is that he has uncanny aim when it comes to chucking socks, shirts, leggings, and so on, into a wooden laundry hamper a dozen feet from his locker. Not even needing to look, he can keep a conversation going and toss the balled-up items right through the hamper's small opening, item after item, with aplomb.

Unfortunately for Hawk and his relatives that day, it was a game where he atypically saw almost no playing time. Playing their nickel defense (five defensive backs, two linebackers) virtually the entire game, the Packers went with lean, fluid linebacker Brandon Chillar instead of Hawk to help cover dangerous tight end Dallas Clark. A former UCLA Bruin acquired from the St. Louis Rams in the offseason, Chillar played a standout game, containing Clark, flying around, making open-field tackles. "He's everywhere!" hailed CBS commentator Phil Simms during the telecast. "We should have talked to that guy!"

On a day when his Colts counterpart played one of the worst games of his illustrious career, Aaron Rodgers completed 21 of 28 passes for 186 yards, with one touchdown, throwing no interceptions and taking no sacks. His passer rating stood at 104.2. He was a machine in the first half, completing 16 of his 19 passes for 147 yards, and that included a clock-stopping spike. RODGERS IS OUR MANNING proclaimed a Lambeau sign.

Ryan Grant helped the ball-control game, gaining 105 yards on 31 carries, his first time breaking the century mark this year. The previous week against Seattle, he'd carried the ball 33 times for 90 yards. His per-carry averages (2.7 in Seattle, 3.4 against Indy) were nothing to write home about but his grinding and Rodgers' accurate throwing (not to mention the secondary's interception returns) were a potent enough blend to fuel a combined 61 points of offense the past two games.

It appeared things were starting to click for the Pack. As special teams coach Mike Stock said after the Colts game, "Dead in the water early doesn't matter. It's how you finish." His punter had only kicked twice but did so for a 55.5-yard average. His unit even tipped an Adam Vinatieri field goal, Johnny Jolly getting enough of the ball to force a miss. Questions about Rodgers' toughness were starting to look silly. In the three games since separating his shoulder, Rodgers' passer rating was 108.5. And through all seven games, while we're reviewing numbers, he was averaging a 98.8 rating. Brett Favre's career best rating was 99.5 in 1995, his first MVP year. In his sixteen Packer seasons, Favre averaged a quarterback rating of 85.8. It would be lost on no Packer fans that while Rodgers was outperforming Manning in Lambeau, Favre, playing at the same time in Oakland, had thrown zero touchdowns against two interceptions for a miserable 47.8 rating. And while the Packers clobbered the Colts, Favre's Jets lost to the lowly Raiders 16–13 in overtime. Just ignore the fact with 1:24 left in regulation and the Jets backed up to their own 5 with no timeouts, Favre completed passes for 31 and 18 yards to set up Jay Feeley's 52-yard, game-tying field goal at the gun. With the loss, New York fell to 3–3. The Pack was 4–3.

The Tennessee game brought the Packers back to earth. *It's how you finish* applies to games, too. The Packers entered the red zone four times, but only had one touchdown to show for it. First-and-goal at the 10; first-and-10 at the 12: they didn't get it across. "We need to finish those drives off with touchdowns," said Rodgers. The bye week gave his shoulder some rest, and he was practicing again, but of his 41 pass attempts, 19 went incomplete, and five were notably off-target.

He'd rethink that bomb to Jennings in the end zone, which was picked off by safety Chris Hope. He was sacked four times, once at the Titans 12, once losing the ball. Most frustrating was the ending, the finish. To have the ball at the Titans 45 on first down with three minutes left, a mere 3 yards from moving inside Crosby's field goal range, and then go incomplete, incomplete, and a 2-yard shovel pass on a blown blocking assignment . . . well, that wasn't getting it done.

Nor would the Packers be heading to Minnesota confident in their run defense. The Titans pounded them for 178 yards on the ground, 54 of those in one explosive burst by locomotive LenDale White. And in overtime, save for a checkdown pass rookie burner Chris Johnson turned into a 16-yard gain, the Titans just ran, ran, ran. And won.

Barber & Jones. Earnest Graham. Michael Turner. Smash & Dash. All trouble. And next on the schedule was Adrian "All Day" Peterson, the NFL's second-leading rusher with 823 yards through eight games and the 2007 Offensive Rookie of the Year.

It's 300 miles from Green Bay to Minneapolis. You cross the heart of Wisconsin on two-lane Route 29 through Wausau, passing roughly forty miles north of the Tauscher farm down in Auburndale. I guess we could call that Tauscher Country.

Outside tiny Colby, birthplace of Colby cheese, thin snow sat in patches along the highway verges and in the bare brown farm fields. Sixty miles west, just before hooking up with I-94 for the last hundred miles to Minneapolis, I stopped at the Golden Spike Saloon across from Altoona's freight yard and railroad tracks. Inside, I asked the bartender, a young, balding guy with thick plastic glasses, dressed in a gray hoodie, whether he knew where Fuzzy Thurston grew up. I'd read somewhere that Thurston grew up near the railroad tracks at this hardscrabble end of Altoona, still a neighborhood of railroad-themed taverns, freight cars on sidings, and auto-body shops. The guy didn't know. I found out later, reading Thurston's memoir, that he grew up just a few blocks away on what was then an unpaved road, and that it was in this very bar, the Golden Spike, where Thurston spoke to his future wife Sue for just the second time ever and on the same day they met, their initial meeting on a beach outside Eau Claire. There were no Thurston photos or mentions in this bar that I could see. But there was a framed drawing of Lombardi behind the bar. And a sign declared, WE BACK THE PACK AT THE GOLDEN SPIKE! I believed it. Despite being just 25 miles south of Bloomer, there were no signs of "Closet Creeper" Vikings fans. There were old-timers in VFW jackets, bikers in black leather, younger guys in Packers caps playing pool or watching one of three different college football games showing on the TVs, and clouds of cigarette smoke. I said goodbye to the Golden Spike. On my way out of town, I stopped at the high-school football field where the Altoona Railroaders play. A weathered sign read FUZZY THURSTON FIELD.

Minutes later, headed to Minneapolis, my car's thermometer read 32 degrees. It was the first time this year the display had shown the freezing mark. On cue, flurries began to fall.

\* \* \*

You've probably heard the Metrodome gets loud. This is accurate. To pump up the crowd during pregame, players run out through an inflatable Vikings ship behind a bearded, fur-clad Norseman on a thunderous motorcycle. Speakers blast Led Zeppelin's "Immigrant Song," that Leif Ericson-inspired anthem about people from a land of ice and snow. Jimmy Page riffs, drums and bass-line pound, and Robert Plant wails *"ayee yaaaaaaa ya!"* Flashpots explode and smoke swirls as the miked motorcycle roars across the artificial turf. Later—every doggone first down, in fact—a Viking ram's horn blows—*ah-ooooooooooo*!—and the public address guy says, "That's another Viking . . ." to which the crowd roars in response, "First down!"

There's tons of Norse tribal drumming, and ear-splitting Metallica and AC/DC. They mix it up with a far different tune when the Vikings score—whether touchdown, field goal, or, um, safety. These guys in '50s-looking collegiate yell-leader outfits (clothes you wear if you're nicknamed "Biff") come running out with huge purple banners on long poles they can barely handle and parade around to this old-timey college pep song type thing that begins chirpily, "Go, Vikings, let's win the game!" For a Packers fan, it's a little bit annoying, but it kind of grows on you, that song. You almost start wanting to see Biff and the guys again. Or maybe you're just waiting for one to trip.

Another song was played that day—twice. "The Safety Dance" by Canadian synth pop band Men Without Hats. First Kevin Williams got to Rodgers and slapped the ball out. Rodgers chased it into the end zone and flung it underhanded toward Tory Humphrey as he hit the turf. The refs flagged him for illegal forward pass, the penalty resulting in a safety. Later, in quarter two, Jared Allen sacked Rodgers in the end zone for another two points. A pair of safeties a dozen minutes apart kind of summed up this game, one in which penalties and poor punting kept pushing the Packers back or shortening the field for the Vikes, one in which the offense stagnated and Rodgers was under hellacious pressure. Midway through the fourth quarter he'd been sacked four times and knocked down an even dozen, the last a crush-job by linebacker Ben Leber who rocketed in untouched. Compare that to the first Vikings game of the season, when Rodgers wasn't sacked once. In the Metrodome he completed 15 of 26 for 142 yards, with no touchdowns and no picks, for a passer rating of 72.9, a mark lower than his 76.7 against Tennessee. Once again he started poorly, throwing short and several feet to one side of Jordy Nelson, who was wide open on the left sideline and might have gone all the way. After a low punt to cap a dismal three-and-out opening series, the Vikes returned the ball 20 yards to the Packers 39. Following a Sidney Rice touchdown on a 3-yard pass from Gus Frerotte, the Packers showed little improvement on their second possession. If anything, this series was even uglier. After two sacks on three plays, they'd gone backwards 7 yards and once again had to punt.

The only reason the Packers were even in the game—and stop me if you've heard this before—was the outstanding play of their secondary, which included three interceptions and yet another "Pick 6." First, Woodson grabbed a short Frerotte pass at the Green Bay 43. Three minutes later, Ryan Grant ran the ball in from the 1. Then just thirty seconds before halftime, Tramon Williams intercepted a deep slant intended for Bernard Berrian and ran it back 19 yards, setting up Crosby's 47-yard field goal as time ran out. In quarter three, Nick Collins charged up from single deep coverage and jumped a cross for the tight end, taking it back 59 yards to the house. Just like that, the Packers were back within four, at 21–17. It didn't seem to matter that the Vikings had gone with seen-it-all veteran Frerotte for this rematch. Then again, no starting quarterback was doing much against the Packers secondary these days. It led the league in both interceptions (15) and passer-rating, holding opposing signal-callers to a 59.9 average. In game one, Tarvaris Jackson rated 59.0. On this day, Frerotte rated even lower, at 53.4.

Despite amassing fewer than 100 yards of offense, the Packers grabbed a 24–21 lead late in the third quarter. It was déjà vu for Vikings punter Chris Kluwe. In game one, Will Blackmon took a third-quarter punt back 76 yards for a score. Here he zigzagged 65 yards, making six Vikings miss, five of them hitting the turf following either a juke or post-juke block. Will the Thrill had one almost whimsical moment when, picking his way through traffic at the Minnesota 35, he sliced laterally then even slightly backward, reducing his speed, short-stepping, before exploding from a thicket of players in a stumbling lean, straightening up, veering left, and cutting back toward the end zone for a high-stepping entry. The Metrodome fell silent. Briefly. Very briefly.

The previous week had been The Chris Johnson Show. Today it was—who else—Adrian Peterson's time to shine. After nearly sinking his team on the previous possession by fumbling on a fourth-and-1 tackle and strip by linebacker Desmond Bishop (himself nearly fitted for goat horns for a whiff on Chester Taylor who turned a swing pass into a 47-yard score), Peterson, who'd vigorously lobbied Vikings coach Brad Childress to go for it on the fourth-and-1, took over the game on a drive in which everything was on the line and only a touchdown would do it.

With 5:56 to go and the Vikings trailing 27–21, Peterson showed why he's one of the league's most dangerous and dynamic players. All he did from this point was run or catch on six of the next seven plays, accounting for 64 of the Vikings' 69 yards. He ran for 40, and caught two short passes for 24 yards. The knockout punch was a 29-yard touchdown run right on an inside zone-blocking play. After one crisp cut through a massive hole, Peterson was off to the races. Sound familiar? It was entirely too much like the 57-yard dash Grant popped on the Vikes in game one. "All Day" finished the game with a season-high 192 rushing yards, a total pushing him above the thousand-yard mark after just 9 games. "Good to beat those people," said Vikings head coach Brad Childress after the game.

It almost didn't happen. After Blackmon returned the ensuing kickoff 31 yards to the Packers 41, Green Bay caught the luckiest of breaks. A tipped short Rodgers pass flew up in the air and dropped into the hands of Donald Driver, who caught the ball in full stride and turned it into a 19-yard gain. At the Minnesota 40 now with exactly two minutes to go, McCarthy's play-calling got conservative—excessively conservative in the eyes of some. He called a pair of Grant runs and a screen pass. Together, they gained 6 yards. Mason Crosby came on to attempt a 52-yarder.

There were thirty seconds on the clock.

I was sitting (make that standing, at this point) at the top of the Metrodome, just nine rows from the ultimate nosebleed row. I had a way better view of the baggy off-white nylon roof and rotating fans that keep it from collapsing than I did of the field and players. My seat neighbor was a Packers fan, Steven Strasser, 20. A soldier in the Tenth Mountain Division, he was here on a visit from Fort Drum in upstate New York. His mother and two sisters were with him. They were raised in Wisconsin but were now living in a Minneapolis suburb. Steven was standing, too. So was a Packer fan ten rows down from us, surrounded by people in purple and shoulder to shoulder with a Vikings fan wearing those pig-tailed Hagar horns. It was an odd-couple sight gag all game long, though there were times I worried about a fight. This hardcore Packers fan had gone mohawk for the game, his head and face painted green and yellow, a Driver jersey pulled over a yellow long-sleeve T-shirt with one sleeve torn off. His bare arm was meaty and tattooed. He stood almost the entire game thrusting that arm into the air while shouting, "Go, Pack, go!"

"*Go—back—home!*" chanted some Vikings fans.

In pregame, I'd watched Mason Crosby bullseye two 60-yard kicks. And truly, this try came painfully close. From where I was standing,

I thought it was good. So did Steven. So did Packer Mohawk Guy. We all thrust our arms in the air and roared. Packers win, 30–28! But no. The kick failed to draw and missed by inches. Vikings win, 28-27. Crushed, I sank back down into my seat with that canned sitcom ode to deflation in my head. *Wuh-wuh-wuh-wuh*. Steven Strasser sank back down into his seat. And Packer Mohawk Guy made the quickest exit in the history of stadium exits. Before he disappeared into the nearest tunnel, I caught a glimpse of his stricken face, his stricken painted face. It looked like one of those ancient Greek theater masks, the ones with the exaggerated frown denoting tragedy.

* * *

After losing two games by a total of 4 points, the Bears were a tonic. In what *Journal Sentinel* columnist Michael Hunt accurately called a "freaky dominating" performance, the Packers crushed the Bears 37–3 on a gray, blustery mid-November day at Lambeau, the temperatures in the low 30s but fan spirits tropically bright. "The Bears still suck!" thundered the crowd late in the game. It was Mike McCarthy's first home win against Lovie Smith, and he couldn't have asked for more out of his Packers. "If there was ever a model for a football game at Lambeau Field," said McCarthy afterward, going on to say that indeed, this performance would be it.

The Pack amassed 427 total yards of offense, the Bears 234. They possessed the ball fifteen minutes longer, a whole extra quarter to run and pass. Rodgers went 23 of 30 for 227 yards and two TDs, his passer rating 105.8. Thanks to phenomenal protection by the O-line, he wasn't sacked or knocked down once—he never even left his feet. This after eight sacks and multiple jarring hits over the previous two games. Huge, too, were his third-down conversions. After going a wretched

1 of 11 against the Vikings converting third downs (alarming given that he'd come into that game best in the league), here Rodgers moved the chains 7 out of 14 times on third-down passes. Also encouraging was his fast start, as he hit on his first seven passes out of the gate in his first cold-weather game.

Rodgers really had only one pass he'd want back, an underthrow to Driver who was open in the deep middle. After darting up the pocket, the mobile quarterback threw on the run. Linebacker Brian Urlacher, back-pedaling, snagged it 30 yards downfield, at the Bears 10, for his first interception of the season. Later I asked Rodgers if that had been a moment where he might have hesitated between running and throwing, as there was a lot of tempting open field before him as he let the ball go. "No," he stated unequivocally, "that was just a straight underthrow. Donald was open. I short-armed it. I should have used all the grass of the end zone."

Another cheering story was the running game. Ryan Grant rushed for 145 on 25 carries. Brandon Jackson chipped in 50 more in a superb, 10-carry game of his own. A combined 195 rushing yards between the halfbacks was impressive, considering how the Bears defense had held Tennessee to a startling 20 rushing yards the week before. And on the season, Chicago was holding opponents to just 74 rushing yards per game. The rushing attack was keyed by stellar O-line play, left guard Daryn College and center Scott Wells doing ace combo-blocking on zone runs to the left. Speaking of run-blocking, Jordy Nelson had a highlight-reel downfield block of his own, marching strong safety Kevin Payne a good 7 yards backward ahead of Grant on a left-side run down to the Bears 1. McCarthy had his team running from the get-go, crossing up the Bears on a second-and-14 a minute into the game by handing off. Grant promptly electrified Lambeau with a

35-yard sprint. Twice more on second-and-long, McCarthy called runs, and both times Grant crashed for 7 yards.

For the first time in a while, Ryan Grant was consistently breaking tackles, making guys miss. The Packers run defense stiffened, too, holding rookie phenom Matt Forte to 64 yards.

"This is the Green Bay Packers team you're going to get every week from here on out," promised Greg Jennings. "The next six games we have a chance to go places," said A. J. Hawk, who did an estimable job as the play-calling middle linebacker in place of Nick Barnett, who was lost for the season after tearing his ACL in Minnesota. With the Vikes losing to Tampa 19–13, the 5–5 Packers now stood in a three-way tie atop the NFC North. After a trip to New Orleans on Monday night, the Pack would host two warm-weather teams—Carolina and Houston—at Lambeau. Thank you, NFL schedulers. Like GM Ron Wolf before him—"Unload the whippets," advised Wolf, referring to lightweight speedsters in Lambeau's wintry weather— Ted Thompson had built his team for cold-weather games. And McCarthy designs his training schedule with an eye to having his team healthy and peaking as they hit the chilly November and December stretch drive. Judging from that Bears beatdown, his design was working. In a game when everything, but everything, went right, Mason Crosby shook off that Metrodome miss and hammered a career-high 53-yarder in the cold on his very next kick. And the defense notched yet another touchdown, a franchise-record seventh. It was a scoop and score by 271-pound defensive end Jason Hunter, showing big-time wheels after collecting a fumbled Kyle Orton snap and motoring 54 yards to the house. His first Lambeau Leap was the icing on the cake. Hunter showed major hops for a big fella, vaulting his whole body into the crowd.

I caught up with O-lineman Daryn College a few days after this historic whupping of an arch-rival. The Boise State tackle turned Packers left guard was, in the words of the *Press-Gazette's* Tom Pelissero, "arguably playing the best and most consistently of anyone on the offensive line, [and] the best football of his young pro career the past two months." Born in Fairbanks, Alaska, his teen years spent on Santa Claus Lane in tiny, nearby North Pole, the third-year lineman had to fight to keep his starting left guard job pretty much from the get-go. He won the job in training camp back in 2006, lost it after his first preseason game, and was back in after a Week 2 injury to fellow rookie and camp roommate Jason Spitz. In 2007, he was benched for three games before reclaiming his spot toward season's end. This year he faced training-camp challenges from Allen Barbre and rookie Josh Sitton. But as the 2008 season opened, Colledge was back beside starting left tackle Chad Clifton. Durable and versatile, Colledge slid over when Clifton had his freak allergic reaction minutes before the Titans game. Drafted No. 47 overall, highest ever for an Alaskan native, Colledge scored a 30 on the Wonderlic, one of the best on the Packers and right up there for NFL linemen. A communications major hoping to work in TV/radio after football (bank on it), Daryn Colledge is a precise, fluent, high-speed talker with an expansive personality that blends warmth, humor, and confidence.

He might be best known nationally for that State Farm commercial where he and Spitz sing a training-table duet version of Nancy Sinatra's "Feelin' Kinda Sunday." He and Spitz teamed up again in the premiere episode of the lineman's interview show, "The Colledge Experience," on the team Web site. As the five-minute show concludes, Spitz says to his buddy, "We've been roommates three years. You act like you don't even know me." "I'm trying to be professional!" Colledge replies. Merry prankster Spitz then scats into his mike, *"skibbidy*

221

*bop!"* It became a Spitz signature. Three weeks later, during Colledge's interview of Aaron Rodgers, Spitz snuck behind the couch, popped his head up right at the end, and let loose another, *"skibbidy bop!"*

Then he couch-tackled Colledge.

Daryn and his wife, Megan, whom he met at Boise State, have two boxers, Duke and Dash. "A brindle and a fawn," says Colledge. He looks a little scary in his Packers team photo—goatee, dark buzzed hair, dark eyes staring a hole in the photographer—but on this day he's got more hair, his chin is shaved, and he's wearing stylish, scholarly-looking spectacles that suit a guy who likes to read novels. Nor can you see the sleeve of tattoos on his right arm, or the wealth of tattoos on his back; he's in a black long-sleeve shirt with silvery swirls.

Against the Bears on Sunday, Colledge added to his crisp combo blocks by surging forward and engaging middle linebacker Brian Urlacher, a four-time All-Pro selection, at the second level. He pulled on a trap toss that gained 7 yards, opened a hole for Rodgers on a third-down draw, and drove Pro Bowl defensive tackle Tommie Harris backwards into the end zone on Grant's 4-yard touchdown run. He wasn't quite this proficient his rookie year, and he still well remembers the challenges of 2006.

"I felt like I got hit by a bus that first preseason," Colledge says. "I came from Boise as a left tackle and happened to move to left guard and to make that transition in the NFL—in this conference especially, with all the quality players on the inside, so many Pro Bowlers—it was a bit of a train wreck, man. I'll tell you what, I got benched after San Diego. I played terrible, but I learned a lot that first season. I'm still learning a lot every day, but the shellshock I think is over. I expect to go out now and do well and compete but in the beginning it was like scratch and claw and survive and hope when the dust settles you're still standing."

Colledge has taken his share of hits from hawk-eyed Packers beat reporters during his three seasons of up-and-down play. But the "downs" are fewer now, and he's become an O-line mainstay, holding down the fort at a position forever associated with Lombardi-era great Fuzzy Thurston. I asked Colledge, with his own media aspirations, how closely he followed Packers media coverage, which is ceaseless, fine-grained, and notably sophisticated, certain Packer writers watching nearly as much game film as Packers position coaches.

"I've tried to calm it down, man. But it's just my nature to follow it," he said. "I like to see what reporters are doing. I like to see the questions they're asking, the angle the media is trying to take with players and the team. But being a player myself, and being under scrutiny every day, it can get hard if you follow what they're saying every single day. I mean, sometimes you don't want to know what people are thinking about you. So I've tried to calm it down a little bit, but there's still a part of me that every day is interested in this side of the game. There's a certain relationship between the media and players that's always going to be there. For some players, it's a love-hate relationship, for others it's a hate-hate relationship. But mostly we realize the media has a job to do and we have a job to do and the fans need the coverage."

Not surprisingly for a guy who makes time to read novels and who absorbs his share of Packers coverage, which references the Packers past, both glorious and inglorious, in every third paragraph or minute of radio/TV commentary, Colledge is well aware of Packers history, and finds meaning in it. Remember, too, that when Packer players walk out of their locker room, Packers history is all over the corridor walls in the form of framed photos and newspaper clippings, and that when they walk down the Packers tunnel toward the playing field, before they enter the stadium bowl bearing the names of 21 Packers in the Pro Football Hall of Fame, they pass over a slab from the original Lambeau tunnel, one predating the renovation, one trod by the Lombardi greats. A nearby sign on the tunnel wall tells contemporary Packers:

PROUD GENERATIONS OF GREEN BAY PACKER PLAYERS, WORLD CHAMPIONS A RECORD 12 TIMES, HAVE RUN OVER THIS VERY CONCRETE TO GREATNESS.

"It's something you think about every day," says Colledge when I ask how much he thinks about Packers history. "You walk by those trophies and you think about the great guys who played here. Especially, for me, the offensive line. Guys like Fuzzy Thurston, Larry McCarren. They're here, they're around. [As a reporter], Larry's in the locker room every day. Amazing players. Amazing history. And look at the teams we play. Chicago, Minnesota, teams with their own deep history. You take pride in that. There's a certain weight placed on you that I think you have to accept and that I'm excited to accept because I have an opportunity to play for one of the great franchises in the NFL. I've spent some time with Fuzzy. Paul Hornung. Bart Starr. Jerry Kramer. Kramer—Idaho guy. We sat down and talked during an autograph session. Talked for a good fifteen minutes. Very intelligent man. It's great to see all these guys still so involved with the team. But I mean that's how it is here, the closeness, like a family. I love that element."

# PART FOUR:
# A WINTER'S TALE

# CHAPTER 10:
# GREEN BAYOU PACKERS

**T**HE TITANS FINALLY lost in Week 11. Who beat them? Brett Favre and the Jets, that's who. 34–13. I wasn't there but still watched it in a pretty good place: Kiln, Mississippi, Favre's hometown. Flying down to New Orleans early for the Packers Monday night game against the Saints, I drove out to Kiln on Sunday, my first trip to this piney, sandy hamlet of country stores and gas stations fifty miles east of the Crescent City. Home to 2,000 people, Kiln sits just three miles north of the Gulf. Before heading over to the Broke Spoke bar, I made a pilgrimage to Brett Favre Field at Hancock High School. A life-sized bronze statue of Favre launching a pass towers atop a base of black marble. A plaque fixed to the base provides Favre's football bio through 2004, when the statue was dedicated. It concludes with a quote from Vince Lombardi: "The good Lord gave you a body that can stand most anything. It's your mind you have to convince."

So this is where it all began. Everything, all the way up to the Summer of Favre and beyond. It was here that the 17-year-old quarterback shook the hand of Mark McHale, then a first-year assistant coach at Southern Miss. There was something about the kid, his confidence, the way he said, "Coach, I can play for you," that stuck with the coach, that made him come back to watch a couple games. Brett Favre hadn't even been on the recruiting list McHale was given, but when visiting this area, high school coaches kept asking him if he'd seen the kid from Hancock North Central. So McHale caught a game, but with Hancock's coach (Irv Favre, Brett's dad) employing a Wing-T offense, Favre mostly just handed the ball off. Still, there was something about this kid. McHale caught another game, saw more handing off, and was fixing to leave when suddenly, on a broken play in the second half, the young quarterback threw a ball that, as McHale told the *Green Bay Press-Gazette* years later, "had smoke and flames coming off it." McHale lobbied the Southern Miss head coach to offer Favre a scholarship. One was offered—the only scholarship Favre received—but only after a late de-commitment by another recruit opened up a defensive slot. Maybe they'd make him a safety, the thinking went. Scratch that. The kid looked good in August, throwing the ball. Favre went from seventh-string quarterback to backup by season's start. Then in game three, with Southern Miss trailing Tulane 21–14 at halftime, Brett Favre got the call and promptly threw a touchdown. He ran around wildly in celebration, then threw another. The 17-year-old freshman led his team to a 31–23 victory. The rest, as they say, is history.

I was alone at Brett Favre Field, as I'd been at Hal Prichard Field in Leonardville, Kansas, three weeks earlier. The weather was just as perfect, sunny and 70 degrees, a few white puffy clouds in the sky. There was a sound of wind in the tall, skinny pines that border the field. In time a couple of Wisconsinites joined me at the statue. They were Jim and Cathy Bloomfield of Beaver Dam, fifty miles northwest of Milwaukee. They were going to the Packers–Saints game, too. After they departed, three more Favre pilgrims showed up, the Hemauers of La Crosse and New Holstein. There was a father, mother, and their forty-something son. The elder Mr. Hemauer was a Packers season-ticket holder who had attended the Ice Bowl.

The Hancock High kid who'd run the Wing-T on this field was playing exceptionally well for the Jets at present, and doing his share of throwing. In his last two games, a 47–3 demolition of St. Louis and a 34–31 overtime victory over New England, Favre was a combined 40 of 52 for 425 yards, with four touchdowns and just one pick. His passer rating averaged out at 119.5. I'd watched the Thursday night overtime thriller at a "Brett Favre—Love Him or Hate Him" party held in the bar of The Woods country club in suburban Green Bay. It was mostly a golf crowd, the links-attired patrons ranging in age from thirty to eighty. At the door, you told the cashier "touchdown" or "interception." You were then handed color-coded tickets entitling you to a free drink depending on what Favre did. I chose touchdown. He threw two of them, against no picks.

When the former Packers quarterback threw a 16-yard pass to Laveranues Coles to move the Jets into field goal range in overtime, a white-haired gentleman in an Irish sweater and tweed cap hugged his forty-something son then kissed him on the cheek. The son, as high-spirited as his dad, proceeded to shout to everyone in earshot, "Brett Favre's the best! He knows how to win!"

The Broke Spoke was a different kind of venue. A biker bar turned Packer mecca following its discovery by Wisconsinites during Super Bowl weekend 1997 ("A Lourdes for cheeseheads," wrote one visiting reporter), the Kiln drinkery occupies a weathered one-story clapboard structure with a bullet-holed wooden sign painted to look like a Confederate flag. The sign rests above a corrugated metal awning stickered with orange stencils bearing the names and hometowns of two Wisconsinites, Todd from Oakfield and Jerry from Sheboygan. More names and Wisconsin towns are written in black Sharpie all over the plank-walled interior, an L-shaped space with a wood floor, pool table, and rear wooden bar. Packers paraphernalia is plentiful, as are ceiling-hung bras. The seats of green and yellow wooden barstools read Go, Pack, Go! A sticker on the low ceiling reads, GREEN BAY: A DRINKING TOWN WITH A FOOTBALL PROBLEM. Over the years, owners Steve and Mabel Haas have gotten to know untold people from Green Bay; during Packer games when Favre wore the Green and Gold, phone lines would connect this place with Titletown bars. Friends a thousand miles apart would knock down simultaneous halftime shots in celebration of the Pack.

Packer fans, many traveling down from Wisconsin, had jammed the bar January 20 during the NFC championship against the Giants (a game played in Green Bay). Dave Ancinic had driven down from Racine in his RV. For years he'd wanted to watch the Pack at the Broke Spoke. When he showed up three days early, Steve and Mabel told him to set up in the gravel parking lot. Just be careful of the wooden outhouse, painted Packer colors, they advised. In no time at all, they made him feel like family. He even helped out in the kitchen, cutting onions for the gumbo. Not only had he never been in on gumbo preparation before, he'd never before had so much as a spoonful.

The Lourdes analogy seemed apt the day I visited. With the screen doors propped open to the beautiful day—no need to worry about bugs this late in the year—an older gentleman in a Packers cap and T-shirt wheeled an oxygen tank around the worn plank floor. I met a group of five down from Eden, a 660-person town just south of

Fond du Lac. They were all wearing long-sleeve green and white shirts reading JET-PACK on the front, FARVE on the back. Yes, one admitted with a laugh, they'd screwed up his name.

Those shirts were the only things in the bar indicating Favre was a Jet, except for what was on the TVs. This place remained a Packers bar; Steve Haas said he had no plans to alter the decor. Still, there was much cheering of Kiln's favorite son as he led New York to victory, completing 25 of 32 passes for 224 yards, with two touchdowns and an interception. He'd done what his former understudy Aaron Rodgers couldn't do three weeks earlier, which was beat the Titans. At 8–3, the Jets were alone atop the AFC East, their win total already doubling that of 2007, a fact Favre supporters were quick to point out. The Green Bay Packers were in first place, too, albeit tied with the Vikes and Bears. They just had to take care of business in New Orleans. The seventy-five or so cheeseheads in here felt good about their chances. Ever since Super Bowl XXXI, New Orleans seemed like a lucky place for the Green and Gold.

After the Jets game ended, the bar cleared out pretty fast. The Eden folks were heading to Pat O'Brien's in the French Quarter of New Orleans. Former Packers center turned Green Bay sportscaster and radio color guy Larry McCarren was taping his weekly Packers TV show, *Larry McCarren's Locker Room,* in the bar's rear courtyard. I hung out a bit more, chatting with two friendly bartenders, Derek and Gina. Steve and Mabel had gone up to Nashville with Brett's brother Jeff for the Jets–Titans game. Dressed in a replica of Favre's crimson Hancock jersey, Derek mentioned that he was a second or third cousin of Deanna Favre. "She was a helluva an athlete herself," said Derek, who was in her year at school. "Real good basketball player." I told him I'd heard the same thing up in Green Bay. I'd met a couple women at the Stadium View (Derek knew the place, of course, the View being a kind of sister bar to the Broke Spoke) who'd played rec-league basketball against Deanna, one describing her as "a fierce competitor."

Derek said I should come back the following afternoon before the Saints game, meet Steve and Mabel, and have some gumbo. I told him I wasn't sure I could make it back, as I would be visiting another small Cajun town a hundred miles west. "Well, then, I'll tell Steve and Mabel you stopped by," Derek said, giving me their card. Then he had an idea. "You ever have moonshine, Phil?" he asked. I said I had not. He went and got some, poured a little on the bar, and held a lighter to it. The flames burned blue. Blue was good, he said; red or yellow, not so much. Seconds later we were standing in a humble rear office, its back door open to the day. Derek was holding a plastic milk jug filled with clear moonshine, preparing to decant it into a pair of Dixie cups. "Ya'll gonna like this stuff," he said, his eyes bright in a merry face beneath a fringe of cherubic curls. "It's the real deal! It'll knock your dick in the dirt!"

We drank. Soon we were joined by Gina and Sammi, another young woman staffer, and then by two more bar staffers, Brad and Dave. For the next twenty minutes we all stood back there and talked Brett Favre, Packers, and Saints. All five Broke Spoke staffers were huge Saints fans. And for the first time in six Saints–Packers matchups dating back to 1993, they wouldn't have to worry about divided loyalties when they watched the big game on the bar TVs the next night. No longer did Brett Favre from Kiln play for the Pack.

At one point, Gina and Sammi grabbed my notebook and started scribbling in it. When they handed it back, I saw one of them had written, "Saints need a pass defense! McKenzie out!" McKenzie was Saints cornerback and former Packer Mike McKenzie, out with a knee injury. Beneath the expression of concern for the Saints' secondary, one of the young women had also penned some choice words for Thompson and McCarthy. All in good fun. Mostly. It was obviously better, much better, for this bar, for these employees, for Steve and Mabel, when Brett Favre was a Packer. Even a retired one. Green Bay, Wisconsin and Kiln, Mississippi—that was the bond; that was the special union.

Before heading back to New Orleans, I made one last stop, just down Kiln Road from the Broke Spoke. I pulled into Dolly's, a gas station and convenience store. Painted upon a concrete wall facing the road was a giant yellow Packers helmet and a salute to "SUPER BOWL XXXI." As in the bar across the way, cheesehead pilgrims had been writing their names and hometowns on the wall for years, along with expressions of thanks and affection. Ben & Dawn. Joe, Kim, Jolee, and Nathan. The Leiblings. I stood there for a while, looking at all the names, sunlight slanting gently in from the west, shadows deepening. Hundreds of Packers fans from Wisconsin had parked, gone over to the wall, and found a spot to leave a record of their visit. It seemed every town in my home state was represented on that wall, many of them places I knew only from highway signs or high school sports results. Kewaunee, Chilton, and Spooner. Mayville, Lodi, and Ashland. Ladysmith, Nekoosa, and Little Chute. Tony Romo's Burlington was up there. And Becky Van Kauwenberg's Seymour. And tiny Reedsville, where Packers director emeritus Bernie Kubale grew up above his dad's bar, the Kubale Tavern.

"Thanks Irv and Bonita—from WI," read one inscription thanking Favre's parents. "Aaron and friends ♥ Kiln," read another. "Thanx for 16 great years," read a third.

* * *

Napoleonville, Louisiana, is a bayou farm town of about 650 people located fifty miles west of New Orleans. It's where Packers cornerback Tramon Williams hails from. The second-year player won the starting nickel-back position out of training camp then took over at right cornerback for four games while Al Harris was sidelined with his ruptured spleen. With Harris back, Williams returned to the nickel role, but against Chicago, with Green Bay playing nickel virtually the entire game, he played 49 of 54 snaps, and played well. Williams was sure to see a lot of action against the pass-happy Saints as well. His four interceptions had him tied with a number of defenders for second-best in the NFL, trailing only his teammates Charles Woodson and Nick Collins, who had five apiece.

After a bit of meandering on tiny country roads in this land of bayous and sugarcane, I finally found Napoleonville (also the hometown of Williams' Assumption High School teammate Brandon Jacobs, now a star running back for the New York Giants). A tornado had touched down here a few weeks earlier and ripped away half of a two-story building in the five-block downtown, furniture still sitting in an upper room cross-sectioned by the twister. It blew out a fine century-old stained window in the Cajun Corner Café, a wonderfully atmospheric place with a pressed-tin ceiling, plank floor, and antique-farm-implement decor. As I enjoyed a bottle of beer and my first crawfish burger, I spoke to the proprietors, husband and wife Rob and Marlene, whose dream it was to open this café, and in the process save a fine, historic corner building, much like Jordy Nelson's parents had saved those equally historic buildings in the even smaller farm town of Leonardville.

When I asked Williams about the size of his hometown, he said, "Well, it's got some people in it." The wording of his answer became clearer when I learned, after stopping by the public library and talking to staffers, that Williams actually grew up a few miles outside town, in an even smaller community, at the end of a lane wide enough for only one car, in a home a football's throw from a turtle farm, the pond giving way to sugarcane fields. Welcome to a place smaller than Aaron Kampman's eighty-person Kesley. To find it, I had to stop at a tiny post office on a bayou road. The helpful clerk phoned a mail carrier familiar with the neighborhood. She gave me directions and still I took a couple wrong turns. A gray horse stood in a small corral as I inched down the lane in my rental car. A couple of dogs started woofing. Williams' parents were already in New Orleans, getting ready to watch their son take on Drew Brees and the NFL's top passing attack. Parking beside the turtle farm, I walked back down the lane to a small neat brick home with a satellite dish and weathered metal marker commemorating a young man's high school graduation: AHS 2001 GRAD TRAMON.

Mrs. Evans, an elderly woman in a housecoat and ruby-red headscarf, appeared in the doorway of the home across the lane. Then a relative of Tramon's, Dixie Williams, came out of her little house and joined us. "Tramon never wanted to stand out. He wasn't someone who always needed to be up there," said Mrs. Evans, holding her hand high and flat, like a stage. "Yeah, he was kinda quiet growing up," Dixie Williams agreed. "But Tramon, if he says he's gonna do something, he'll do it. You can be sure about that." Nodding, Mrs. Evans added, "One thing about Tramon, he was always wanting to throw that ball around. Running up and down, all day long, throwing and catching that ball."

Tramon Williams wasn't drafted coming out of Louisiana Tech. He didn't go to Tech on a football scholarship, or even plan to play football there. After starring at Assumption, he decided to focus on his education, and picked Tech for its electrical-engineering program.

Practical and hard-working, he hit the books. His hoped-for degree was something that would open up opportunities for him and end his days of stocking supermarket shelves, shoveling coal and cleaning machines at the power plant, cleaning tractors, working construction in Baton Rouge, and planting on his uncle's farm. But a future in football was not his goal. Then, during his first semester at Tech, he attended a Bulldogs football game against Boise State. Watching the defensive backs, he suddenly wanted to be out there, and thought he could play with those guys. Trying out that spring, he was the only walk-on invited to camp. Head coach Jack Bicknell Jr., now an assistant with the New York Giants, happened to be walking through the weight room when the vertical jump was being tested, and the explosiveness of Williams caught the coach's eye. Bicknell asked to see Williams leap like that again. Then he asked the young man's name, already feeling that he was looking at someone with uncommon athletic ability. Happening upon a young man with that kind of athleticism was "like Christmas," Bicknell later told Lori Nickel of the *Milwaukee Journal Sentinel.*

Packers defensive backs coach Lionel Washington noticed the same gifts when Williams joined the team's practice squad in November 2006 after being signed as an undrafted free agent by Houston before being cut at the end of Texans training camp. "Athletic-wise, he's just a freak of nature," Washington told the paper. "He's a high flyer; he can really get up and run at you. He can go up and attack the football, has excellent ball skills. [Plus], he's got a toughness that's unbelievable."

Before leaving Napoleonville, I stopped by Assumption High. A large, partly wind-damaged sign in front of the school proclaimed HOME OF THE MUSTANGS, but I didn't see a football field. As I stood there searching, a woman in an SUV pulled up and rolled down her window. "Can I help you?" she asked. I told her I was looking for the football field, and explained my purpose. Lighting up at the mention of a book, she introduced herself as Ruth Blanchard, one of the school librarians. She knew both Williams and Brandon Jacobs from their days at Assumption. About that time, the skies opened up. Lisa told me to hop in, and drove me around back to the football field, where she parked. As rain pounded the car, she told a story about a game played there in 2000, played in rain like this, the whole game. Assumption was squaring off against their big rival, Plaquemines High. Tramon and his friend Brandon were the team's stars. Nobody left the stands, despite the bucketing rain.

It rained hard before the Saints–Packers game, too. But tailgaters and fans streaming toward the Superdome came prepared. Out came ponchos, slickers, and plastic garbage bags. Tailgaters crowded beneath the tents they'd erected in the parking lots, still laughing, drinking and chanting, "Who dat say dey gonna beat dem Saints?" the New Orleans equivalent of "Go, Pack, go!" Getting soaked, I hustled inside the Superdome. On my way through a stadium concourse, I passed Triple B's Cajun Corner, its menu listing crawfish pies, jambalaya, and alligator sausage. You couldn't get that stuff at Lambeau.

My seat neighbors were Jerry and Verna Everett of Biloxi, Mississippi. They make the ninety-mile drive to New Orleans often, as they're season-ticket holders and Jerry's job, as a transportation coordinator for movie and TV shoots, brings him to the city on a regular basis. Jerry's coordinated on a bunch of movies, including *Dead Man Walking*, *Monster's Ball*, *Ray*, and a terrific New Orleans movie, *A Love Song for Bobby Long*. These weren't their season-ticket seats. It's a good thing they weren't, as we were sitting toward the top of the lower level off one end zone where the low, overhanging upper deck squeezes your field of vision. Punts and long passes flew up and out of sight before dropping back down into view. Being generous parents, they'd given their good seats to their son and a friend. Until meeting Jerry, I thought Derek Peterson, bartender at the Broke Spoke, was the jolliest human being I'd ever met. Now I'm thinking it's Jerry. He's got a great wit, and about the easiest laugh in the world. And when he's not laughing he's smiling. Maybe he wouldn't have been so jolly if the Packers were winning, but that's a big maybe. And honestly, it wasn't until the Saints were ahead by 30 points that Jerry finally let himself believe a victory was at hand; he wasn't even close to being comfortable when the Saints had a three-touchdown lead. Speaking on behalf of all diehard Saints fans, Jerry said they'd had their hearts broken too many times in the past, by big leads given up, promising seasons gone bad. It's a kind of fatalism I'd only seen before in Red Sox fans prior to 2004, in Cubs fans, and, yes, in Jets fans.

The Saints won 51–29. They shellacked the Pack. It became a Monday night laugher. Jerry was happy, but he's got a good heart, and he tried to limit his jubilance in my presence.

The Saints were only up 24–21 at halftime. And the score might have been dead even had the Pack not given up a 62-yard kickoff return with under two minutes to go, a momentum killer following an 83-yard march capped by a 10-yard Rodgers touchdown scramble on third-and-6 to tie the game. Kick returner Courtney Roby's dash through ineffective arm tackles put the Saints on the Packers 31. After Nick Collins watched an interception chance go through his hands in the end zone right in front of where we were sitting, Garrett Hartley kicked a 30-yard field goal with two seconds left in the half.

The Saints had been answering Packer scores all day. After opening three-and-outs by both teams, Will Blackmon returned a punt 27 yards to the Saints 37. Following three tough Grant carries gaining 28 yards, fullback John Kuhn vaulted over the top for a 1-yard touchdown.

But on the Saints next play from scrimmage, wideout Lance Moore caught a short pass and rocketed 70 yards up the seam for a score. As Charles Woodson blitzed from the slot, Brees made his hot read, hitting Moore just 4 yards downfield before the receiver pivoted away from a frozen Atari Bigby and was gone.

*He looks pretty fast*, I remember thinking. *That's a whippet you don't want to unload.*

Moore and Brees did it again—answered a Packers TD—in the second quarter. The Pack had just marched 72 yards, the big plays Donald Driver's 24-yarder and a 7-yard Jennings touchdown grab off a play-action fake to tie the score at 14. But on the ensuing Saints possession, Lance Moore caught an 11-yard out that a diving Woodson missed by inches. After tight end Jeremy Shockey hauled in a 19-yarder over the middle, Moore once again turned into a helmeted blur, snagging a short cross and speeding away from Woodson and Collins for a 14-yard touchdown. Brees was 11 of 11 on his team's three touchdown drives. This was supposed to be an epic battle between Drew Brees and the Packers vaunted secondary, but it was starting to look like Brees might have the upper hand.

He did. He threw two more touchdowns in the third quarter, a 16-yarder to tight end Billy Miller on a seam route, and a 70-yarder to wide receiver Marcus Colston on an out-and-up. Brees had pinpoint accuracy, time to throw, and mixed up his passes to his fleet receivers with great rhythm. It was like a 'Nawlins version of "The Greatest Show on Turf." Who needed Reggie Bush? Brees ended his night 20 of 26 for 323 yards and four TDs, posting a passer rating of 157.4 (just shy of the highest possible mark, 158.3). For his part, Rodgers lacked his characteristic accuracy, despite facing a secondary playing backups and average pressure. Rodgers finished 23 of 41 for 248 yards. His three interceptions helped drop his passer-rating to 59.8, only slightly better than his season low of 55.9 at Tampa, when he also threw three picks.

It was gone. All the momentum coming out of the Chicago game had vanished. And that talk about being the best secondary in the NFL was on hold, too. The Packers had just surrendered over 50 points, something they hadn't done since 1986. The last team to post that many on the Pack was the Bill Parcells-coached Giants led by Phil Simms and Lawrence Taylor, the future Super Bowl champs rolling Forrest Gregg's four-win squad 55–24.

At least Tramon Williams had a sterling night, with his parents in the stands. He didn't allow a single completion. Neither did Al Harris. You'd think that would author a different story when two of your cornerbacks play shutdown games against a pass-first team. Yet Packers fans would wake to a *Milwaukee Journal Sentinel* headline reading "Road to Destruction," while ecstatic Saints fans would enjoy their chicory coffee and beignets in the golden glow of an enormous *Times-Picayune* headline reading "Unstoppable."

For cheeseheads in my section—and there were a more than a dozen—insult was added to injury when a very drunk, red-faced guy in a Saints jersey spotted a Packers fan in an A. J. Hawk jersey sitting 10 seats off the aisle. The Saints fan—on his way up the steps—decided to give the cheesehead hell. He began yelling, at unbelievable volume, "You need Brett Favre! Without Brett Favre, you suck! It's the truth! It's obvious! You know it! We rule! You suck! We rule! You suck!"

It went on like this for another half a minute. The cheesehead ignored his harasser. Numerous Saints fans told the guy to shut up. Finally the drunk just started chanting, even less creatively, "Brett Favre, Brett Favre, Brett Favre, Brett Favre!"

"Someone needs to Taser this guy," Jerry said.

# CHAPTER 11:
# "I AM A MADMAN"

**F**LASH BACK TO January 12, 2008. It's snowing at Lambeau Field. Seahawks tight end Marcus Pollard catches a 3-yard pass in the right flat to open the second quarter, and before he can even turn his head to start upfield—*boom*—strong safety Atari Bigby drills him, the ball pops loose, and Aaron Kampman recovers at the Seattle 18. Three plays later, Brett Favre throws a fade to Greg Jennings from 2 yards out. The Packers take their first lead, 21–14, after falling behind 14–0.

Big play, that hit. Big game for Bigby. He'd finish with a team-high seven tackles, six of them solo. "Wow, did Atari Bigby close on that play and deliver a big hit when he got there," hailed Fox commentator Daryl "Moose" Johnston, the former Cowboys fullback who knows a thing or two about delivering and taking hits. "That's a 15-yard running start, Moose," observed sideline reporter Tony "Goose" Siragusa. "He closed fast, Goose," Johnston added.

There was more. On Seattle's next possession, Bigby raced in again and smashed wideout Bobby Engram, who did well to hold onto the ball after a 9-yard reception. But the 213-pound Bigby stopped him short of the first down.

"Engram took a big hit from, guess who, Atari Bigby," said play-by-play man Kenny Albert. "That's why they call them *strong* safeties," added Siragusa. After Albert referenced Bigby's selection as NFC Defensive Player for the Month in December, Johnston remarked, "Boy, he's got great range. He's hitting guys in full stride. He's not breaking stride."

One play later, the Seahawks punted. A roughing-the-kicker penalty promptly gave them the ball back. No matter. Matt Hasselbeck threw to Pollard racing down the left side inside the Packers 10 and—*slap*—Bigby knocked the ball down just as it arrived.

"Bigby again with a big play on the ball," said Johnston up in the booth. "Watch the timing, right as the ball gets there . . . Bigby's doing a great job of reading Matt Hasselbeck's eyes, seeing where he's throwing, seeing the receiver he likes, and getting to the right point when the ball arrives."

After the game, Packers secondary coach Kurt Schottenheimer praised Bigby's technique on the pass disruption. He noted Bigby's use of his left, or upfield, arm, pointing out that had he used his right, he might have shoved Pollard or been too twisted out of position to make the tackle had the ball been caught. "Huge play for us, and the way he made it, too," said Schottenheimer. "It was a well-thrown pass, and it was absolutely picture-perfect technique and finish on the play."

Bigby wasn't done, though. Four plays later, with the Seahawks threatening on third-and-7 from the Packers 10, Hasselbeck threw to wideout D. J. Hackett up the middle just shy of the end zone. Hackett heard footsteps and dropped the ball—then flew through the snowy air, having been blown up by a human missile. That would be Bigby. Still photos show Bigby in launch mode, rocketing at Hackett, then Hackett being blasted off his feet and enjoying some air time.

"That play was caused when Bigby hit Marcus Pollard or when he hit Bobby Engram," said Johnston. "Everybody is going to be looking for No. 20 the rest of the game."

"I'm watching him," quipped Siragusa. "Make sure he doesn't come to the sideline and hit me . . . I'll tell you what, Atari Bigby—the way he's flying around, big hits, going at the ball—I mean he's really the driver of this Green Bay defense."

Pollard never caught another pass that day. He dropped two, one in the end zone in the third quarter, one on fourth down in the fourth. He said he had trouble seeing the ball in the snow but was there some kind of Bigby Effect? Charles Woodson certainly thought so.

"Big plays. Anytime the secondary makes those receivers a little jumpy out there, catching the ball, it pays dividends," said the five-time Pro Bowl corner.

It wasn't only receivers Bigby was jacking, either. Just a minute into the game, he dropped running back Shaun Alexander for a loss on second-and-3 at the Green Bay 26. In doing so, he'd done what he'd been doing all season, helping stop the run. He finished the 2007 regular season third on the team in tackles, his 121 stops (95 solo) the most recorded by a Green Bay defensive back in nineteen years. Against the Giants at frigid Lambeau January 20, the Jamaican-born, Miami-raised Bigby once again led the team in tackles, his nine stops (eight solo, twice anyone else's output) tying him with lineman Corey Williams. Bigby didn't register an interception in these two games, his first postseason action, but during the regular season he led the team with five, including four in December, coming on strong late in the season. His three forced fumbles tied for the team lead. And he proved to be a workhorse. After being a projected reserve and special teamer coming into '07 ("He will contend for a backup safety role, and special teams prowess should help in that quest," said the team Web site), Bigby won the starting job in training camp and ended up playing 94.9 percent of the defensive snaps, tops on the team.

But 2008 had been very different. Bigby severely sprained his ankle in the third exhibition game against Denver and was slowed the rest of the season, though he managed to start six games. He also hurt his hamstring in the first Detroit game September 14 and didn't return until after the bye seven weeks later. When he was in there, he was nowhere near top form. He injured his shoulder in game 12, missed the next two games after that, and finally was placed on injured reserve. The day after Christmas, he had ankle surgery. Six months later, he still wasn't a full participant in June minicamp, through by late July he was ready for training camp.

I met with Atari Bigby at Tony Roma's by the Green Bay airport on a chilly Friday night before the team headed to New Orleans for the Monday night game. Bigby, 27, came in wearing a loose-fitting gray sweatshirt and roomy jeans, with work boots on his feet. He's listed as 5-11, so he doesn't really dominate a room, and the loose sweatshirt gave little hint of his powerful frame, a build that had the Packers thinking they might convert him to linebacker when he first joined their practice squad in 2005. To see him crossing the Roma's floor this Friday night, it was almost hard to believe this was the same guy who could de-cleat 250-pound tight ends, flat-out stone 230-pound running backs, and give magic-carpet rides to wide receivers. If you watch film of that Seattle playoff game, it becomes apparent that Bigby's a Da Vinci of the hit, his mastery of impact physics a thing of beauty. Beyond that, he was on fire with his reads, timing, and angles. He was having a defensive back's "peak experience," everything working in perfect rhythm, not having to think. He was judging slices of time down to the millisecond. When Hasselbeck threw that short pass to Marcus Pollard, there was no one within 10 yards of the tight end. For viewers of the telecast, there was literally no Packer in the picture. Then, *boom!*

Bigby was named by his grandmother, whom he lived with for a time in the gritty Liberty City section of Miami, shuttling between her and his mother. A media member asked his grandmother about the name when he was starring at Central Florida University in Orlando. She said she didn't name him Atari after the video game, she just liked the Japanese word, which has connotations of both hitting a target and hitting the lottery. Born in Falmouth, Jamaica, not far from Montego Bay, Bigby doesn't have much information about his father. He and his mother and older sister left Jamaica when he was four.

He began dating his wife, Jill, while at Miami Senior High School, an athletic powerhouse. Texans receiver Andre Johnson was a high school teammate. Bigby ran track, lettered in soccer his freshman year, and played three years of football, on both sides of the ball, posting 500 receiving yards along with 72 tackles his senior year. Jill ran track and played basketball. It was a forty-five-minute bus ride from home to the school (movie fans, it's where they filmed *Porky's* in 1982), but that ninety-minute daily commute introduced him to big-time athletics, brought him together with his future wife, and showed him life outside of Liberty City. Named for its housing projects and known nationally for stories of unrest, drug wars, and, most recently, terrorist plotting (would-be bombers reportedly met in a rundown neighborhood warehouse), Liberty City earned a sunnier shout-out from native son Chad "Ocho Cinco" Johnson during the

2008 Summer Olympics. "Where I'm from—Liberty City—I know a couple of people who can beat [swimmer] Michael Phelps right now," Johnson told hosts Tony Kornheiser and Michael Wilbon of ESPN's *Pardon the Interruption*. "Seriously. I'm telling you. And I'm one of 'em." He then named a Liberty City pool.

Bigby and Jill have two daughters, Michelle, eight that day, and Leenah, five. "We have a son on the way, too," says Bigby, his wife seven months pregnant at the time. A Rastafarian since age 14 ("My mother encouraged me to make my own decisions, to follow through on the way I saw things, in terms of religion."), Bigby hasn't eaten meat or cut his dreadlocked hair since the ninth grade. His wife and daughters live in Miami, and Bigby says it's not always easy, the separation. "We've been doing the back and forth thing for three years now," says the Rasta Packer, whose large, sleepy-lidded, wide-set eyes and long eyelashes create a slight Bambi effect, a football doe whose Web site is called AtariHitsBig.com and bears the slogan, "Hit hard or go home!"

His older daughter Michelle struggles a little with the back and forth, Bigby tells me, and wishes her dad could be around more. "Hopefully one day I'll get her a nice contract from the Packers so I'll know where I'll be for a while," he says, while a song from the 1960s counterculture musical *Hair* plays loudly on restaurant speakers. It works, that song, given Bigby's shoulder-length dreads. I thought he might get some glances—not too many people in Green Bay look like him—but no one does any rubbernecking, neither the Roma patrons, who see him around town as they see other Packers, nor the staff, who see him weekly. "I come here *all* the time," he says with a grin. That squares with my opening minute here, when I told the hostess I'd be interviewing a Packer. "Atari?" she asked. Then three different staffers said hi to him as he crossed the restaurant. "I sit at the bar by myself and order the same thing every single time," Bigby says in a self-amused way. "I only eat fish and the grilled salmon's good."

It's a window on a player's life, a player whose family is 1,600 miles away, having dinner alone at the bar at Tony Roma's by the airport. It wasn't snowing this evening, but it would snow heavily within days. December 2008 would go down as the single snowiest December in Green Bay history, with 46 inches burying the town, obliterating the 110-year record by an astounding nine inches. And it was the second-snowiest month in the history of the city, just a couple inches shy of March 1888. Once or twice during the endless snowstorms, I thought of Atari Bigby, sitting at the Roma's bar, snow falling thickly outside the windows. A Rastafarian from seaside Jamaica by way of inner-city Miami, here in Green Bay, Wisconsin. The hand of professional sports—it works in mysterious ways sometimes.

I ask Bigby what he does for fun during the season. "I bowl. Al likes to bowl, too," he replies, referring to fellow dreadlocked Packers defensive back Al Harris. "Probably 90 percent of the team likes to bowl." Bigby goes on to say a little more about the then 33-year-old Harris, someone with whom he watches five to six hours of game tape a week during the season, sessions Bigby calls "homework." "This year after games, I'd go over to Al's house a lot," says the Packers strong safety. "Me and Al spent a lot of time together, because we've both been hurt this year. That kind of brought us closer together. And we both came back at the same time."

"As far as just relaxing at home," he says in response to another question, "to be honest, I'm a big National Geographic, Discovery Channel guy. *Man vs. Wild*. I could watch shows with alligators, crocodiles, snakes, all day long. I'm the same way with people. I like to watch what makes people tick. I'd say I'm sensitive to people's moods, to their vibe, their vibrations. I can meet someone, talk to them, shake their hand, and tell if they like you." Bigby's manner is genuine, gentle. There's no hint of bravado, no effort to project toughness. Like so many Packers I've met, Bigby knows he's tough and doesn't need to advertise it. But in his thoughtful manner there's also a sense of what he's been going through, his struggle with the injuries. When your body's not working, there's only so much you can do. Toughness only goes so far.

"It hasn't been a pony ride," Bigby says of the season so far. Keeping faith with his team's wishes, he keeps the major injury private, just saying it's not his hamstring anymore. "I was really looking forward to this year, too. Now that I have a lot more experience. It's been tough. Some mornings, to be honest, I'll be in bed and just . . ." Bigby trails off, shaking his head. "Whatever you see me doing now, on the field, it's extremely painful. And the fact that I'm out there and teams can't really pick on me, even though physically I'm not where I want to be, that just shows that mentally I know what I'm doing. Like if you lose your eyesight, your hearing picks up. Mentally I know what I'm doing."

Ten days after this Week 12 Friday night, Bigby will ask the team's video staff to cue up every play he'd been involved in this year. Alone with a remote-control in the defensive backs meeting room, he sat in the dark and studied his performance. "What I had to do," he told Jason Wilde of the *Wisconsin State Journal*, "was say to myself, 'Am I really good? Or was I lucky last season?'" He was hoping to banish the fear that he was merely a one-year wonder. He reviewed the play where he got burned by Lance Moore in New Orleans, a sequence that earned him a seat on the bench, only to return later in the game when backup safety Aaron Rouse himself went out with an ankle injury. Then he watched a similar play from the Carolina game the following week, a receiver running the same route against a blitz. This time,

Bigby made the tackle. "I feel like I'm a good player that was playing injured," he will conclude. "I'm only dealing with an injury. I don't think I'm dealing with proving that I can play."

Someone like Bigby, who essentially came from nowhere to become a conference defensive player of the month and postseason star saluted by Moose and Goose, has no deep resume of elite-level NFL play to fall back on when times are tough. There's not much distance between Atari Bigby "the driver of the Green Bay defense" and the Bigby who didn't get drafted out of Central Florida, who got signed and then cut by his hometown Dolphins in summer 2005, signed and then cut by the Jets weeks later. The Packers sent him to Amsterdam to play in NFL Europe in spring of 2006, cut him after training camp a few months later, then signed him to the practice squad for the second time in two years. He'd gone into that camp with high hopes after excelling in Europe but broke his hand in the Family Night scrimmage.

It wasn't very long ago that Bigby thought he was through with football, or football was through with him. It's a story he's never told before, and he's excited to tell it. "The 2005 season had started," he begins, "and I'd been out of football about a month after being cut by the Jets. I was looking for a job, anything. We had two little kids. I have a college degree, liberal studies, but I couldn't find a job—you know, the hair, different reasons. Jill was like, 'You can still play. So either you call the teams, or I'm gonna call the teams.' So I started calling and e-mailing every team in the NFL. I called and e-mailed every Canadian team. I didn't get a single response. Nothing. But I'd held onto this business card I'd picked up at the combine. It's like my mom always said, everything happens for a reason. The card was from Joe Baker, the Packers defensive backs coach at the time. So I gave Joe a call and said, 'Look, man, I'm in a jam. I don't even want a contract.

I just want a workout.' Joe said, 'Okay, I'll forward your number to our scouting department.' And I got a call. They wanted me to come up for a workout. My flight to Green Bay was on Halloween. The next day they signed me to the practice squad."

Promoted to the active roster on December 22, Bigby made his Lambeau debut on Christmas Day against the Bears, playing on special teams and recording one coverage tackle. He'll never forget the experience. It was his first time down on the field, since practice squad players watch games from above in a team box rather than from the sidelines. One thing he remembers is the temperature—his first time playing in serious cold. "I was shocked when I walked out there! Shocked! Up until then my experience of Green Bay cold had pretty much been walking back and forth to my car. You're in the box during games, you practice inside. But I was also in awe. Wow, I'm in Lambeau, I remember thinking. Green Bay, Dallas—probably the two biggest teams in America. And I'm at one of 'em now. And it's not a closed stadium—that brings more to the game, being outside. It makes it a little more, you know, vibrant. I remember running down on kickoffs, in awe. That whole day for me . . . I was in awe. I was thinking, 'I can't believe I'm livin' out my dream. If I don't ever play again, I've lived out my dream.' I'm very appreciative of the things I've gotten, the things that I've seen because of football."

I ask Bigby what it was like coming back from Europe to a place where football, American football, is the only game in town. He laughs. "Green Bay's even different from the *American* places I've been!" he says. When I ask how so, he replies in an animated voice, "The fans. The fans. The fans. They know your name from day one of training camp. They know you when you're on the practice squad. Little kids—five, six years old, calling your name!"

Is this really the same Atari Bigby about whom secondary coach Kurt Schottenheimer said, "He's a very physical, very violent player. He truly wants to hit people. He doesn't slow down to hit anything. If it's moving, he's going to hit it." When I ask Bigby if he hits hard because that makes plays or because he enjoys laying the wood, he thinks a moment then smiles.

"What if I told you that . . . I don't know my own strength?" he says. "I'll make one of those hits and I'm like, 'Did I do that? Was that me?' I have to be honest with you. The guy you see on the field is not the guy you see off the field. Well, I mean, everybody has their ego, from guys in the medical profession to Mr. Trump—everybody has that. But I'm not normally someone who wants the spotlight off the field." What does his wife Jill think of his punishing style? "She wants me to tackle harder!" he says with a laugh. "She watches on TV down in Florida and when we talk she'll tell me to pick it up a little bit. She'll tell me I might have been dialing back when I tackled some player. She'll be watching the New Orleans game. Watching me!"

After football, this hard-hitting, nature-show-watching Packer strong safety, a guy who's learning Bob Marley songs on his acoustic guitar, wants to "be a full-time dad. Just spend time with my kids. I'd also love to own a business. I like seeing things from start to finish."

Nine days hence, Bigby's season would be over. He'd hurt a shoulder on one of the defense's many goal-line plays in the Carolina game. And that night, heavy snow would fall.

* * *

Sportswriter Bob McGinn brought the hammer down on the Pack after the New Orleans debacle. His column ran in the *Journal Sentinel* the morning of the Panthers game, November 30. The twenty-year veteran of the Packers beat told readers that the essay—and at 900 words, it was more essay than column—originated in response to the Saints drubbing, a "matchup of two 5–5 teams from the same conference both motivated by a chance for a berth in the postseason. The Saints played with urgency; the Packers played without energy, almost like zombies." McGinn's thesis—a tough one—traced what he saw as a lack of energy and urgency to the "buttoned-up" climate favored by Packers management. The "controlled, conservative atmosphere" promoted by Thompson, McCarthy, and Murphy, McGinn contended, had filtered down to the coaching staff and locker room. "Pack's Cool Ways Yield Tepid Play," read the headline. "Thompson and McCarthy are flatliners, particularly Thompson," read McGinn's most arresting sentence.

McGinn called Thompson's "composed and even-keeled" leadership style both a blessing and a curse. He suggested McCarthy may have gone too far in curbing his own more naturally spirited personality, citing McCarthy's use of the bland word "disappointing" to describe the play of his defense in New Orleans. "It's almost as if the motto for this organization should be: *Never let them see you sweat*," wrote the dean of Packers beat reporters.

Drawing on years of Packers observation, McGinn contrasted the present management's style to the "far more open" Packers under the leadership of Bob Harlan, Ron Wolf, and Mike Holmgren. Harlan set a lively, informal tone; Wolf and Holmgren spoke their minds, even going off "if they deemed it appropriate"; media-relations policy allowed greater access to coaches and players. For Packers fans, the most troubling element of McGinn's piece was his contention— debatable but provocative—that the Packers management style actually influenced team personality. "They don't have much fire," wrote McGinn. "The Packers don't appear outwardly to play with emotion and they generally play without an intimidating style."

Of course Bigby would be an exception, but Bigby was sidelined. McGinn didn't mention No. 20, but as Jason Wilde wrote days later, "Bigby brought an attitude and toughness to the [defense] that seems to have been lacking for most of the season." This year there was no Bigby Effect, no streak of receivers dropping balls out of fear of dreadlocked detonation. "The presence of one man wouldn't have turned around the Packers woeful defensive fortunes," Wilde observed, "but how much better would the defense have been [with] a healthy Bigby?"

"We don't have that Ray Lewis–type guy," said Greg Jennings in McGinn's piece, referring to the Baltimore linebacker known for being vocal, intense, fierce, and, yes, intimidating. "Most of us are more reserved, quiet, trying to lead by example."

But was there enough leading going on? McGinn argued no; in fact, he cited a leadership "void." And this was too bad, for McGinn believed the Pack had the talent to win the NFC North "going away." He quoted a Titans personnel man who said the Packers were the best team they'd played through eight games, a man puzzled why they weren't playing better. Was the lack of a "winning edge" quarterback-related? McGinn said no, that going with Rodgers was the right move. Admittedly, they were young. For the third straight year, the Packers were the NFL's youngest team. The two players voted team leaders in a January player poll, Brett Favre and veteran long-snapper Rob Davis (now working in player development), were no longer suiting up. But the youth excuse went only so far. McGinn admitted a risk in writing so critical a column spurred by just one disastrous game, the "first time since December 2006 that one of McCarthy's teams had collapsed in a game that meant anything." It might be that the Packers would rebound this very day and beat the Panthers, a team with a reputation for toughness, a team with intimidating Julius Peppers and fiery Steve Smith, Smith a guy who had punched a teammate in the face during training camp. McGinn would be happy to eat his words if the Pack went out and won a hard-nosed victory.

Brett Favre's former Super Bowl teammate Mark Chmura, co-host of a Sunday morning football show on Milwaukee's 540 ESPN Radio (the station still running the "Is Ted Thompson Satan?" teaser), also perceived a leadership and ferocity deficit. "They have no identity," said the former All-Pro tight end. "They're like the Russian hockey team [in the 1980 Olympics]. I don't see enough anger. Where's the personality? You don't have to be Terrell Owens or Chad Johnson. Just show some fire. Maybe someone needs to throw a fit." And he told a couple stories about Mike Holmgren going off.

Former Packers safety Johnnie Gray weighed in, too. Every Friday afternoon during the '08 season, Gray co-hosted a two-hour Packers radio show on WDUZ from the floor of Brett Favre's Steakhouse. Like McGinn and Chmura, Gray had concerns about the team's lack of fire. "Good teams usually have a McNasty or two," he said. "That's what I call them. McNasties. It doesn't mean they're thugs, it just means they have an edge. They have an attitude. They bring it onto the field. They might not be choir boys in life but they play hard, tough, with an edge."

Would the Packers make these guys recant? Would they go toe-to-toe with the Panthers and push their faces into the Frozen Tundra?

Nope. Not really.

Steve Smith is fast. Turbocharged. In pregame warm-ups, he showed a frightening ability to switch gears, going from 0-to-60 in an eye-blink. That might be useful on a football field.

He put on a skills show for early Lambeau visitors. Under a gray sky threatening snow, with temperatures in the mid 30s, he and quarterback Jake Delhomme began with some fastball catches in the north end zone. From eight yards away, Delhomme fired one bullet after another at Smith, who caught them high, low, left shoulder, right shoulder, right hip, left hip, back turned, and even sitting down, doing some stretching as Delhomme whipped balls at him point-blank. They were having a good old time, laughing beneath their helmets. Peppers was having a good time, too, greeting Carolina fans down by the rail, then running sprints with scary burst.

Meanwhile, Packer fans, not to say Packer players and coaches, were a little less ebullient than these 8–3 Carolina Panthers. The Packers were 5–6. They needed this game. Big time. The Bears and Vikes, both 6–5, would square off that evening on *Sunday Night Football*. If the Pack lost, they'd trail one of those teams by two games. It was only a slight exaggeration to say that the season was on the line.

Delhomme and Smith moved on to another startling display. With faint echoes of the egg toss game, where you and a cohort see how far apart you can get while still being able to catch an egg lobbed back and forth barehanded, the challenge here seemed: *How far can Jake lead Steve before even Steve can't rocket forward and snag the ball?* Delhomme kept tossing it further out in front of Smith and Smith kept streaking under the ball and hauling it in. As it happened, I was watching with a Carolina fan, a Tar Heel in his late teens who'd moved to Green Bay with his mom just a month earlier. It was ace timing for his first game at Lambeau. Together, we watched Delhomme loft a ball about 20 yards in front of a slow-jogging Smith. To my eye there was no way on God's green earth "Lil' Playmaker" was going to be able to sprint beneath that rainbow and make the catch.

Oh, he made the catch. Suddenly appearing like he was in a sped-up video, Smith shot forward, blazed beneath the ball, and snagged it in one outstretched hand. Then he decelerated almost instantly, like a parachute popped behind him. I turned to the kid from Carolina, standing with his girlfriend at the yellow barrier rail. "That's not human," I said. "Steve does that all the time," the kid replied.

Steve Smith didn't display his receiver version of a nitro-fueled dragster in the game, but he did something just as stunning. The Packers actually shut him down in the first half. He didn't catch a single ball. But a half remained. And he didn't start doing his damage until three minutes into the fourth quarter. His first big catch was a leaping, tumbling 36-yarder down to the 1 on a post route with Tramon Williams in one-on-one pursuit following a defensive breakdown. Smith, 5-feet-9 at most, timed his jump perfectly, using his body to shield Williams off the ball. Tailback DeAngelo Williams finished what Smith started with a 1-yard touchdown run to even the score at 28. The quick, short drive was set up by a Mark Jones 51-yard kickoff return. Jones also had two other deadly returns of 42 and 45 yards that day. If you're guessing field position was once again a problem for the Packers, you guessed right. The longest of five Panther touchdown drives was 55 yards; the shortest went just 17. Late in the first half, Packers center Scott Wells suffered a concussion but it wasn't detected. Woozy, he shotgun-snapped the ball way up over Rodgers' head from the Packers 36. Panthers lineman Charles Johnson recovered at the 17. With thirty-four seconds remaining in the half, DeAngelo Williams punched it in for the second of his four 1-yard TDs.

Panthers 21, Packers 10.

The Packers rebounded, though. They reeled off 18 unanswered second-half points, taking their first lead with 13:43 to go in the game.

The 76-yard drive featured a nifty 23-yard pickup by Jordy Nelson on third-and-15, a stutter-go-stop down the left sideline with a post-catch spin move to gain extra yardage. Then Jennings beat cornerback Ken Lucas (a.k.a. the guy Steve Smith punched in the face) for a 21-yard touchdown on a zone-blitz bullet up the middle from Rodgers. This drive followed an even more impressive one, an eight-play march of 95 yards, the Packers' longest of the season. It began spectacularly, with Rodgers throwing a 45-yard bomb out of the end zone to Driver on a go. On the first play from scrimmage, Driver smoked cornerback Chris Gamble, dove like Superman, and made a fingertips catch. Connecting on his next five passes, Rodgers added 16 more yards with a tight-roping scramble along the right sideline. The touchdown came on a 5-yard touch pass to tight end Donald Lee. As Rodgers faked a handoff, Lee slow-blocked, then released, and caught a perfectly lofted ball. A two-point conversion on a Jennings out tied the score at 21.

When the Packers went up 28–21 on the blitz-beating Jennings seam route, Lambeau exploded. We were starting to believe! My bench neighbors were Bob Glasspiegel, a Hartford, Connecticut, resident raised in Milwaukee, and his son Ryan, a student at the University of Wisconsin in Madison. Bob wore a Rodgers jersey on top of his layers. Ryan did the same with a Nick Barnett jersey. Sitting in front of us was the *We're at the game* guy in his grass-green ski hat with the little tassel. With so gripping a comeback, he and his four friends were no longer playing a drinking game where he bought his buddies beer if and when "One-Cut Grant" made more than one cut. Because Grant is such a straight-ahead runner—even more so this year, it seemed—the guy didn't end up buying that much Miller. At any rate, he was locked into the drama now. We all were.

Enter Lil' Playmaker. His first big catch on that post route handed Carolina an easy 1-yard score with 11:10 to go. But again the Pack had responded. Rodgers led an impressive 16-play, 79-yard drive that devoured nine minutes and thirteen seconds, the longest fourth-quarter Packers drive in thirty-eight years. Rodgers to Gumby for 17! Rodgers for 6 on a third-and-4 scramble! Jennings for 17! Driver for 13! With Rodgers going 6 of 6 on the drive, the Packers reached the Panthers 9-yard line with 3:52 to go. And right on cue, snow began falling. *Have some white stuff, warm-weather Panthers! How's that snow feel, Lil' Playmaker? Get much of that growing up in Los Angeles?*

The rhythm didn't last. First, the Packers were flagged 5 yards for delay of game. Then Rodgers was flushed sideways out of bounds at the 14. But wait! Julius Peppers hammered him—you could hear the crunch fifty rows up. The personal foul gave the Packers a first down at the Carolina 7. On the next play, Brandon Jackson ran it down to the half-yard line. The second-year man out of Nebraska was having a breakout game, gaining 80 yards on just 11 carries (Grant, by contrast, had 39 on 12). Jackson had broken tackles, shaked and baked. And thanks to that last run, the Packers had just 18 inches to go to take a touchdown lead at the three-minute mark.

Eighteen inches. The season more or less hanging in the balance. *Gak!*

On second down, Jackson ran at right tackle and lost half a yard. On third down, John Kuhn ran up the middle for no gain. The Packers had to settle for a 19-yard field goal, putting them up 31–28 with exactly two minutes to go. Now it was up to the defense to hold the lead. This time they would stiffen, right?

Wrong.

Special teams did the D no favors on the kickoff, as Mark Jones caught a perfectly good Crosby effort at his own goal line and promptly returned it 45 yards.

Uh oh.

Ryan Glasspiegel turned to me after turning to his father, worry in his face. He was right to be worried. On the Panthers' very first play from scrimmage, the snow thickening, Delhomme looked left out of the shotgun, gave a tiny pump, and with Brady Poppinga right in his grill lofted a moon ball off his back foot. I threw my arms skyward and cheered—just as I'd done in the Metrodome when Crosby attempted his game-winner. *That thing is so* intercepted! I thought. *Go up and get it, Charles!* Charles Woodson, playing safety in place of Bigby, was stride for stride with Smith running another post route. Woodson has four inches on Smith. The pass traveled so high, it looked like a punt. It was almost comical, the way the ball hung up there forever in the snow. "Jake shouldn't have thrown the ball," said Panthers radio analyst and former Packers safety Eugene Robinson later. Exactly! Ripe for the picking. Game over!

Not today. Just as Woodson went to jump, Smith gave him a crafty little tap in the chest, enough to throw off Woodson's launch, both men running full speed. Smith then vaulted skyward, arched his spine, and reaching back behind his head, his body looking a bit like a wedding-cake ballerina, or a dunker doing a reverse slam, snagged the absolute end of the slippery ball, David Tyree-like, in cupped, gloved hands. Then he hit the ground, somersaulted, popped back up, and got tackled at the 1. Woodson lay flat on his stomach back at the 10.

Ryan Glasspiegel held his head in his heads, his mouth agape. He resembled a Lambeau version of Edvard Munch's painting *The Scream*. And he wasn't alone. All over Lambeau Field, people gripped their heads, their mouths wide open. All over Lambeau, *The Scream*.

*That didn't just happen.*

It happened.

After DeAngelo Williams punched in his fourth 1-yard rushing touchdown of the day, the Packers got the ball back on their own 17 with 1:30 to go. On first down, Rodgers sailed a pass to a wide-open Jennings running an out that would have gained at least 20. Then he rolled away from pressure and tried an on-the-run bomb to Driver. Underthrown, the pass was picked off by retreating linebacker Jon Beason at the Carolina 39. Game over. Panthers 35, Packers 31.

That was one glum trudge down the chilly concrete stadium ramp. Left turn, left turn, left turn around the girder supports. "Brett wouldn't have lost that game," said a guy in the slow-moving crush. "Yeah," snapped a nearby stranger, "Brett woulda been covering Steve Smith."

Out into the snow we went. Among the masses of people spilling into the flake-swirled parking lot, a young woman, her tone plaintive, asked, "Is Brett on?" the question aimed at no one in particular. "It just started," replied a helpful forty-something man walking nearby. He meant the Jets–Broncos game. Maybe that's what it would come down to for some Packer fans. Brett and the Jets looked headed for the playoffs; the Packers season appeared to be doomed. But all was not lost because at least they had Brett. They could always watch Brett.

And people did watch Brett on TVs at the Stadium View. Denver beat New York 34–13 in the rain at Giants Stadium, the loss dropping the Jets to 8–4, stalling the momentum they had gained after beating Tennessee and New England. At one point, Brett Favre even held his helmeted head in his hands. Jerricho Cotchery had just dropped a 30-yard pass. Brett stood there in the rain, his hands on his helmet.

When I got home that night, I went to a window and watched the snow. I watched it whiten the roof of the tavern across the street. I watched it cover the tavern parking lot. Traffic was light on the Mason

Street Bridge, its undercarriage lit a soft blue, blue a hue of note in a city of so much green and gold. At least it wasn't Panthers teal.

Fifty years ago, almost directly below this window, disgusted Packers fans hanged team president Dominic Olejniczak in effigy during the tail end of Scooter McClean's 1–10–1 horror show season. As it happened, the 2008 Packers had something in common with their 1958 brethren. By giving up a combined 86 points to New Orleans and Carolina, this team had surrendered more points in consecutive games than any Packers team had in half a century. You had to go back to the '58 Packers and the 91 points they surrendered to the Colts and Eagles for a parallel.

I thought of going over to my bed and punching it like Santiago Gardner had done after January's NFC championship game. Instead I just watched the snow. I stood at the window a long time. At some point I would turn on a light. And maybe my eyes would travel to a pair of index cards taped to a wall above my writing table. They each bore a quote. One was by Vince Lombardi, as quoted in Jerry Kramer's *Instant Replay*. "A few plays decide each football game," Lombardi had said. The other came from former Packers GM Ron Wolf's book *The Packer Way*. "In the dark hours after a loss," wrote Wolf, "I am a madman."

# CHAPTER 12:
# SHOVELERS NEEDED

---

**T**HE HALF DOZEN reporters observing the Packers practice Wednesday, December 3, their first session since the loss to Carolina, kept a close eye on kickoff coverage work. Mark Jones had torched the Pack for 155 yards on four returns. And it wasn't just him. Through twelve games, the Packers were giving up an average of 24 yards per kickoff return. Since 1950, they'd had only two seasons where they yielded 24 yards or more on kickoffs. Special teams were a concern for another reason, too. The Packers were looking for a new punter, having cut Derrick Frost two days earlier. In the previous five games, including two played in domes, Frost had averaged just 34 net yards on his punts, hitting rock-bottom with a 30.8 net in New Orleans. Against Carolina, his net average was 32.3, thanks to a couple more low, easily returnable kicks. By contrast, Panthers punter Jason Baker, a journeyman playing for his sixth NFL team, had averaged 42.3 net on Sunday.

Frost's season gross (42.1) and net (36.1) averages ranked him twenty-sixth in the NFL. The punter he'd replaced, Jon Ryan, had caught on with Seattle, and was currently seventh in the NFL in gross (45.9) and sixteenth in net (37.3).

Reporters were also questioning another special teams move. In early October, the Packers cut linebacker Tracy White, who just weeks earlier McCarthy had called their best special teams performer in '06 and '07. The Packers wanted to hold onto practice-squad linebacker Danny Lansanah, whom the Dolphins wished to sign to their active roster. To keep him, they cut 27-year-old White and activated the rookie. Tracy White had been something of a special teams leader, motivating on the field and encouraging unit players to study film. His leadership might have made a difference in recent weeks.

The Packers practice facility, the Hutson Center, is named for the world-beating Packers receiver Don Huston, a man who earned the sobriquet the "Copernicus of Football" for inventing pass patterns such as the Z-out and buttonhook. Nine stories high at its apex, the facility boasts a pair of 60- and 70-yard FieldTurf fields at right angles to each other, one set of goalposts, and two high observation platforms with video cameras to record practice. Weight-training equipment and exercise balls fill the southeast corner, and Packers championship banners hang high on the south wall. On this December morning, a practice-squad lineman thumped a big tractor tire against the same south wall. Weight plates banged, machines clanged. Linemen slammed tackling sleds against a wall. When game drills commenced on the two fields, four refs officiated. Horns blew, coaches yelled, zebras whistled. All session long, football language filled the air. "Pennsylvania Zeus, wide-in!" "Blue 58, blue 58!" "Flip it over! Right hash!" "High and tight!" "Build a wall! Build that wall!"

The guy yelling "Build a wall," as you might guess, was offensive line coach James Campen. "Blue 58" came from Aaron Rodgers, who maintained a cheery, sprightly, comradely presence during the 45 minutes I observed. He smiled. He joked. He cracked up when 6-foot-4, 305-pound, lion-maned offensive lineman Allen Barbre came at him like Frankenstein, arms out, complete with loud groaning roar. He and Ruvell Martin did their aerial shoulder bump, but at comically reduced intensity. A walk-through shoulder bump. Between plays, Rodgers spun a football sideways on one finger, casually, perfectly. After a catching a fade pass for a touchdown, tight end Donald Lee trotted back and gave Rodgers a friendly pat on the backside.

Seeing the quarterback's rapport with teammates, I was reminded of how during spring preseason Rodgers hosted catered meals at his house each week for his fellow Packers. The idea was to build relationships with the players he'd be leading. This is the same QB who told a reporter he liked giving teammates nicknames because they helped forge a connection.

The practice highlight, at least from an offensive perspective, was a silky flea flicker. Rodgers handed off to Brandon Jackson, who flipped the ball back to Rodgers, who hit Jordy Nelson in stride for a 30-yard TD. Would we see that baby on Sunday against Houston?

"Okay on the leverage! Good job on the split!" shouted 69-year-old special teams coordinator Mike Stock during the kickoff coverage session. An 18-year NFL coaching veteran in his third season with the Pack, the white-haired Stock moved a bit stiffly in his gray sweats and ball cap but was vigorous and animated in his instruction. He continued calling out, teaching, encouraging. "Make sure you buddy up!" he shouted. "Take your angles! Don't make it hard!"

"Let's go, let's go, let's go, let's go, let's go!" hollered assistant special teams coach Shawn Slocum, 43. "Maintain! Maintain!" Between kickoffs Stock counseled newly signed defensive tackle Alfred Malone, who'd be covering kicks Sunday. "Whatever happens here, you want to be on two levels, Alfred," he said. "Establish center, come back on the one."

Just before the horn blew, Stock shouted some final instruction.

"You're gonna have to haul ass to get your angle back!"

It snowed that night. Six inches. Thursday morning, the *Press-Gazette* ran a notice announcing that "Lambeau Field Needs Shovelers." The Packers required 300 people, age 15 or older. Those interested should assemble at the stadium's west gate at 10 A.M. The work paid $8 an hour, shovels would be provided. When I arrived at 10:20, there was already a line of 200 bundled-up hopefuls waiting outside in the coldest weather of the season so far. I was told 250 shovelers had already been admitted. A dozen of them had arrived at 6 A.M. and stood in the 10-degree cold for four hours.

The logic behind joining this line was two-fold: Some shovelers might only work an hour, and when one left, a new person was admitted; and not everyone would be able to stand the cold and boredom. Indeed, nearly every minute a person walked away. It was sunny and there wasn't much wind but it was still barely 12 degrees and when you're not moving, that's cold.

The line kept thinning out and before long we were actually "inside" Lambeau, but all we'd really done is move out of the sunshine a few feet into the just-as-cold gate area. I stood in that line for two hours. It's the coldest I've ever been in my life. I hadn't worn enough layers, and I didn't have any chemical heat packs in my boots and gloves, as many around me did.

What made the cold bearable was conversation. I talked to two linemates, Scott Reek of Neenah and John Koeller of Appleton, the entire time. Scott is a teacher and a competitive Frisbee golfer. He told a story of playing a winter tournament in Kalamazoo in Ice Bowl–like temperatures, the worst cold he's ever experienced. Still, to maintain touch on the disk he had to keep his throwing hand bare. A former member of the military stationed in Guam and Southern California, Scott lived in Alaska for eight years and has "overnighted" in every state save Maine and Delaware. Wisconsin's tourism board should hire Scott. "I could live anywhere but I choose to live here," he said. "The seasons. The people. You're never more than a mile from a river or a lake." John is a freelance computer programmer. He plays cello, sax, acoustic guitar, electric bass, and keyboards in his spare time. His pride and joy is a '76 Corvette that he's worked on for two years, fitting it with an engine and 4,000-watt sound system in the process. Come June, he'd be taking it to Dropfest 2009, one of the Midwest's biggest custom car shows, at the raceway in Kaukauna, Wisconsin. Hydraulics, stereo power, donut-driving, and drifting were only some of the competitions scheduled for Dropfest.

Scott and John each drove thirty-plus miles to Green Bay for the experience of shoveling Lambeau. "I'd be here for free," Scott said. "Lambeau is like my Graceland." That quote went up on my wall. It sat beside the Lombardi and Ron Wolf quotes during my last three weeks in Green Bay.

They both come up to Lambeau on game days just for the tailgating. "I like soaking up the Mardi Gras–meets-Oktoberfest feel," said John. Scott and his wife drove up for the tailgate scene on October 19, when the Packers played the Colts. They slipped inside the Hutson Center to watch the University of Wisconsin marching band rehearse for their halftime show. They typically drive up and tailgate, go to the Packers Pro Shop, eat at Brett Favre's Steakhouse, then head home in time to beat the traffic. "I try to approach Lambeau from a different route every time I come up," Scott said. "I park on different streets, at a different house. Just to get a new perspective. I like meeting the different people, the homeowners. Everybody's got a different personality, a different style, when it comes to lawn parking."

"Sue, we got a parker!" hollered one of those homeowners early Sunday morning before the Houston game, the little ranch home's lawn cleanly shoveled to make it vehicle-friendly. The forty-something woman who hollered was wearing a Santa hat, as it was the last Packers home game before Christmas. Most of these Oneida Street houses north of Lombardi Avenue sported some kind of holiday decoration. Just down the street at a corner house another cleanly shoveled lawn bore white stakes stapled with small signs reserving parking spots for today's game. WALLY, WABENO, WI. BARBARA, MADISON. CHUCK – ROSCOE, ILLINOIS.

Scott, John, and I finally got into the Lambeau bowl about 12:20 P.M. We had been among the last people in line, and when three folks handed in their shovels, away we went. By now the temperature had risen to a balmy 20 degrees, the sky china blue. Sun glittered on the snow-covered field. Two long aluminum slides ran from row 60 at the top of the bowl all the way down to the field, one on the visitors' side, one on the home side. You shovel a bench or concrete row, take your snow to the slide, dump it, then go back and get some more as a bulldozer removes the snow below. Once your crew clears a section, you manually move the slide—*All together now! Lift!*—to the next aisle. Eventually the two slides meet in the south end zone and Lambeau is ready for a game.

Unless, of course, it snows again.

After several minutes of shoveling, I finally began to feel my fingers and toes. I wasn't sure if Scott or John had noticed, but I was barely able to speak during our last half hour in line. My face was numb. The concrete floor we were standing on might as well have been the Arctic shelf, and seemed to send up waves of subzero air. When John asked where I'd be sitting Sunday for the Houston game, I pointed up to the press box. The heated press box. I was okay with that.

An hour later I was in the Packers locker room talking to our new punter, Jeremy Kapinos, 24. A linebacker-looking guy at 6-1, 235, broad-backed with a shoulder tat, the Virginia-raised Kapinos was a four-year starter at Penn State, where he totaled more yards than any punter in school history. Undrafted in 2007, he was signed by the Jets that summer. Cut after training camp, he worked maintenance on a golf course for three months before rejoining the Jets and punting in one game in December. He spent the offseason with New York but had been let go before camp.

In a tryout both inside and outside the Hutson Center the previous day, Kapinos outperformed the two other punters the Packers brought in and won the job. Consider what he was facing: In four days he'd be punting at sold-out Lambeau Field in single-digit temperatures for a team whose special teams had been under a microscope for weeks. The previous punter was booed and blamed (and cut). Oh, and this game was an absolute, 110 percent must-win for the Packers to maintain even a prayer of going to the postseason. He had two days to practice. Welcome to Green Bay!

When we spoke, he'd just come back from a non-punting visit to Lambeau. He didn't hide, in either his words or bearing, the weightiness of the moment, the newness. I asked him what it was like punting outside on Clark Hinkle Field during his tryout. "It was pretty frozen," he said, then pointed toward the players' showers. "It was hard as that tile in the bathroom."

What about Lambeau itself? "It was awesome," Kapinos said. "I'll probably go back there Monday or Tuesday to take some pictures.

It was good to get a feel for it, instead of just walking in Sunday for the first time. It was definitely cold. It's gonna be cold. And windy. But I've punted in cold at Penn State. Plus, I've been hearing Frozen Tundra stories, Lombardi stories, from Coach Paterno for five years now."

My next stop was rookie cornerback Pat Lee. Lee was born in Miami, lives in Miami, and played his college ball at Auburn University in Alabama. I asked him how he was doing in this cold.

"Oh, it's all right. I just layer up."

"Have you bought a parka yet?"

"A what?"

"A big winter coat."

"Not yet. Probably order online."

"Are you asking anyone for cold-weather advice?"

"Little bit. They're just saying it's gonna get colder. I think I'm gonna get one of those big North Face jackets that can handle anything. It's funny, I remember me and my buddies at the combine, we were joking about getting drafted by Green Bay and going to all that cold. And here I am."

Plowed snow was already banked high in the Lambeau lots. Mini avalanches were sliding down the big-top tents covering the Tundra Tailgate Zone. The players' lot beneath the windows of Curly's Pub was slippery with patches of snow and ice. You could sit in Curly's and watch players come out after practice. Most of them walk slowly, carefully, not wanting to slip, their legs tired from practice, some nursing leg injuries, a number of them raised in warm climates. They come out holding thick playbook binders, meals in Styrofoam containers, bananas, often talking on their cell phones. A few players, including Pat Lee, had remote starters. White exhaust would suddenly shoot into the frigid air from a parked Escalade or Tundra pickup; a few minutes later the player would baby-step through the lot to their warmed-up vehicle. The players could look almost vulnerable, almost frail, from above, testing their footing, puffing ivory clouds from their mouths. But one Packer stood out for the quickness, even the jauntiness, of his trek across the lot. Aaron Rodgers. The Californian. He'd bop out of Lambeau in blue nylon sweats, warm-up jacket, white sneakers, and a white knit cap (his "bonnet," according to the less favorably inclined), with a leather courier bag slung across his back. Even on the wintriest days, he seemed to have a spring in his step, like there was summer in his heart despite the ice below his feet.

It was 3 degrees at kickoff. Hats off to a few brave Texans fans I'd seen walking cheerily around the tailgate scene as early as 9 A.M., dressed in their brand-new winter clothes and saying, "Howdy." I saw at least three Houston backers in ten-gallon hats, two of them wearing winter boots but one guy rocking the cowboy boots. Unfortunately for the Packers, the Texans players seemed just as unaffected by the cold as their hearty, loyal fans. They marched into polar Lambeau and scorched the Packers for 549 yards, the most given up by the Pack since 1983. Quarterback Matt Schaub—in a knee brace, returning after four games on the shelf following a Jared Allen love tap—passed for a franchise record 414 yards. Throwing short, medium, and long, rolling right and left, he was a bootleg maestro on a bum knee. Rookie Steve Slaton piled up 120 yards on the ground. Turnovers were the only reason the Packers were ever in the game. Houston fumbled at the Green Bay 1 and 18, muffed a punt at midfield, and saw Tramon Williams pick off a pass at their own 28.

After three quarters of so-so play, Rodgers finally caught fire. Throwing some pinpoint passes, he led a pair of fourth-quarter touchdown drives. With the Packers down 13–7, he arced another exquisite rainbow—perhaps his most exquisite all year—to Jennings on a 63-yard play-action pass, the ball traveling an equal amount aerially, moving the Packers all the way to the Houston 6. With a corner and safety blanketing him, Jennings ran a post with a deft corner fake and split the defenders for the catch. Grant then dashed 6 yards off right tackle to put the Packers up 14–13.

Down again 21–14 with six minutes to go, the Packers tied it up thanks to a 9-yard Rodgers-to-Nelson hookup. Putting all his practice time against bump-and-run veterans Al Harris and Charles Woodson to superb use, Nelson lined up against second-year nickel back Fred Bennett. While Houston corners played 7 yards off Jennings and Driver on the left, Bennett lined up mere inches away from Nelson on the right, licking his chops, ready to jam the rookie. Rodgers signaled Nelson to change his route. At the snap, Bennett thrust both hands toward Nelson's throat, but Nelson beat Bennett's arms away with a powerful upward swing of his right arm, surged around him to the right, and accelerated. Rodgers lofted a perfect touch pass to the rear right corner of the end zone. A lunging Bennett tried his best to disrupt the catch but Nelson's grip was iron and Bennett bounced away and fell down. It was Nelson's first touchdown since Week Two at Detroit, and it was a huge one.

As fans rejoiced, Nelson tossed the ball downward—a seemly spike—then took off for his first Lambeau Leap. He showed big ups, cranking a 180-degree turn in the air and landing cleanly on his rear on top of the wall. Showered with love, he lingered there for a couple of seconds, then hopped down and trotted back to the Packers sideline. Moments later he sat wrapped in a big quilt-like parka.

Up in the press box, reporters on the Packers side exchanged looks of brief, guarded approval. Maybe this would be the game where the Packers would pull one out. The team had started the game horribly, and the hushed, muffled environment of the press box went from library quiet to funereal silence. ("No cheering in the press box," intones a voice over the PA system. "Violations could result in credentials being revoked.") On the game's third play, in the brutal cold, the field scraped of snow, Matt Schaub went long for wideout Kevin Walter, who caught the ball and scored. A 58-yard touchdown pass, 90 seconds in. The lightning-quick score was bad enough, but the details and context were downright grisly. Just like Brady Poppinga got to Delhomme on his 54-yard pass to Steve Smith—just two opponent passes prior—here Aaron Kampman hit Schaub as he threw, causing an underthrow. Walter ran a hesitation-and-go down the left sideline against Tramon Williams. Outplaying Williams for the ball, Walter made the grab, then juked hard-charging safety Nick Collins, who promptly smashed into Williams, taking out his legs. Williams did a full flip, a perfect aerial that could have passed for an Olympic tumbling routine. Williams was down. Collins was down. Kevin Walter jogged untouched into the end zone. It was an ugly, slapstick, crushing way to open a game. And it came fresh on the heels of the Steve Smith Miracle.

Not to invoke the Keystone Cops again, but there's a silent-movie quality to watching a Packers game from the Lambeau press box. Even when the crowd is roaring, you can barely hear it. The crystalline glass enclosing the vast, ultra-modern Lee Remmel Press Box, so clear it seems to magnify the view, is nearly soundproof. It feels hermetically sealed up there, and it's very high—so high, at the summit of the stadium, that from its windows you can see east all the way past Interstate 43 to the horizon. You can see houses, smokestacks, little cars moving on the highway. And little distant football players, fallible, helmeted human beings, running around down there, crashing into each other, making mistakes. The view's an Olympian one.

I was seated in the second of three tiers, directly behind five *Journal Sentinel* scribes (Michael Hunt, Bob McGinn, Tom Silverstein, Lori Nickel, Greg Bedard). Just left of the Milwaukee quintet were Tom Pelissero, Rob Demovsky, Pete Dougherty, and Mike Vandermause of the *Green Bay Press-Gazette*. The AP's Chris Jenkins sat in my tier. At my elbow was Martin Hendricks, who writes for the *Journal Sentinel*'s weekly supplement, *Packers Plus*. These are pros who supply skilled, elegant stories for the most ravenous, Xs and Os intent audience of newspaper-reading football fans in the country. How many papers would do as the *Journal Sentinel* did last September and run an 1,800-word story on a defensive lineman's techniques and philosophy? The text occupied every inch of a newspaper broadsheet, except for its illustration diagramming "Defensive Alignment Designations." Here's a taste of Bob McGinn's Kampman treatise:

> *What Kampman is trying to avoid is being "washed" inside the C gap (between tackle and tight end) that is his responsibility. Most of his "washed" plays, according to Kampman, occur when he's asked to stunt into the C gap and, without a proper base, gets angle-blocked by the tight end. . . . From the 7- or 8-technique, Kampman will engage the tackle by his third step. In obvious passing situations, he will be in a 9-technique outside the tackle or, if there's a tight end, outside him. Often his stance will be angled toward the quarterback. "Then it can be four, five steps to the junction point, or where the party is going to start," he said. "Some tackles that really float, that feel comfortable handling power, won't even make contact until the fourth step or more."*

Readers of Monday's *Journal Sentinel* would find six pages of equally sophisticated coverage, including a weekly feature called "Play of the Game." Arrows diagram movements of key players on both sides of the ball. Crisp analytic text breaks down "The Formation," "The Play," The Reaction," and "The Aftermath." The featured play from the Houston game would be a 27-yard reception by former Badger tight end Owen Daniels with 50 seconds left in the game, the score tied at 21.

Here's maybe 10 percent of the extensive play breakdown:

*Woodson is halfway between playing back as a Cover 2 safety and being up near the line. Blackmon blitzes from his slot position with the hope that Brown will over-commit to helping on Poppinga, who attacks inside rather than around the corner. . . . Even though it wasn't a great call, Bishop is still in proper position to make the play. All he has to do is maintain his leverage and then break when the ball is thrown. But Bishop jumped the stop move and allowed Daniels to break out the backside.*

Come Tuesday, another critical play would be anatomized in the "Play of the Week" feature, and McGinn would publish a 1,500-word position-by-position evaluation of the Packers. Not to be outdone, Monday's edition of the *Green Bay Press-Gazette* would devote seven full pages to dissecting the Houston game, including a half-page column, "By The Numbers," by Packers historian Eric Goska. "The Packers," Goska will write, "are in danger of fielding their most generous fourth-quarter defense in the last 56 years and perhaps of all time."

Like Jordy Nelson, Jeremy Kapinos did his best to keep the Packers in the game. After a miserable first effort, a 25-yard side-of-the-foot shank that got him booed ("I deserved it; I gave myself a punch in the face on the sidelines," he told me after the game), he punted seven more times for a 41.6 gross average, dropping three balls inside the Houston 20. Several punts drew huge cheers, as had a few booming pregame punts. Kapinos came out for warm-ups and promptly blasted a pair of 55-yarders in his opening minute at Lambeau Field. Then he slammed a 63-yarder that bounced off the back of a Texans coach, much to the delight of early-arriving fans.

But when he shanked that first meaningful Lambeau punt, he jogged off the field shaking his head, his shoulders slumped. The left-footed punter would bounce back, however. Five minutes later, he had to punt again and thumped a 48-yarder with a solid 4.09-second hang time. Four minutes after that, he rocked a 49-yard spiral that landed at the Houston 1, just barely bouncing into the end zone for a touchback. If only the offense would get it in gear, he wouldn't have to keep going out there. He'd punted three times and it was still the first quarter.

The offense finally did get it in gear. After that Nelson touchdown catch tied the score at 21, the Packers defense forced a three-and-out. They had the ball at their own 16 with 4:37 left and a chance to win the game. And the drive could hardly have started better. On the very first play, Rodgers hit Driver on an intermediate crossing route that he turned into a 59-yard catch and run, thanks in part to a great downfield block by Jennings. One 3-yard run later, Grant pounded ahead for 8 more and a first down. Correction. Tony Moll, in for Mark Tauscher who was carted off with a knee injury, was flagged for holding, the penalty wiping out the gain and moving the ball back to the Houston 32. "I didn't see the penalty. I didn't think Moll held

276

him at all," said Steve Tasker on the Fox telecast as Coach McCarthy vigorously protested the call.

On second-and-17, McCarthy called for a screen. But blitzing linebacker DeMeco Ryan beat Daryn Colledge and sacked Rodgers for a 9-yard loss. Just like that, the Packers were out of field-goal range. Counting the erasure of Grant's first-down run, they'd gone 27 yards backwards in two plays. On third-and-26, defensive end Mario Williams beat Moll and got to Rodgers, who flipped the ball to Donald Lee for three yards to avoid the sack. Kapinos came on to punt, and kicked a beauty. A civilian on Tuesday, the new Packer punter banged a high, pinpoint spiral with a hang time of 4.56 seconds. It landed at the Houston 2, bounced straight up, and was downed at the 3 by linebacker Spencer Havner, elevated from the practice squad just days before.

Houston took possession at their own 3 with 1:49 to go. It was windy and bitter cold. The score was knotted at 21. But a funny thing happened on the way to overtime.

After Slaton gained 3 yards and Green Bay called a timeout, Schaub faked a handoff to trigger play-action. Linebacker Brady Poppinga bumped fullback Vonta Leach off the line, then read run and spun back inside. Now wide open in the right flat, Leach hauled in a 5-yard swing pass with one hand before advancing it another 17 yards on the ground. After Schaub recovered his own fumbled snap on the next play, wideout David Anderson caught a 17-yarder across the middle. Following a 4-yard pass to Anderson came "The Play of the Game." Houston was at their own 48 with fifty seconds to go. Defensive coordinator Bob Sanders called a second consecutive cornerback blitz. But Will Blackmon got a late start off the line and Schaub had time to hit Owen Daniels up the middle on a stop-and-go that burned linebacker Desmond Bishop. As Daniels hesitated, Bishop dashed forward. Daniels ran by him, veered right, snagged a 7-yard cross and took it another 20 yards upfield. In a minute's time, the Packers had given up pass plays of 22, 17, and 27 yards, squandering Kapinos' pin-back punt.

It was a tough reversal for Bishop, who to that point had given the Pack real energy and punch at linebacker in a fill-in start for Brandon Chillar. In the second quarter, he saved a touchdown by chopping the ball out of Daniels' hand at the 1. Before that, he shot through the line and tackled fullback Cecil Sapp for a 3-yard loss to force a punt. He had a team-high 11 tackles, the Packers' only sack, and a quarterback hit. Call it an up and down day.

Houston stood at the Green Bay 25 with 28 seconds left. Schaub spiked the ball to kill the clock. Slaton rushed for 3. On came Kris Brown, who booted a 40-yarder at the gun.

Houston 24, Packers 21.

The Packers fell to 5–8.

It was a lugubrious elevator ride down from the press box in a car full of Packers beat reporters. It was a frigid walk on a concrete mezzanine above an unheated concourse just inside the west gate above throngs of miserable, exiting fans. Down in the media room at the bottom of Lambeau Field, beat reporters were grim and silent, waiting for Coach McCarthy. "From the Packers' standpoint," Tom Silverstein would write that evening from his post in Lambeau, snow once again falling on the stadium, "it might have been the worst-conceived game plan, worst-executed performance, and worst attempt at defending a home field that a defense has come up with in a long time." His colleague Michael Hunt would lament the "latest last-second abomination" and "insanely repetitive" nature of the mistakes and failures, going on to say that his notes from the Carolina game look almost identical to the notes for this one. And Bob McGinn would go ahead and type the phrase, "One of the most disappointing seasons in franchise history."

At last a stone-faced head coach entered the room. After Kris Brown's game-winner, McCarthy had torn his headset off and hurled it to the ground. But there'd be no verbal equivalent of that here. He was "frustrated, very frustrated," he said. He said the team would come in tomorrow and "correct our mistakes." Asked what was left to play for in the last three weeks of this broken season, McCarthy replied—notes of pride and anger entering his voice—"We're the Green Bay Packers." He meant his was a franchise with a proud tradition of winning and playing hard and it wasn't about to change now. "We're going down to Jacksonville to win a football game," the coach stated gruffly. "We need to win a game around here." After that, the room was silent. "Is that it?" asked a PR staffer.

That was it.

# CHAPTER 13:
# "THE BEARS STILL SUCK"

**T**HE PACKERS LOST to Jacksonville 20–14. And with that December 14 loss, they were officially eliminated from the playoffs. At 5–9, they were guaranteed of a losing season for only the second time in seventeen years, joining the 4–12 Mike Sherman–coached club from 2005. I watched the game at home, in the quiet of my hotel apartment. It seemed okay to do this—to stay home, instead of going somewhere—as it wasn't like I was in a completely meaningless place, a place without Packer echoes. I reminded myself that the view out these windows—the Mason Street Bridge, the frozen Fox River, the brownstone former train depot—was once Vince Lombardi's view. I'd be watching the game mere paces from where he used to sit alone and study film.

I'd already been out that morning anyway. I walked two snow-covered blocks to St. Willebrord's, "Vince's Church." A soaring, steepled edifice built of red brick in a Gothic style by Dutch immigrant

Catholics more than a century ago, it was here Lombardi came every weekday morning for 8 A.M. Mass. I sat in a rear pew and took in what surrounded him for years of church-going: the dark wood, white plasterwork and high, vaulted ceiling. Later that day, I drove four miles downriver to his former home at 667 Sunset Circle. A custom-built brick ranch on a curving, quiet lane just yards from the river, it was here where Lombardi celebrated with family and friends after winning the "Ice Bowl" in 1967. The occupied residence bears no special marker. But just a few feet away stands a fire hydrant painted green and gold.

After Sunset Circle, I drove south a mile, crossed the Claude Allouez Bridge, and parked on the snow-locked campus of St. Norbert College. With exams ending Friday, the place was deserted. I walked past the dorm where Aaron Rodgers had been playing cribbage with teammates when he got the news that Favre had been traded to the Jets. I continued on to a neighboring red brick dorm, three stories high and modern as well. SENSENBRENNER HALL read the tablet sign. It was here where Jerry Kramer and Paul Hornung, Fuzzy Thurston and Max McGee, Ray Nitschke and Bart Starr, once bunked. It was here where Herb Adderley and Jim Taylor, Jim Ringo and Bob Jeter, Willie Wood and Forrest Gregg, played cribbage games of their own, cribbage the "national pastime" of Packers during camp, according to Kramer. It was here where Willie Davis and Boyd Dowler, Carroll Dale and Dave Robinson, Henry Jordan and Bob Skoronski spent summer nights for years. Here was where Vince Lombardi called out, "Good morning, sisters!" to a pair of strolling nuns one fine morning in 1964. I stood on the same path, plowed of snow and lined with leafless trees. Melt pellets had been sprinkled to help with ice.

I hadn't planned on a Lombardi day. It just happened. Had the Packers won, I might have crossed Crooks Street to the South End Pub

& Grill to have a beer with fans more relieved than merry. Or maybe I'd have gone to the other corner tavern, the Fox Harbor Pub & Grill. Housed in the beautifully restored 1896 Freimann Hotel Building, it sits just a hundred feet down from where Augustin Langlade and son Charles, Wisconsin's first permanent settlers, had their riverfront home. The Fox Harbor Pub is where, back on October 19, I witnessed one of the most joyous sights I saw during my three-month stay in Green Bay. A young man in a Rodgers jersey began dancing with a young woman in a Peyton Manning jersey to John Mellencamp's "Pink Houses" playing on the pub speakers. It was just the two of them, dancing on the otherwise empty hardwood floor before river-facing windows, and though I think they'd just met, for a moment there they looked like they were in love. They looked like the happiest people in the world. When they got back to their respective tables, the guy with Packer fans, the woman with Colts fans, each high-fived their friends. The music, the moment, had called them.

But the Packers didn't win. They lost their fourth straight and fifth in six games. They went down to Jacksonville and couldn't get one yard in three tries at the Jaguars 44 as the fourth quarter began. First, Ryan Grant was stopped for no gain on an inside toss. Then Grant was stopped for no gain on a stretch play right. Then John Kuhn was stopped for no gain on a dive play that literally never got off the ground. He needed only a foot and a half.

Still, the Packers were up 13–7. But then Jaguars' wideout Dennis Northcutt continued his best-receiver-in-the-NFL impression—with a little help from his opponents. In the first quarter, he caught a 31-yard touchdown on a stutter-and-go, beating both Blackmon and Collins. Here in the fourth, after the Packers' short-yardage debacle, he snagged a 17-yarder up the middle on third-and-18. Quarterback David Garrard then gained 4 yards on a fourth-and-1 draw play and tailback Maurice Jones-Drew took a short pass 14 yards into the end zone.

The Northcutt/Jones-Drew combo gave the Jags their winning score, too. On the first play from scrimmage after a Packers field goal made it 16–14, Northcutt ran a post route then bent it back toward the corner for a 41-yard reception. He veered into open space beyond both Harris and Collins playing a Cover 3 zone. All told, Dennis "Packer Slayer" Northcutt, subbing for injured Jerry Porter and suspended Matt Jones, caught five balls for 127 yards, the second-best total of his nine-year NFL career. From here, Garrard and Jones-Drew did the rest. Garrard dashed 14 yards on a third-and-4 draw, then added two more when Blackmon chopped the ball out of the QB's hands but it bounced right back to him. Moments later, Jones-Drew rushed for a 2-yard touchdown.

When the Packers got the ball back, they were trailing 20–14 with 1:50 to go. Rodgers opened with a pair of incomplete passes, one a checkdown dropped by Brandon Jackson, then connected on three straight to move the Pack 32 yards from the 16 to their own 48. Unfortunately, he couldn't make it four in a row. On second-and-2 with 48 seconds left, he barely overthrew Donald Lee on a 25-yard seam route. The pass was picked off by free safety Reggie Nelson and that was all she wrote. Garrard came on for a game-ending kneel-down, a well-deserved one after completing 21 of 33 passes for 238 yards and rushing for another 31 yards on five carries. His 105.4 passer rating marked the fourth straight game that an opposing quarterback had exceeded a rating of 100.0 against the Pack. Compare that to the first ten games of the season when not a single opposing signal-caller topped the century mark.

Even with another tight, winnable game going down the drain, a loss setting in stone both a losing season and a spot in any future statistical columns listing NFL teams who missed the playoffs after going 13–3 the previous year, there was some small but not insignificant solace possible if the Packers could beat Chicago eight days hence on Monday night. For that game, I went somewhere. I went to Scottsdale, Arizona. On more than one cheesehead Web site I'd run into mention of "an ultimate Packer bar in the desert." When I worked out my travel arrangements a month earlier, I had no way of knowing that I'd be leaving Green Bay in the midst of its snowiest December ever. It was a cold one, too. At 10 A.M. the day I left town, Sunday, December 21, it was 4 degrees below zero. I flew to L.A., rented a car, then drove 350 miles across the desert to Phoenix and a few miles northwest to neighboring Scottsdale.

Mabel Murphy's was a trip. It sits rather incongruously on gallery-lined Main Street in Scottsdale's Old Town "Arts District." The spot began as a happenin' disco joint in the '70s (a small glitter ball still hangs above what's left of the dance floor), but for the past dozen years, it had been owned and run by Oshkosh native and Packer fan Ron Felker. The exterior is Southwestern enough to blend in on this Spanish-style, palm-lined street—white stucco walls, green-painted awning, patio parasols, plants; only the green Packer flag beneath the awning hints of a cheesehead paradise within—but pass through the door beneath a sign reading WISCONSIN SPOKEN HERE and you might mistake the joint for a bar in Green Bay or Sheboygan. Headquarters of the thousand-strong "Arizona Pack" fan club, Mabel's is all Packers, all the time, décor-wise. Photos of Lambeau-, Lombardi- and Holmgren-era players cover the brick walls, along with framed paintings of Lombardi, Favre, and receiver Robert Brooks, Arizona Pack pennants, a "Title Towel" from the '97 Super Bowl, endless Packer signs, and Arizona Pack charter-member nameplates bearing names such as Ron Wolf and Fuzzy Thurston. A framed Lombardi inspirational quote hangs by the front door. Even the wooden condiment holders are tagged with names like Starr, Canadeo, and Nitschke. Until recently, a Packer fan in her seventies ran a mini pro shop, the Packer Deli, out of a closet-sized nook toward the bar's rear.

Moments after I arrived, I met a woman called Judy who turned out to be the Arizona Pack fan-club coordinator. Dressed in a Packers sweatshirt, in her late sixties, Judy introduced me to numerous club members, all Wisconsin natives. I met Dr. Michael Brennan, team physician for the Arizona Cardinals and Diamondbacks. I met Green Bay native Fred "Fast Freddie" Rauch, someone whom Judy called the bar's "grand pooh-bah" and a good friend of retired *Journal Sentinel* Packers beat reporter Cliff Christl. And I met Scottsdale police officer Rick Roystan. Rick, from Wautoma originally, looks just like Ray Nitschke. He was wearing a Nitschke jersey, gets called "Ray" all the time, and is often asked by Packer fans visiting Mabel Murphy's to join them in photos because of his resemblance to the legendary linebacker.

Rick, his wife Mary, his 28-year-old son Brett, and Brett's girlfriend Elizabeth Quijada were my company for the Bears game. Brett was in a Nick Barnett jersey, Mary in a green and gold Packers jacket, and Elizabeth wore a green and gold pullover. Elizabeth is a born and bred Arizonan. So is her dad. But somehow her dad became a lifelong Vikings fan in his youth. After dating Brett for three years and coming to Mabel Murphy's for every Packers game, Elizabeth had become a major cheesehead, much to her dad's chagrin. "Would he ever come in here?" I asked. "No!" both her and Brett exclaimed. "They can't even watch a Vikings–Packers game together," Brett added.

We sat in a row of white plastic patio chairs arrayed on the sunken dance floor beneath the glitter ball relic. There were two more rows of patio chairs spread across the floor, wooden TV tables to put food and drink on, a pull-down movie screen onto which the game was projected, and pans containing sauerkraut lined a nearby table, the kraut waiting to be spooned onto bratwurst. Like many of the people in here, the Roystans and Elizabeth Quijada ordered fried cheese curds as appetizers and Johnsonville brats for their entrée.

Twenty minutes before kickoff, our Oshkosh-born bartender cranked "The Bears Still Suck Polka" on the bar stereo. Everyone knew the lyrics and clapped and sang along.

A favorite stanza:

*If you drive to Soldier Field they make you pay a toll.*
*For cripes' sake they only won one lousy Super Bowl.*
*They make fun of Wisconsin, but we don't get upset.*
*Where do you think they're all headed every chance they get?*

During the game itself, Officer Rick Roystan was Nitschke-intense. "Nothing but luck!" he roared late in quarter one when blitzing safety Danieal Manning deflected a slant meant for Driver. The ball popped up and dropped neatly into the hands of defensive end Alex Brown at midfield. "Now tackle the son of a gun!" Rick hollered on the next play, watching the dangerous Devin Hester catch a 9-yard pass. But Rick had fun, too. At halftime, with the Packers leading 14–3 after amassing 221 yards while handcuffing the Bears' offense to the tune of 50 total yards, Rick turned to his son Brett and said, "On further review, the Bears still suck."

This line was repeated many times in singing form during the half when the bartender again blasted "The Bears Still Suck Polka." It was a happy halftime, though with that kind of yardage domination, Rick and I agreed that the Packers should have had a bigger lead. Certainly the mood was lighter here in Mabel Murphy's than at Soldier Field,

287

where bundled-up Bears fans had watched Kyle Orton pass for 36 yards and rookie running back Matt Forte rush for just 14. The 2-degree weather marked the coldest for a Bears game since record-keeping began in 1963.

The Mabel's merriment slipped a notch in the third quarter, which ended with the Packers ahead just 14–10. The Bears scored following a play that had Rick pretty steamed. With 13:13 left in the third, the Packers sacked Orton to force a punt. But Brad Maynard's 42-yard effort bounced off Packer blocker Jarrett Bush after he was pushed into the path of the ball by a Bears special teams player. Five plays after the Bears recovered the ball at the Green Bay 27, tight end Greg Olsen easily caught a 3-yard slant for Chicago's first touchdown.

But it was midway through the fourth quarter when the smiles in Mabel Murphy's really began to dwindle. First, Devin Hester returned a low, 33-yard Kapinos punt 23 yards to the Chicago 49. Then on the opening play of the series Matt Forte popped a 28-yard, tackle-breaking run. The rookie ran four more times for 16 yards before Hester snagged a 3-yard pass on third-and-4 at the Green Bay 7. Making a sensational wrap-up tackle, Brandon Chillar brought Hester down short of the first-down marker. It was fourth-and-1, with 3:41 remaining on the clock. The Bears went for it. And like Chillar, nose-tackle Ryan Pickett stepped up big-time, turning man mountain—stone wall—Forte running right into him and bouncing back. Out came the chains. The spot gave the Bears a first down by inches. By the nose of the ball. On the next play, Forte ran it in from 3 yards and the extra point was good, knotting the score at 17.

Beat the Chicago Bears, and workdays feel shorter, clothes fit better, colors look brighter in Packer Land. "It almost didn't matter if you had a losing season," '50s-era Packers tight end Gary Knafelc once said in an NFL Films documentary, "as long you beat the Bears." Knafelc, host of a pioneering Packers television show, *Packerama,* and the public-address announcer at Lambeau Field for a full forty years after that, helped his 1957 team beat the Bears 21–17 in the first-ever game at Green Bay's new west-side stadium. With 8:21 to go and the Packers down 17–14, he caught a 6-yard Babe Parilli pass to put the Pack on top for good. And Vince Lombardi got off to a bright start with the Green Bay faithful in '59, beating the Bears 9–6 in his debut as Packers coach. Down 6–0 with seven minutes to go, Jim Taylor scored on a 5-yard run. After Max McGee kicked a 61-yard end-over-end punt to pin the Bears at their own 2, lineman Dave "Hawg" Hanner tackled Bears QB Ed Brown in the end zone for 2 points. It was a time before "The Safety Dance," alas.

Beat the Chicago Bears, and, frankly, it would be a better Christmas holiday for the people here in Mabel Murphy's tonight. The season had been one long, painful continuous noogie, but some small salvation was at hand. Beat the Bears, and it would be a better holiday for the Neuhaus family, and Santiago Gardner of San Diego, and Dan and Cheryl Nielsen of Fond du Lac. It would be a better holiday for the Tulsa Packer Backers, and Indy Packer Backers, and the Cheddarhead Pack of Houston. It would be a better holiday for Packers fans watching tonight at the Australian Pub in Pacific Beach, and Kettle of Fish in New York City, and the Rocky Flats Lounge on a windswept Colorado highway between Boulder and Golden, a no-frills roadhouse opposite the now-shuttered Rocky Flats nuclear bomb factory. The building used to be the bomb factory's payroll office; now it's a Packers bar with a Brett Favre shrine and a Friday night Wisconsin-style fish fry featuring perch and walleye. This is where my dad, mom, and younger brother Joe, a Denverite, were for Bears Game 1, that 37–3 Lambeau stomping. "It was wall-to-wall cheeseheads," my dad said of the Rocky Flats Lounge. "You could barely move in there. Within three or four seconds you swore you were in Wisconsin."

Beat the Bears, and it would be a better holiday for the dynamic New Yorkers, Wisconsin natives both, who run the incisive, sophisticated Packers Web site CheeseheadTV.com out of the Big Apple. And it would be a better holiday for Packer-loving fans in Stockton, California. One of them, Jeff Bleyl, in recommending a local Packers bar called Stockton Rocks, posted the following to a Packers-fan Web site a few years back: "25 fans show up each week. I like to close my eyes and hear all of the Wisconsin accents. I feel like I am home again."

It looked good there for a moment, too, beating the Bears. Beating them again. After Will Blackmon returned a short Robbie Gould kickoff 32 yards, an out-of-bounds hit by the *other* Adrian Peterson tacked on 15 additional penalty yards. In one fell swoop, the Pack leaped all the way to the Chicago 35 with three minutes to play. The opportunity was at hand. After six close losses by 4 or fewer points, the Packers had a golden chance to break this tie score, win a tight one, bring holiday joy to cheeseheads everywhere, and get the monkey off the back of Aaron Rodgers, a monkey its owner had cheekily outfitted in a Brett Favre Packers jersey. There would be no better time for Rodgers to throw a couple sweet balls and end this thing.

His first pass missed a wide-open Ruvell Martin about 12 yards downfield on the left side. His second pass was a quick-hitter out on the left edge to Jennings for a mere 2 yards. There was a whole lot riding on this next down, a third-and-8 from the Bears 33. And Rodgers came through. In the bitter cold, he whistled a strike to James Jones on a 9-yard comeback along the left sideline. The target window was tiny, the margin of error tinier. Jones leaped, closed two strong hands on the ball as cornerback Corey Graham punched at it, and came down with just enough yardage for the first down. In doing so, Jones shone brilliantly, just as he'd had on four separate plays the previous week against Jacksonville, catching a quartet of balls for 132 yards. Despite a sprained posterior cruciate ligament that plagued much of Jones' season and left him with just 20 catches after 47 his rookie year, the San Jose native ran a route and made a catch that could hardly have put more stress on his knee, and after giving his all on this play, he had to come out of the game.

There were two minutes to go. The Packers enjoyed a first-and-10 at the Chicago 24. McCarthy called three straight runs, causing the Bears to burn their last timeout. Grant gained 1 yard, 4 yards, then lost a yard. Out came Mason Crosby onto the Chi-town tundra. This time, he didn't miss by inches like he did against Minnesota. Instead, something else happened. As if someone had placed a curse on the 2008 Packers, or had voodoo dolls of mid-line Packer blockers and stuck pins in them at the snap, the Bears got fantastical penetration and blocked the kick. The booted ball flew right into the white-gloved paw of lineman Alex Brown, who was falling forward, not jumping, and if it hadn't hit Brown's hand, it would have hit the hand of linebacker Jamar Williams, whose flanking hand was up even higher.

The *thump* of leather into palm tells that story, just as a *plink* tells another story, or at least part of it. That plink was the sound of a flipped coin hitting the frozen helmet of Bears linebacker Brian Urlacher, standing at midfield puffing steam with two other Bears captains and three Packer captains, including A. J. Hawk, who called tails at the start of overtime. After the coin hit Urlacher and bounced, the three Bears kind of scurried out of the way and the steam-puffing ref went in pursuit of the stray coin. It just added a few seconds to the drama—

in Soldier Field, in the living rooms of Bears and Packer households everywhere, and in Mabel Murphy's. Finally the ref had retrieved the coin and was ready to announce the result. "Heads," he said.

"We can't even call the damn coin!" shouted Rick Roystan.

Just like in the Tennessee game, it was all over rather quickly. On the very first play of overtime, tight end Greg Olsen caught a play-action pass in the left flat and took it up the sideline. His 17-yard gain netted 32 when safety Aaron Rouse horse-collared Olsen on the way out of bounds and was flagged for a personal foul. Just like that, the Bears were at the Packers 35, at the edge of kicker Robbie Gould's range. Getting nowhere on two Forte runs, the Bears faced third-and-9 at the Packers 34. Forte then caught a swing pass in the right flat, A. J. Hawk slipped, and the rookie sprinted another 8 yards to gain 14. Two nothing runs later, Gould came on and nailed a 38-yarder to win it, 20–17.

"There is no reason to lose this game if you're the Packers," said Ron Jaworwski on the *MNF* telecast. "You've dominated them." "A combination of terrible luck and terrible special team play," added Tony Kornheiser. The Packers outgained the Bears 325 yards to 210 (just as they'd outgained the Panthers 438–300). Orton's QB rating was a dismal 48.7. The Packers sacked him twice, and picked him off twice on back-to-back Bears possessions just prior to that late fourth-quarter scoring drive capped off by the Forte touchdown. First Charles Woodson read Orton's eyes and stole a midfield checkdown pass to Peterson, taking it back 22 yards to the Bears 30, a play setting up Crosby's 28-yard field goal to make the score 17–10. Then four minutes later, Nick Collins grabbed a deep red-zone ball intended for Hester and ran it back 28 yards to the Green Bay 39. Unfortunately for the Pack, they ended up punting from their own 42, and Hester finally did some damage with his 23-yard return of the low, short Kapinos punt.

Field position—the Bears began that late touchdown drive at midfield—helped neutralize the Orton picks. This loss was not on the Packers run defense. Yes, Forte's 28-yard dash hurt, but on the day the Packers limited the rookie sensation to just 76 yards for a 3.2 per-carry. The comments of Jaworski and Kornheiser pretty much said it all. The Pack should have had this one.

Mabel Murphy's emptied out fast, Rick Roystan leading the way. The bartender cued up Johnny Cash singing "Get Rhythm," a fine choice for downcast cheeseheads with its refrain of "Get rhythm, when you get the blues." He followed that with "Man of Constant Sorrow" from the twangy soundtrack to the Coen Brothers' comedy *O Brother, Where Art Thou?* It had rained lightly during the game and Old Town's Main Street was pretty this evening, raindrops glittering in the glow of white holiday lights spiraling up the trunks of tall palm trees and the half-lit windows of art galleries revealing colorful paintings, statues on stands, and Southwestern ceramics. Directly opposite the bar was a store selling vintage movie posters. Spotlit in the window was a *Breakfast At Tiffany's* poster. "That daring, darling Holly Golightly!" it read.

A rain-slick street. Windows of art and celluloid dreams. A mournful fiddle from the soundtrack floating out of the bar, its door propped open to the 60-degree night. Holiday-decorated palm trees. And cheeseheads lamenting the ending of a Packers–Bears game, walking to cars and pickups with Packers stickers on them, here in Scottsdale, Arizona. It was all a little surreal. So was driving back to L.A. the next day, passing through a landscape of thick-armed saguaro cacti while still dwelling on that frigid game. It was getting a little old, a long drive following another close loss, the Packers playing just well enough to lose agonizingly. 850 miles home from Kansas after the overtime loss to Tennessee. 300 miles back from Minneapolis after a 1-point loss to the Vikes. 350 more miles back to L.A., my once and future home, after another overtime loss. Posting its seventh defeat by 4 points or fewer, the 2008 Packers established a new team record and crept within one squeaker of the snakebit '84 Cleveland Browns, holders of the NFL mark for close-loss frustration. And there was still one game left to be played.

* * *

It was cold back in Wisconsin. Christmas morning in Green Bay it was zero degrees. It was zero down in Milwaukee, too, where I spent the holiday. Neither place has a patch on Rice Lake, Wisconsin though, when it comes to cold. That Monday of the Packers–Bears game, the temperature in Rice Lake dipped to 19 degrees below zero, a new record. The low was set at 7:55 A.M., just in time to greet people on their way to work. On December 31, the mercury would again dip to 19 below, setting another record, this one recorded at 8:35 A.M. Located on the upper fringes of Fuzzy Thurston Country, 8,000-citizen Rice Lake sits sixty miles north of Altoona. To Rice Lakers, Green Bay's cold is not quite as bad as what they're used to. Maybe that helps explain why two of the sunniest tailgaters I met during my time in Green Bay hailed from Rice Lake. Paul and Carol Radloff were jolly and convivial even on the frigid morning of the Houston game. And they were just as cheerful on the December 28 morning of the Lions game, a day 20 degrees warmer than that last home contest against the Texans but one sitting at the bitter end of a crushing season featuring a game between the no-playoffs Packers and the 0–15 Lions. Season-ticket holders, Paul and Carol make the 250-mile drive between Rice

Lake and Lambeau, arrive early, and always park in pretty much the same place in Tailgate Row near their tailgate buddy and master of ceremonies Scott Schwartz, owner of a home renovation firm in Pulaski, twenty miles northwest of Green Bay.

A retired paper-mill worker, Paul has bright blue eyes behind steel-frame glasses and had a beard for half the season until he shaved it off. His wife, Carol, laughs as much as Paul does, which if you know Paul, hardly seems possible. I met them back when the weather was perfect, sunny and 65 degrees the morning of the Falcons game. Tailgate Row runs east-west along a central walkway between the Tundra Tailgate Zone and the Oneida Street lot. Paul and Carol and Scott and another dozen regulars in their gang always set up down at the stadium end of Tailgate Row, as opposed to the Oneida Street end. No one in what you might call "Schwartzville" drives one of those crowd-favorite Packer Mobiles, but they still have a heck of a time. The Packer Mobiles tend to line up closer to Oneida Street, and I got a kick out of the sight of them every single time, all eight pre-game tailgates. The green-painted "Pulse of the Pack!" former ambulance van. The bright yellow, Packer logo-ed Titletown Oil Corp. truck. The green "Packers Party Bus." The repurposed EMT truck that flies donated women's bras above its roof strung between two mast-like poles. All these vehicles and another four or five like them have ample wet bars and battery-powered televisions and stage-show-sized speakers to blast rock and country music.

I spent a few minutes in Schwartzville for a final time that brisk, sunny morning of game 16. There was Paul in his black leather Packers motorcycle jacket with a scarf and modified-jester's stocking cap. There was Carol in her green and yellow Packers coat and yellow tasseled ski cap. They were laughing as usual. They were good people to meet in a season like this, as you always walked away feeling better about things. And there was Scott in his Packers jersey worn over multiple layers, serving drinks from the well-stocked bar he sets up, an actual big wooden bar resting atop sawhorse-like supports. The front face of the bar is decorated with donated Packer-fan license plates, like the GOPACKGO tags from Minnesota and Ontario fans. And there behind Scott's bar were the young ladies dancing on lowered tailgates as usual, dancing and singing to songs by Tom Petty and Kid Rock and the Rolling Stones.

The snowbanks ringing the Lambeau lots were gigantic now. Some were a good fifteen feet high. The bronze statues of Curly and Vince seemed to have permanent beanies of snow. The backyards of Packers party houses off the Oneida lot's southern border were fenced fields of white. And everywhere this late-December morning, hordes of merry tailgaters stood talking and drinking on a parking lot surface glazed with snow and ice.

A few days earlier I learned the hard way why Packers players stepped so carefully across their unroofed lot to their vehicles. We'd had a brief thaw then another deep freeze then an inch of light powdery snow on top of the ice. I set out for one of my evening jogs to Lambeau, the stadium always a wonderful sight all lit up in the winter night. To add an extra mile, I ran north to the Nitschke Bridge and came across it and planted my foot on an ice-glazed curb and flew up into the air, momentarily horizontal, then crashed back down hard. The unseen ice had body-slammed me. What made it even better was that three motorists stopped at a red light saw the whole thing. Being a slow learner, I kept going and it happened again. Another fly-up-in-the-air, banana peel wipeout. No one saw that encore performance, though. Defeated, I walked back home, baby-stepping every inch of the way. The next morning my hip and ribcage were sore from where I'd smacked the pavement.

The main thing to know about game 16 itself is that the Packers were only ahead 24–21 with 7:32 left on the clock. The 0–15 Lions had just marched 80 yards for a score in four plays, the big gainers a pair of 36-yard passes from Dan Orlovsky to John Standeford against Al Harris, Standeford doing his best Dennis Northcutt impression. A hush descended on Lambeau, all of us bleacher folks sitting on benches still caked with a little snow and ice from the last storm.

The contest had begun in such a crowd-pleasing way. Barely six minutes into the game, reserve Packers running back DeShawn Wynn scampered for 73 yards and a score, a run-blocking clinic freeing the tailback to take a toss and go untouched up the right sideline. Another young Packer, 21-year-old rookie tight end Jermichael Finley, also sent a charge through the crowd with a pair of dynamic first-half grabs. It took all season, but Finley and Rodgers finally made it happen on a short fade. The former Texas Longhorn beat a defender's jam out of the slot, raced for the rear right corner of the end zone, back-pedaled briefly, then snagged a 3-yard pass for a first-quarter touchdown. Like fellow rookie Jordy Nelson, Finley did a quick, howdy-folks Lambeau Leap, his first. In quarter two, Finley hauled in a 26-yard touch pass down the left sideline, looking uncommonly fast and smooth for a 6-foot-5 tight end, and showing those hands both Rodgers and McCarthy had been singling out for high praise. In full stride and with perfect timing, the rookie put his hands out, caught the ball as softly as if it had been placed there by someone standing next to him, brought the ball down, and kept running until he was pushed out of bounds.

Packer-killer Calvin Johnson kept the Lions in the game with a pair of touchdown catches in the second and third quarters. First he used his height and spring to out-jump Al Harris on a 9-yard fade. Then, blazing into the middle off motion on second-and-13, he caught the ball on the 9-yard line, sidestepped Nick Collins, and sped into the end zone. That tied the score at 14. Lambeau was pretty quiet then, too.

After a 36-yard Crosby field goal aided by a 21-yard Ryan Grant run to start the fourth, the Pack followed that with a 5-yard touchdown toss to John Kuhn, the fullback the beneficiary of a slick Rodgers fake-handoff to Grant and a nicely lofted pass into the end zone. But then John Standeford caught his two balls for 72 yards, and Lions running back Kevin Smith dashed 9 yards for a score to make it a 24–21 game. Enter Donald Driver. On the very first play from scrimmage after the Packers got the ball back, "Drive" ran a hesitation-and-go route down the right sideline. Cornerback Leigh Bodden bit on the fake and Rodgers launched another perfect long ball. The Packer nicknamed "Quickie" in his youth received it at the 30, juked a diving Bodden, then took it the rest of the way for a touchdown.

The 71-yard pass yielded more than a game-sealing score. On the throw, Rodgers surpassed 4,000 passing yards for the season, making him only the second quarterback in NFL history to eclipse that mark in the same year as his inaugural start. The first was Kurt Warner. The TD pass also gave Rodgers 28 on the year, fourth-most in the NFL, and far exceeding his total of 13 interceptions, not one of which occurred in the red zone. The bomb also boosted Driver above 1,000 receiving yards for the fifth straight season and sixth overall, both Packer records. These were bright spots in a dark season, as was the fact that the Pack didn't lose to the Detroit Lions, who set a new benchmark for NFL futility with the loss. The final score was 31–21.

After the game, I went to Fuzzy's #63 Bar & Grill west of Lambeau Field to celebrate Fuzzy Thurston's 75th birthday, an event open to the public. A one-room bar with a retro cocktail lounge feel, Fuzzy's is first and foremost a Packers shrine, decorated with Packers pennants, framed photos going back to the first Lombardi championships, and Packers-themed license plates representing almost every state. Waitresses wearing denim shorts and bright golden tees reading I TAILGATED WITH A LOMBARDI LEGEND serve Lombardi Hotdogs and Fuzzy Burgers, the latter a bratwurst-burger combo. Staffers Mary and Gwen have worked there since Fuzzy's opened in 1999, and before that worked for years at Thurston's previous Packers bar, Shenanigan's. A couple of firecrackers in the wit department, Mary and Gwen seem to know virtually everyone who enters the bar. As Thurston wrote in his 2005 memoir *What a Wonderful World: Fuzzy Thurston, A Story of Personal Triumph*, Packers home games are like "reunion weekends for customers and staff alike," since the same out-of-state fans drop by the bar every time they're in town.

Before Thurston came out to greet the crowd, our gray-mustached karaoke jockey sang Bob Seger's "Turn the Page." Then a sixty-something woman with a bloom of sprayed hair and a dusky smoker's voice gave us a fine version of The Doobie Brothers' "Long Train Runnin'." Finally our emcee Jerry, a fifty-something bespectacled African American man wearing a golden Fuzzy's tee and cherry beret, did justice to Smokey Robinson and the Miracles' "Tears of a Clown." By now the bar was full. Surprisingly, hardly anyone was paying attention to the Jets–Dolphins game showing on the TVs. If the Jets lost or Baltimore kept its big lead on Jacksonville, these could be Brett Favre's final minutes in the NFL should he retire for good. I didn't see any Favre jerseys on the backs of patrons either. There were two Rodgers jerseys and three No. 63 Thurston jerseys, though.

Thurston came out and took the mike with about a minute left in the Jets game. As people shouted, *"We love you, Fuzzy!"* and *"You'll always be 63 to us, Fuzzy!"* the TVs showed Favre standing on the sidelines while the Dolphins tried to run out the clock. Frederick

"Fuzzy" Thurston—a guy who loved to sing, talk, and laugh—was diagnosed with cancer of the vocal chords in 1980. Surgery to remove his chords and larynx saved his life, but gone was the voice that future wife Sue heard for the first time that summer of 1956, on a beach near Eau Claire, and later that night at Altoona's Golden Spike Saloon. The youngest of eight children raised by a widowed mother in a frame house on a dirt road near the railroad tracks, the boy nicknamed Fuzzy by a sister saw athletics as a way to get an education, and to escape Altoona's poverty. A story that ends with Thurston winning five NFL championships playing for Vince Lombardi begins with a 12-year-old boy shooting baskets on a hoop erected at a nearby gas station owned by an Altoona family man called Darrell Woodington, who encouraged the athletic Thurston.

Back then Altoona High didn't even have a football team. Thurston, a slender 6-foot-1 basketball shooting guard, was overlooked by the state school in Eau Claire but did get an offer from Valparaiso in Indiana. Credit an assistant football coach for changing Thurston's life. Thanks to a summer hefting 250-pound blocks of ice at the Altoona rail yard's icehouse, loading the slabs onto a chute that sent the ice down into a train's refrigeration car, Thurston had packed on fifty-plus pounds of muscle by his sophomore year and was still getting bigger. The coach saw an agile, rock-solid athlete who could easily high-jump six feet, throw the shot-put and discus, and run. He saw a football player, perhaps an offensive lineman. Coach Walt Reiner suggested Thurston try out for the team. Fast-forward three years. Fuzzy Thurston was selected by the Philadelphia Eagles in the fourth round of the 1956 NFL draft. The road got rougher from there. Before catching on with Lombardi's Packers in 1959, Thurston was twice cut by the Eagles, traded by the Bears in preseason, served twenty-one months in the Army, and spent a week in Winnipeg preparing to play for the Blue Bombers of the Canadian Football League. When he was signed to the Colts' practice squad in 1958, he still hadn't seen a minute of regular-season NFL game action. Activated in time to play on special teams in the "Greatest Game Ever Played," the Colts' classic 23–17 overtime win against the Giants in the 1958 NFL championship game, Thurston was traded to the Packers for linebacker Marv Matuszak at the start of camp in 1959. He'd driven from Madison, where he'd been living with his wife and their two young children, arrived in Baltimore, was told about the trade, and headed right back to Wisconsin.

Thurston had grown up rooting for the Packers. His family and many friends lived in Wisconsin. His only concern? He was going from a championship team to a club coming off a 1–10–1 season, the Scooter McLean–coached squad his 1958 Colts had beaten 56–0. And the Packers' new head coach, Vince Lombardi, had never before held an NFL head-coaching job.

But it worked out all right. Lombardi made good use of Thurston.

Standing in his Mason Street bar forty-nine years later, Thurston held the microphone close to his mouth and said in a whispery, high-pitched voice, "Thank you all for coming. I really appreciate it. I love all of you. God bless you all, and God bless the Green Bay Packers." He was dressed in a white sweater over a red polo, his head fringed by white hair, glasses magnifying his blue eyes. After returning the mike to Jerry, he headed into the crowd, bear-hugging, kissing cheeks, even delivering a couple fist-bumps. I shook Fuzzy Thurston's hand and it's big and strong. His wife Sue, her figure trim in a pink polo, stood smiling nearby as he greeted everyone. His dancing ability had helped win her heart, he revealed in his memoir. "Not to brag," Thurston wrote, "but I am a really good dancer. I'm a big guy but light on my feet."

Strong but light on his feet—perfect attributes for an offensive lineman running the Packers Sweep. Pull at left guard and arc out toward the right sideline behind right guard Jerry Kramer, halfback Paul Hornung gliding a half step behind, his left hand sometimes even touching your hip, then—*boom*—set a block on the next tackler to appear after Kramer sets his block. In 1962, Thurston received more All-Pro votes than any other player in the NFL. Not bad for a guy who didn't even play football until his junior year of college.

Having greeted every last well-wisher, Thurston sat down to a Packer-decorated birthday cake and a can of Miller Lite. He couldn't have been happier. He was surrounded by family and friends, he had his health at 75, and his beloved Packers had won earlier that day. What a wonderful world. "With Fuzzy," wrote friend and memoir collaborator Bill Wenzel, "the glass isn't half-full, it's overflowing." One of the book's many pleasures is the collection of teammate reminiscences. Jerry Kramer sums up Thurston's eternal positivity, his sunny outlook despite the cancer and loss of his voice, despite being wiped out financially in the 1970s. Kramer compared Thurston to a five-year-old who gets a bucket of horse manure for Christmas and goes, "Yippee!" Why so happy? people ask. The kid says, "With all this manure, there's got to be a pony around somewhere."

Other teammates recalled Thurston's solicitude. "He has a big heart," said Hall of Fame safety Willie Wood. "What can you say about a guy who has everybody's feelings at heart?" Thurston was "color-blind" when it came to race, remembered linebacker Dave Robinson. "Fuzzy smoothed the waters for us," he noted. "He was one of the guys black players gravitated toward." Added Hall of Fame defensive end Willie Davis, "Fuzzy was great at creating togetherness. He was the essence of what you would consider a good teammate."

As Thurston enjoyed his cake and beer, a 50-something woman with big hair, long crimson fingernails, and a curvy figure handed him a present. Unwrapping it, Thurston removed a pair of pink polka-dot boxer shorts and joke-store "beer goggles," a pair of cardboard sunglasses with lenses shaped like beer bottles. Matchlessly deadpan, Thurston put the boxers on his head and set the goggles over his glasses and went back to eating his cake. His pretty wife Sue took it all in with a "*There he goes again—that's my Fuzzy*" look on her face.

A Miami punt with 28 seconds left was the only thing that saved Brett Favre from ending another season, and possibly his NFL career, on an interception. The pick came with 5 minutes left to play and the Jets down 24–17. They had a first down at the Miami 29. Favre went no-huddle, perceived disarray on the Miami side, quick-snapped and threw short to Chansi Stuckey. Except Stuckey had barely moved. The ball flew over his head right into the hands of cornerback André Goodman. It was Favre's third pick of the day, putting an exclamation point on what had been a dreadful slide since the heights of mid-November, when No. 4 led his team to consecutive victories over New England and then unbeaten Tennessee. When all was said and done, Favre's last five games would feature 9 interceptions, 9 sacks, just 2 touchdown passes, and a passer rating of 55.4. Later we'd get medical details about a torn biceps tendon in his throwing shoulder, an injury affecting his accuracy and strength on certain throws. But just now, the focus was Favre's home-stretch slide, and the Jets' collapse.

After Tennessee, there was that 34–14 loss to Denver in the Meadowlands rain. Favre went 20 of 43, with no touchdowns and a pick. In the second half, he threw incompletes on third-and-1, third-and-3, and fourth-and-3. In a 24–14 loss to the 49ers the following week, Favre went 20 of 31 for 137 yards and no touchdowns. Against the Bills in Week 15, he threw more two picks and one touchdown, posting what would be his highest post-Thanksgiving passer rating, an underwhelming 61.4.

He slid further. In a 13–3 loss to the lowly 3–11 Seahawks, Favre threw two picks, no touchdowns, took 4 sacks for 37 lost yards, and rated 48.7. And on this day against Miami—a game the Jets lost 24–17, if you'll forgive the spoiler—Favre's interception hat trick gave him a league-leading 22 picks, bringing his interception total on the season equal with his touchdowns.

The Jets easily could have lost all 5 of those games. They received a gift against Buffalo when a sacked J. P. Losman fumbled at the Bills' 11 with 1:54 to go and his team up 27–24. Lineman Shaun Ellis scooped and scored for a 31–27 miracle win. Not to put too fine a point on it, but the Jets' collapse was the Packer organization's good fortune. Had Brett Favre stayed in mid-November form, the Jets certainly would have made the playoffs. Imagine if Favre had sparkled in January. Cheeseheads would have been tuned in en masse. Hits to the FireTedThompsonNow.com Web site would have crashed the server every other day. Maybe every day.

But that's not what happened. Just like the Packers, the Jets lost four of their last five games. And Aaron Rodgers' numbers in this stretch were decisively better than the man he replaced. While Favre threw for 1,011 yards in that stretch, Rodgers amassed 1,439. Rodgers passed for 11 touchdowns against just 4 interceptions. His 100.02 passer rating nearly doubled Favre's 55.44 mark.

It's ironic, I suppose. In a Packers season plagued by injuries (Mark Tauscher's torn ACL in the Houston game only the last in a distressing list), it may have been an injury to a player on another team, not a season-ender but still significant, that kept cheesehead pitchforks in the shed.

After a Miami punt, the Jets got the ball back on their own 1-yard line. They had 17 seconds to work with and no timeouts. To go 99 yards would require 100 times more Favre magic than he'd ever conjured before. Taking a shotgun snap in his end zone, his left leg coming up in that familiar rhythm hitch, he threw a crisp short spiral in traffic to halfback Leon Washington. Advancing past the 10, Washington flipped the ball backwards. And who should catch it? Brett Lorenzo Favre. Dashing out of the end zone, he did a small boyish leap, snagged the lateral, ran a couple yards, then flipped it forward to Jerricho Cotchery a split-second before he was demolished by Dolphins safety Yeremiah Bell, the hit sending Favre to the turf. When he popped back up after a complete roll, he saw that he'd been flagged for an illegal forward pass. Would this, then, be it? Our last moment of Favre? If so, it kind of had it all: a zinger of a pass, a moment of improv, big-time toughness. Coming off the field, Favre undid his chinstrap as we'd seen him do countless times over the years. Then his hand reflexively rose to do the same thing, falling a moment later. He remained on the sideline for a final Jets lateral-fest, five men in kelly green touching the ball before it was all over. When it was, the helmeted quarterback jogged quickly for the tunnel, chased by photographers. "There goes the iconic figure of Brett Favre," said CBS Sports play-by-play man Jim Nantz. "He's retired a couple of times only to come back. But this, very possibly, is it."

Maybe it was the moonlight on the snow on the frozen river. Maybe it was being up on that bridge, the Mason Street Bridge, with a view of all downtown, a city of bars and spires, as someone once wrote of Green Bay. There was the steeple to "Vince's Church," all lit up. There were the smokestacks releasing steam into the night. There were the riverfront mounds of coal, covered in snow, moonlit. Or maybe it was spending time in the presence of Fuzzy Thurston, a man who, as Jerry Kramer says, finds the good in everything, and in everyone. But as I made my way home, over the river, I was remembering only good things, my favorite things, about Favre's career. I was remembering a 22-year-old Favre's 35-yard pass to Kitrick Taylor with 13 seconds left that beat the Bengals 24–23 at Lambeau back in 1992. I was remembering his audible to open Super Bowl XXXI in New Orleans, a little glance left then a lofted ball to Andre Rison for a 54-yard touchdown. I was remembering December 22, 2003, the night after his father Irv died. With Deanna watching from a booth, her husband threw for 399 yards and 4 touchdowns against Oakland. There was a sky-touching rainbow to Javon Walker, the receiver grabbing the ball between two defenders and tumbling into the end zone for a touchdown.

I was also remembering stories. I'd heard them in the Stadium View. Favre in his beat-up *NYPD Blue* T-shirt dropping by the Van Kauwenberg dairy farm to get hay for his deer blind. Favre pranking Mike Holmgren on a trick-or-treat night in 1995, wearing a ghoul's mask and a Don Beebe jersey. Holmgren didn't know it was him, nor did he recognize a masked Beebe and Frank Winters. He said he was out of candy. The players laughed all the way to their cars.

And as I came down off the bridge, nearly home, I was remembering another Favre story, a small one, but one that stayed with me. It was in Favre's early years in Green Bay. Deanna was playing a rec-league basketball game. Favre came to watch. He sat in the stands, wearing a ball cap, a pinch of snuff between his cheek and gum. After the game, one of the players on the opposing team, the woman who told me the story, went to her gym bag and got her Packers cap and went up to Brett Favre and asked him to sign it. Favre signed her cap. Then he walked out into the night.

# EPILOGUE:
## SAME TIME NEXT YEAR

**I** **JOGGED TO LAMBEAU** a final time the evening after the Lions game. I joined a line of 600 other Packer fans waiting to get into the Legends ballroom on the Atrium's Club Level for the 6:30 P.M. live broadcast of *Larry McCarren's Locker Room*, at 19 years Green Bay's longest-running Packers TV show. "Welcome to 'The Guiding Light with Larry McCarren,'" joked the guitarist for house band Third & Short during pre-show banter. In how many other football cities in America would you get hundreds of people, many of them parents with children, to come out on a frigid late-December night to watch the filming of a thirty-minute football show hosted by a former NFL center there to highlight a game pitting a 5–10 team against an 0–15 opponent?

I arrived at 5 P.M. and the line already stretched down a long hall to the escalators. I was told some people had arrived as early as 3:30 for one of the first-come/first-served seats. Proving once again that Wisconsinites will find any excuse to get festive, beer was being served in plastic cups at a Club Level bar. Adults in line happily sipped and joked. "I see you've got your refreshments," McCarren said when he arrived with his wife and came down the hall, marveling a little at the size of the line after so dreary a season. Though maybe that was one of the reasons for the turnout. Like Fuzzy Thurston, another beloved former Packer with comic gifts, Larry McCarren had a light touch, a reliably humorous take on pretty much everything. A last dose of Larry, as most everyone around here called him, might do the spirit good before heading into the long, cold, Packer-less winter.

McCarren, drafted with the 308th pick out of Illinois in 1973, earned the nickname "The Rock" for his streak of consecutive starts for the Packers, ultimately starting 162 games over twelve seasons and earning a pair of Pro Bowl selections. Arguably the hardest-working man in Green Bay show business, the bearded Illinois native has been head sportscaster at WFRV since 1988, winning Wisconsin's Sportscaster of the Year award four times. Now 59, his busy schedule also includes providing color commentary during Packers radio broadcasts and co-hosting the weekly *Mike McCarthy Show*, shown statewide.

Jordy Nelson was McCarren's guest for this season-ending *Locker Room*. As Third & Short played loud, rockin' theme music and audience members waved green and gold pom-poms and yellow foam "We're No. 1" hands passed out by staff, Nelson came down the aisle high-fiving kids who stood for the chance to touch a Packer. Third & Short had already warmed up the crowd with a peppy Beatles number and Cheap Trick's "Surrender." And McCarren had led a hip-hip-hooray for a birthday girl, then took a moment to salute a couple celebrating their 46th wedding anniversary. McCarren joked with the husband about getting off cheap.

Already it had been worth the wait in line. And the time went fast. I spent it talking to brothers Tom and Larry Van Straten, cabbage farmers from Shiocton, and their families. That sauerkraut you put on your brats? It might have originated at Tom's farm. Or Larry's. Big fans of McCarren, the brothers regularly make the thirty-mile drive in to catch a *Locker Room* broadcast.

After Nelson took a seat, his host asked whether he was getting a little tired of cameras and microphones, and if he might appreciate some downtime back in Kansas. Nelson grinned and said, "A little bit. It'll be fun to get back home, get on the farm."

They went to a segment called "In the Huddle," one where McCarren "dissects a play with the player who made it." The play was Nelson's 45-yard kickoff return to open the Lions game, one matching the longest Packers return of the season. "Now Jordy," said McCarren, "this is kicker man right here. And you got blocker man right here. Are you thinking, 'I'm going the distance?'"

"Honestly," Nelson replied, "I'm thinking don't get tackled by the kicker."

Introducing the next segment, McCarren said, "Jordy, I know you're a receiver and catching passes is your thing but I used to be a center before you were born, and so we talk a fair amount about blocking on this show. Folks, I want you to watch Jordy's block on this play against Chicago, taking on a Chicago Bear and just destroying him. Put that dude on skates!"

We watched Nelson lead Ryan Grant nearly into the end zone, pushing safety Kevin Payne backwards 7 yards. McCarren teased the low-key Kansan by saying he should have sprung up, stomped on the

Bear, and flexed his muscles. Next he played a clip of Nelson setting a block during DeShawn Wynn's 73-yard touchdown run the day before. "There you are there, blocking down on a full-grown defensive end," McCarren said. "Now Jordy, when you get down there in the box, that's not wide receiver territory. Is that strange territory?"

"It is a little strange," said the rookie receiver. "You're hoping the guy's not expecting you to block him and he wasn't. I kind of had an angle on him. If you can get a big hit on your guy to knock him down, kind of a kill-shot, that's good, but the main thing is not to let him get penetration on you and bubble back."

A Daryn Colledge block-o-rama on the Wynn run was the focus of "Larry's Chalk Talk." Once again displaying his versatility, Colledge had shifted from left guard to right tackle to take the place of injured Mark Tauscher. Still, what Colledge did in terms of pulling, blocking, running, and staying with a play would have made former Packers guard Fuzzy Thurston proud.

"I've been watching this stuff a long time," said McCarren, "but yesterday I saw something that may have been a first. Here's DeShawn Wynn's big run. The Packers do a good job of sealing the perimeter. They've got folks pulling, and one of those folks is Daryn Colledge, playing right tackle yesterday. Let's watch him." As the clip ran, McCarren telestrated the play while the band's guitarist noodled a solo. "First of all, he knocks that Lion into another Lion. He stays on his feet, comes downfield and cuts down not one but two Lions. Let's roll that back and see how many folks Daryn Colledge blocked all by his lonesome!" As the highlight re-started, McCarren said, "Count along with me. It'll be fun. Okay, here's Colledge. There's one Lion! Two Lions! Keep going. There's three Lions! And there's four Lions! Four blocks on one play by one guy! Unbelievable!"

As fans came out the glass Atrium doors and walked past the statues of Curly and Vince into the Green Bay night, they were feeling pretty fine thanks to Larry. He'd reminded everyone that there was much to look forward to in 2009, not least more touchdown catches by Jordy Nelson, more run-springing blocks by Colledge, and more pinpoint spirals by Aaron Rodgers. Many of these people would be back to watch the season opener of *Locker Room*, the show's twentieth anniversary. Many would also hit the other weekly Packer TV shows, like Monday's *Inside the Huddle with Donald Driver*, broadcast live from The Bar on Holmgren Way, and *Tuesday Night Touchback*, a live hour from the Legends brewpub in De Pere. Thursday nights fans could attend the taping of *Inside Lambeau*, shot inside Curly's Pub and co-hosted by Wayne Larrivee, McCarren's Packers radio partner. I caught shows featuring Will Blackmon, Mason Crosby, Nick Collins, Tramon Williams, James Jones, Jason Spitz, Pat Lee, and the player selected by his teammates as 2008 Packers rookie of the year, Jordy Nelson.

One *Inside Lambeau* guest would not be back. The eloquent, gentlemanly, always interesting defensive lineman Colin Cole, who gave generously of his time talking to me in the locker room, signed a five-year, $21-million contract with Seattle during the offseason. Like another child of Jamaican parents, Atari Bigby, Cole had a pregnant wife and was hoping to sign a long-term contract for the stability it would bring his family. When we last spoke in late December, he delivered something of an ode to the Packers organization, one shading into valediction, for as much as he wanted to stay in Green Bay, he sensed a multi-year contract might not be in the cards for him.

"I really love this place," said the 335-pound lineman one day after practice. "Up and down the organization, you have such good people here, from the coaches to the players to the equipment managers to

311

the trainers, everyone. It's a business, but it doesn't feel like a business. If I end up leaving, I'll miss these guys—everybody here—and I think they'll miss me."

Seattle acquired Cole on March 1. By then, massive change had come to Green Bay. What happened was a stark reminder that the Packers, like any NFL team, are a business in the end, and when performance slips below a certain level, jobs are in jeopardy. One week after the season ended, on Monday, January 6, Mike McCarthy fired five defensive coaches and his strength coach. Let go in the largest mass firing in the team's history were defensive coordinator Bob Sanders, 55, secondary coach Kurt Schottenheimer, 59, cornerbacks coach Lionel Washington, 48, defensive tackles coach Bob Nunn, 43, defensive ends coach Carl Hairston, 56, and strength coach Rock Gullickson, 53. Schottenheimer, Hairston, and Gullickson were men McCarthy had known for years, the first two as colleagues in Kansas City in the '90s, strength coach Gullickson a man McCarthy had worked alongside for five years in New Orleans.

The firings followed by three days the team's announcement that 69-year-old special teams coordinator Mike Stock had retired. Ultimately, McCarthy would elevate Stock's second-in-charge, Shawn Slocum, 43, to the top spot.

The axing of five defensive coaches mere days into January left little doubt where McCarthy thought the source of the team's struggles originated. The seven-game plunge from 13–3 to 6–10 set a new Packers record, an ignominious one. How easily, though, things could have been different. Had Crosby's kick in the Metrodome drawn another foot to the left, and his kick in Chicago not met a gloved palm, and had Woodson reached a hand just a little further as Delhomme's moon ball arrived, the Packers likely would have had three more wins and gone 9–7. And if that late-game pass to Nelson in Tennessee hadn't been slightly redirected . . .

Couple inches here, couple inches there. That's the difference between 6–10 and 10–6 in the NFL.

Two weeks after the mass firings, an even bigger change arrived. What's bigger than letting go five coaches on one Black Monday? How about radically overhauling your entire defensive system by switching from a 4-3 scheme to a 3-4? On January 19, the Packers announced the hiring of former Carolina and Houston head coach Dom Capers as defensive coordinator. He would set about transforming the Packers defense into a base 3-4 alignment, his specialty. Coach Capers left perhaps his deepest mark on the NFL running the vaunted 3-4 Pittsburgh Steelers defense under head coach Bill Cower from 1992 to 1994. Pittsburgh still uses the 3-4, as does Baltimore, and statistically these two defenses were the NFL's best in 2008.

Instead of four linemen and three linebackers arrayed behind them, the Packers in 2009 will line up three stout, space-eating linemen and four linebackers, at least one outside backer big enough to play defensive end in a 4-3 scheme. McCarthy is hoping the blitz-heavy defense will bring more pressure on quarterbacks, and better stop the run. One player the new scheme may benefit if his health returns in '09 is strong safety Atari Bigby. Bigby has a chance, analysts argue, to become a kind of "Packers Polamalu," a Green and Gold version of Pittsburgh's fleet, attacking, heavy-hitting interception machine Troy Polamalu.

If you were one to believe, with Bob McGinn and Johnnie Gray, that the Packers could have done with a little more fire in '08, you would not have been displeased when Capers brought on board five-time Pro Bowl linebacker Kevin Greene, third all-time on the NFL sack list, as his outside-linebackers coach. Greene, 46, known for his fierce, aggressive style as a player, along with his flowing blond hair and stint as a pro wrestler, will focus on helping the linebackers transition to the 3-4, a scheme Greene thrived in playing for Capers at Pittsburgh and Carolina.

In April's 2009 NFL Draft, the Packers continued their defensive reboot. With the No. 9 overall pick they selected Boston College nose-tackle B. J. Raji, a 6-2, 337-pound agile behemoth. When the team's first turn arrived, Texas Tech wide receiver Michael Crabtree was still on the board. Some observers had Ted Thompson hewing to his BPA ("Best Player Available") philosophy and taking Crabtree if he could, despite possessing a well-stocked receiving corps. Crabtree would give Rodgers another deadly weapon, and Donald Driver couldn't play forever.

But Thompson went with defense and the 3,000 Packer fans jamming the Lambeau Atrium for the annual Draft Party loved the Raji pick. Hoorays for a nose guard! Huzzahs for a run-stuffer! It was a striking change from the last two years, when attendees booed the GM's selection of Jordy Nelson and defensive tackle Justin Harrell. When a reporter informed Thompson that he hadn't been booed this year, the dry-witted Texan replied, "They must be getting soft."

It appeared the GM had selected for need this time around. And soon enough he again went outside what we thought of as the Thompson playbook, trading up to get USC outside linebacker Clay Matthews with the No. 26 overall pick. Going all in for potentially rapid defensive improvement, Thompson surrendered his second-round pick and both third-round picks to secure Matthews.

There was more rowdy Atrium applause. Who knew Ted Thompson could be so daring?

Depending on how the 2009 preseason goes, Packers fans may see Clay Matthews lined up at right outside linebacker opposite left outside linebacker Aaron Kampman this fall. Yes, that Aaron Kampman. No Packer is being asked to change more than "Kamp," a player who mastered left defensive end through constant, even obsessive, focus. By the time you read this, a verdict of some sort concerning the success of this dramatic transition should be in.

I originally ended this book with a scenario, one that looked plausible through the spring and first half of the summer, though one that not very long ago at all would have seemed the purest fantasy, something as likely to happen as swine taking wing, as Michael Hunt might say. The scenario was linebacker Aaron Kampman intercepting a Brett Favre pass on November 1, 2009, at Lambeau Field. Favre was wearing Vikings purple. Extending the scenario, I had Kampman blitzing on the Vikings' next possession. And yes, he got to the quarterback. He sacked No. 4.

And Lambeau roared.

But then Favre decided not to join the Vikings for the start of training camp. Still, Aaron Kampman will indeed play linebacker in 2009. The sight of him grouped with A. J. Hawk and Desmond Bishop, Brady Poppinga and Jeremy Thompson, Brandon Chillar and rookie Clay Matthews, all taking instruction from new Packers linebackers coach Kevin Greene, was one of the most defining images from day one of training camp 2009. And Greene, Kampman, and Matthews all figured into my favorite moment from that sunsplashed Saturday afternoon at the new and improved Ray Nitschke Field. After Kampman blew up a short pass play, he came toward the sideline. Greene loved what he saw. Matthews, the former USC Trojan, his fair hair worn long not unlike the way Greene wore his hair during his playing days, stood beside Coach Greene, swigging Gatorade. Greene let Kampman know how pleased he was. He slapped Kampman's shoulder pads. He hollered, "K, that play fired me up! That play fired me up good!"

This, maybe more than any other moment that first day of camp, spoke to the new season. The new year. Last year was over. This year was just starting. It had me fired up.

# AFTERWORD: THAT'S MORE LIKE IT

**W**ITH JUST UNDER two minutes remaining in the first half of Super Bowl XLV, the Packers leading the Steelers 21–3, cornerback Charles Woodson went airborne. And came down hard. He'd sprinted stride for stride with blazing Steelers wideout Mike Wallace down the left sideline, then launched into a full-out dive as the ball arrived, successfully defending the pass but cracking his left collarbone on impact. The thirteen-year veteran, playoffs co-captain, and 2009 Defensive Player of the Year spent the rest of the game on the Packers sideline, left arm in a sling.

Pittsburgh scored five plays later. Juking to get open as Steelers quarterback Ben Roethlisberger danced away from onrushing B. J. Raji, Hines Ward caught an 8-yard toss in the far right corner of the end zone with 41 seconds left. As the teams headed in for half, massive high-def video board in the new Cowboys Stadium displaying a 21–10 score, every Packer fan on the planet wanted to see Green Bay come out in quarter three and light up that board with a bunch more points, just to be safe. Yes, their 3-4 defense under coordinator

Dom Capers ranked second in the league in points allowed, trailing only these Steelers, but Pack fans well remembered Roethlisberger whistling a final-play 19-yard touchdown pass to this same Mike Wallace back on December 20, 2009, the rookie dragging his toes before toppling out of the end zone. Steelers 37, Packers 36. Nor had they forgotten Super Bowl XLIII, when Roethlisberger hit Santonio Holmes for another toes-dragging, toppling TD to beat Arizona 27–23, that clutch 6-yarder occurring with just 35 seconds remaining.

So yes, a bunch more points would be good. Come out after the Black Eyed Peas did their halftime thing and fill that 40-million-dollar flatscreen with images of Packers boogie-ing and shoulder-bumping in the end zone. It didn't happen. What happened was four possessions, four punts. A dropped slant that if caught might have been six. A James Harrison sack of Rodgers. Three 3-and-outs. 31 total yards. As the third quarter ended, the score was 21–17, Rashard Mendenhall's 8-yard run at the 10:25 mark pulling Pittsburgh within four.

And it wasn't just Charles Woodson watching from the sideline. Twelve-year Packer Donald Driver, appearing in his first Super Bowl here in his home state, had suffered a high ankle sprain midway through the second quarter and was also done for the night.

Enter Kevin Greene. Stepping to linebacker Clay Matthews on the sideline, Greene quietly summoned all his considerable intensity, put his face close to the helmeted Matthews, chin jutting out, and in a gripping moment captured by NFL Films, using a nickname for Woodson and a bleeped word for emphasis, said to the blond-haired 'backer with brilliantly controlled fire: "*Everybody looks up to Wood as being a leader. He's gone. Nobody's standin' up and rallying the troops. It is time. It is time.*"

Cue the very first play of quarter four. Clay Matthews, runner-up to Pittsburgh safety Troy Polamalu for 2010 Defensive Player of the

Year, barked to lineman Ryan Pickett, "Spill it, Pickett! Spill it!" just before the snap. As Mendenhall took a handoff, Matthews and Pickett surged forward and met the running back in a coordinated backfield slam. (The Malachi Crunch, I remember thinking, mind zipping back to *Happy Days*, demolition derby episode, the Malachi brothers teaming to crush a target car from both sides.) The ball popped loose, Desmond Bishop recovered, advanced it 7 yards. The Packers were back in business at their own 45.

Would they convert? They'd turned two first-half interceptions into touchdowns, the first coming barely 20 seconds after Jordy Nelson got the Pack on the board with a 29-yard touchdown catch on a right-sideline go route. Backup nose tackle Howard Green jarred Roethlisberger's arm as he threw, causing a duck that safety Nick Collins plucked near his right sideline and ran back 37 yards for an electrifying first-quarter score. And in quarter two, dimeback Jarrett Bush darted forward and stole a midfield pass intended for Wallace. The pick set up a 21-yard scoring missile, Rodgers to Jennings down the seam, safeties Polamalu and Ryan Clark converging a split second too late to defend a pass airborne a scant .85 seconds.

Quarter three had swung the momentum to Pittsburgh. A score here would return it to the Pack. Watching the game alone in a Long Island farmhouse, standing up the entire time, too tense to sit, I was starting to think the Packers might just do this thing. Seal the deal. That this would be the year, as opposed to the previous two, when things went right for Green Bay right down to the clock's final tick. Charles Woodson and Donald Driver out? Rookie defensive back Sam Shields with a newly dinged shoulder? Nick Collins needing I.V. fluids before halftime? Par for this season. To come this far, to the very brink of securing the Lombardi Trophy, the Pack had to overcome a league-high fifteen players on injured reserve, among them

Jermichael Finley, Ryan Grant, Nick Barnett, and outside linebacker Brad Jones, replacement for Aaron Kampman, the pride of Kesley having signed with Jacksonville in March 2010. They'd had to win their last two regular-season games, then three straight road playoff games. That snakebit feeling that plagued 2008—one revived during Aaron Rodgers' first playoff start against Arizona in January 2010 when cornerback Michael Adams flew in and knocked the ball out of Rodgers' hands, the QB's flailing foot kicking the ball straight up while Adams grabbed his facemask in a baffling no-call (a Karlos Dansby snatch and score ended the Packers season a moment later, the 51–45 overtime loss wasting a sensational 422-yard performance by Rodgers and ensuring endless replays of clipboard-holding Mike McCarthy dropping to his knees and gasping "No!" at the nightmare)—that snakebit feeling I remembered Ed too well was, just maybe, ready for retirement.

Of course it didn't exactly feel that way early in 2010 after the Packers lost nail-biters to Chicago, Washington, and Miami by a total of nine points in a 4-game stretch, a last-second or game-ending field goal the difference in each contest ('Skins and Fins in overtime, no less). Packer fans flashed right back to '08, and had the team suffered a couple more of these tight-margin defeats, talk of Rodgers and McCarthy failing to win the close ones would have flared up again. Beating Brett Favre's Vikings 28–24 at Lambeau a week after the home loss to Miami helped, though it should be said even that contest went down to the game's final seconds, Favre slipping, jumping up off the grass, rolling right, and firing a 20-yard fourth-down pass into the back of the end zone that sailed too high for a leaping Randy Moss (a Viking again for four tumultuous weeks in 2010). Having played out-of-his-mind well against the Pack in two Viking wins in 2009 (41 of 59 for 515 yards, 7 touchdowns, not a single interception or sack,

QB ratings of 135.3 in Minnesota, 128.6 at Lambeau), here Favre was nowhere near as sharp, nor were the Lambeau boos quite as deafening, though they were still loud.

Until Favre chucked that disastrous interception at the end of the NFC Championship against the Saints in January 2010, it had been a remarkable season for the grizzled forty-year-old, who joined the Vikes midway through training camp, a week after I had to turn in this book. Posting arguably his best ever stats, he threw 33 touchdowns against just 7 picks for a career-high passer rating of 107.2. I watched Favre do what he did for Minnesota while set up in that same Quality Inn apartment above Lombardi's first Packers office in downtown Green Bay. By chance, it had opened up again, and I grabbed it. Jason Vanden Heuvel and Peter Burkel were still working the front desk. I still popped across Washington Street for pizza and beer at the Fox Harbor Pub & Grill. One September Sunday, instead of catching the Bengals game at Lambeau, I went to Fuzzy's #63 and watched it with Sue Thurston, Fuzzy's wife. She cheered loudly, expressed disgust, and swiftly analyzed problems with the Packers offensive line. I visited Tailgate Row and hung out with Paul and Carol of Rice Lake, and Steve Schwartz at his license-plate-decorated bar in "Schwartzville." I joined Jon Neuhaus and his tailgate gang when everybody flew in for the Dallas game. Crisscrossing Wisconsin to promote my book, I was in a Borders in Eau Claire telling the audience about Skeeter Stolt when suddenly a voice rang out from the back row: "Hey Phil, it's Skeeter!" He'd driven down from Bloomer. I signed four copies of the book for him.

The Packers went 11–5 in 2009, a good year despite the shocking playoff conclusion. Yes, some fans pointed at what Favre did for the division-winning 12–4 Vikings, but in Green Bay and around the state I was running into fewer people who questioned Ted Thompson and Mike McCarthy's momentous decision to go with Aaron Rodgers. He'd set a Packer playoff record for passing yards against the Cardinals (posting a jaw-dropping 318 yards in the second half, nearly equalling Lynn Dickey's franchise record of 332 playoff yards in just two quarters), and a few weeks later, Brett Favre—as Packer fans weren't shy to point out—ended another team's season with an interception. 2010 did not go well for Favre, with issues on-field and off. Slowed by injuries, he threw just 11 touchdowns against 19 picks for a career-low passer rating of 69.9. As the Vikings limped toward a disappointing 6–10 season, a sprained shoulder ended Favre's astonishing streak of 297 consecutive regular-season starts on December 13.

I'd moved from Los Angeles to Titletown in 2008 hoping for a dream season under Aaron Rodgers.  Something else happened. I returned to Green Bay in 2009, saw Favre play the Packers in a purple helmet, saw the Pack take on the look of a team that could do some damage in the postseason now and into the future, led by their phenomenal young quarterback Rodgers, aptly deemed "a man of accuracy" by eighty-six-year-old Packer fan Gertrude Behnke. "Aunt Gert," as she's known, coined the phrase in a January 2011 webcast interview with her grand-nephew Corey Behnke and his CheeseheadTV.com co-founder Aaron Nagler.) Then in 2010, as I watched from the east coast, it seemed that dream season might happen. Oh, there were moments of doubt. Take that embarrassing 7–3 loss to Detroit in early December, for instance. But the very next game, the Packers nearly beat the Patriots in Foxboro behind backup quarterback Matt Flynn, losing 31–27 with Rodgers sidelined following a second concussion. From there they notched must-wins against the Giants at home and Chicago at Soldier Field to edge into the playoffs as a No. 6 seed. Powered by Rodgers, who threw for 404 yards and 4 touchdowns for a 139.9 passer rating against the NFL's second-ranked pass defense, Green Bay demolished New York 45–17. They then got by the Bears 10–3, a late Nick Collins interception of Jay Cutler providing the "dagger," as Packers radio announcer Wayne Larrivee would say (and probably did).

To reach pro football's pinnacle, they had to do what no NFC playoff team had ever done—run the table as a sixth seed. And they did it. Packers 21, Eagles 16. Packers 48, Falcons 21. Packers 21, Bears 14. The No. 1, 2, and 3 seeds, sent packing. Rookie sixth-round draft choice James Starks set a franchise rookie playoff rushing record with 123 yards against the Eagles. Napoleonville's Tramon Williams, the undrafted free agent whom the Packers signed to a 4-year, 33-million-dollar deal in November, leaped high to seal the victory with an end zone pick of Michael Vick, the league's eventual Comeback Player of the Year. It was Tramon again against the Falcons, vaulting skyward to grab a Matt Ryan pass intended for Michael Jenkins in the end zone. With ten seconds left in that same second quarter, recognizing a formation, Tramon jumped a sideline pass intended for Roddy White and took it 70 yards back to the house, his first pick-6 at any level coming at a most opportune time.

*"When are teams going to realize,"* tweeted former Packers beat reporter Greg Bedard, now covering the NFL for the *Boston Globe*, *"that Highway 38 is a road to nowhere?"*

And how did Aaron Rodgers do against the top-seeded Falcons? Not too bad. 31 of 36 for 366 yards and three touchdowns, a passer rating of 136.8. Matt Flynn said simply, "That's as well as I've ever seen a quarterback play. He looked like a possessed man."

I watched the Bears game in Brooklyn with a bunch of Wisconsin transplants who'd all met at that great Manhattan Packer bar Kettle of Fish. In the borough of Lombardi's birth, a couple miles as the crow flies from a Broadway theater whose hit play *Lombardi* was into its fourth month, we watched the Packers win the NFC Championship. One of the heroes? Punter Tim Masthay. Yes, you read right. A special teams star. Five of Masthay's punts were downed inside the 20, tying a franchise playoff record, and a sixth just scooted into the end zone. Speed-merchant Devin Hester managed only 16 yards on three returns. Masthay's final punt traveled 57 yards, leaving the Bears behind third-string QB Caleb Hanie needing to march 71 yards to tie the game. Sam Shields put an end to that with his second INT of the game, leaping to snag a red-zone pass intended for wideout Johnny Knox.

We—the merry cheeseheads—all burst out onto a snow-covered building terrace to celebrate the victory, chanting, drinking, smoking stogies in the cold. Someone got festive music going. Someone did an imitation of 337-pound Raji intercepting a Hanie pass and running it in from 17 yards out for the Packers' final score. This same person busted out Raji's shimmying touchdown dance. Bear with us neighbors, we just beat the Bears! We're going to the Super Bowl! It felt a little different from that December 2008 overtime loss to Chicago, the Scottsdale night as I came out of Packer bar Mabel Murphy's (shuttered now, sadly) considerably warmer but the mood melancholy at best and the song spilling from the bar "Man of Constant Sorrow."

3,000 miles to the west of Brooklyn on this January night, Jon Neuhaus was celebrating the Packers win with Santiago Gardner, "Santy" had driven up to Los Angeles from Tijuana, where he'd returned to take care of his mother. Jon and Santy met via this book, the same way the two of them got to know Bob Fisher, the Green Bay resident I met during training camp who told me Packer stories from the sixties. They all met up for the 2010 Neuhaus Tailgate, and will do so again in 2011. I plan to be there as well. I want to hear in person Santiago's story of the Bears fan/border guard who talked a little trash when Santy explained the purpose of his visit, sitting behind the wheel dressed in his Aaron Rodgers jersey.

Jon, his mom Kathy, his sister Sarah, Sandiago, Tampa dentist Kevin Snyder, and Kevin's eighteen-year-old son Connor all attended the Super Bowl together, sitting in a sea of Steeler fans. "My dad and I always thought we'd get to see another Super Bowl," Jon told me afterward, remembering his late father Lee, with whom he'd seen both the '97 and '98 games, but it was not to be. Jon was glad Kevin got to bring his son. Kathy couldn't watch the tense last couple minutes. While everyone around her stood, she stayed seated. She said some prayers, Jon says.

Quarterback Ben Roethlisberger got the ball back with 2:07 left and the Steelers down six. The score was 31–25. What a convenient deficit. Packer fans did not want to see a certain movie again, the one where Big Ben drives his team down the field and throws a last-second TD, leaving only an extra point to send the Lombardi trophy to Pittsburgh. But at least the Steelers did need a touchdown. Mason's Crosby's 23-yard field goal moments earlier made sure of that. His kick nearly wasn't needed as a 5-yard touch pass on third-down skimmed off the fingertips of Jordy Nelson, diving full-extension toward the right rear corner of the end zone. We found out later he'd injured his left knee a short time earlier and couldn't get full push-off. After the game, his knee was so swollen he couldn't walk and used crutches to get around for interviews.

Jordy definitely had things to talk about. He and his more garrulous receiving teammate Greg Jennings both had outstanding games. It was Jennings who made sure the Pack converted that Mendenhall fumble into points early in the fourth quarter, losing Polamalu with a break toward the end-zone's far right corner, where he gracefully gathered in an 8-yard pass. And Jordy? All he did was record nine receptions for

140 yards, setting a new Packers Super Bowl receiving record that had stood since Max McGee racked up 138 yards in Super Bowl I. Had the Kansas native caught that short pass for a touchdown at the end of the game, or hauled in a rainbow Rodgers tossed him in the first quarter, he likely would have been the game's MVP. As it was, his QB Rodgers (24 of 39 for 304 yards and three touchdowns, including a 31-yard laser up the seam to Jennings on 3-and-10 to extend the Packers' final drive) won the award, the Camaro, and the trip to Disney World.

You can imagine the cheering in Nelson's Landing as Jordy caught pass after pass. His mom Kim, dad Alan, brother Mike, wife Emily, and another two dozen family members were all in Dallas for the game. But back in Leonardville, the restaurant was packed, people having started reserving seats as soon as the Packers beat the Bears two weeks earlier. Kids, their parents, older folks, people from all over the county. As high as the hopes were for Jordy in this game, I'm guessing no one showing up that night would have predicted that the governor of Kansas would sign a proclamation the following week declaring "Jordy Nelson Day" across the whole state. I'm also guessing at some point during the postgame, maybe at the team's hotel victory party, one or more of Jordy's fellow receivers suggested things might be pretty rocking at Nelson's Landing. They'd all been there, you see. They'd all eaten there. Memorial Day weekend 2010, the whole receiving crew and their wives visited the Nelson family farm, had burgers at Nelson's Landing, played backyard wiffle ball, played a little golf on the 9-hole sand-greens Leonardville Golf Course, and learned a bit about wheat farming and cows. Driver, Jennings, Jones, Bret Swain—all there in small-town Riley and Leonardville. These receivers are, as I said early in the book, a close-knit bunch. Lombardi biographer David Maraniss made note of this closeness in a pre-Super Bowl interview with Don Banks of *Sports Illustrated*, believing it and the closeness of the whole team a key aspect of the 2010 Packers' success. And he said Lombardi would have appreciated this closeness, and would have liked this team: no prima donnas, everyone pulling for each other, guys stepping up when teammates go down. Speaking of *SI*, Jordy and Aaron Rodgers made the cover of the February 14 issue. It captured the two of them doing an aerial shoulder-bump after Jordy scored the game's first touchdown. It's a great shot. Look for it framed on the wall of Nelson's Landing some day.

The two wouldn't have been on the cover if not for the Packers defense, though. The D had to stop Roethlisberger in those final two minutes. Coordinator Dom Capers, coaching in his first Super Bowl after 29 NFL seasons, had to dial up the right coverages, the right pressures. He called for pressure on Roethlisberger's last three passes. All fell incomplete. On the quarterback's final attempt, a 4th-and-5, Tramon Williams brilliantly defended a pass intended for Wallace, leaping, reaching, timing his arrival down to the millisecond. The ball hit the turf. The Packers had won Super Bowl XLV.

# ACKNOWLEDGMENTS

**I** OWE HUGE THANKS to Mike Strong of Regal Literary and Mark Weinstein of Skyhorse Publishing for believing in this book. I'm equally grateful to my parents, Phil Sr. and Mary June, for all their support during my extended stay in Wisconsin. Joe Regal of Regal Literary played a vital role early on, as did Mike Paterniti, who suggested the story could be told with a certain amount of scale. Linda Stevenson was an always-encouraging e-mail presence, as were my brothers Mike, Dan, and Joe. The book would not have happened without the assistance I received from the Green Bay Packers media relations staff and from a host of Packer players. I'm grateful to Rob Crane, my PR point person, and to Rob's colleagues Jeff Blumb, Adam Woullard, Sarah Quick, and Jonathan Butnick. And thank you Will Blackmon, Brandon Chillar, Donald Driver, A. J. Hawk, Spencer Havner, Greg Jennings, Aaron Kampman, Jeremy Kapinos, Pat Lee, Ryan Pickett, and Tramon Williams. I owe a special debt to Atari Bigby, Colin Cole, Daryn Colledge, Jordy Nelson, and Aaron Rodgers for being so generous with their time during weeks when the demands on their time are never-ending.

I want as well to thank Packers assistant strength coach Mark Lovat, Packers director emeritus Bernie Kubale, former Packers executive committee member Pat Quick, and former Packer players LeRoy Butler and Don Beebe for their willingness to help.

I owe a special thanks to another member of the Packers family, Jordy Nelson's mother Kim, for her warm and witty welcome when I visited Nelson's Landing in Leonardville, KS.

It was an honor to spend time in the presence of the superb Packers press crew. Thank you Tom Pelissero, Rob Demovsky, and Mike Vandermause at the *Green Bay Press-Gazette*, Lori Nickel at the *Milwaukee Journal Sentinel*, Jason Wilde at the *Wisconsin State Journal*, and Martin Hendricks of *Packers Plus*. Greg Bedard at the *Journal Sentinel* supplied valuable transcript material, and I relied on his excellent reporting in the aftermath of the tornado that hit Parkersburg, Iowa, as well as his vivid portrait of Coach Ed Thomas of the A-P Falcons, who was tragically taken from us on June 24, 2009. I didn't get to meet Bob McGinn and Tom Silverstein of the *Journal Sentinel*, but went back to their superlative work again and again. And I always found inspiration in the elegant, clear-eyed, laugh-out-loud-funny columns of their colleague Michael Hunt. I benefitted as well from the top-flight work of national football writers John Clayton, Peter King, and Michael Silver, and from West Coast scribes Ira Miller and Matt Burrows. On the radio side of things, I never tired of listening to Larry McCarren, Wayne Larivee, Dennis Krause, Steve "The Homer" True, Mitch "It's All Thunder" Nelles, Bill Michaels, Bill Johnson, Drew Olson, Dan Needles, Johnnie Gray, Chris Havel, Bill Rabeor, Rookie, Mark Chmura, and Craig Karmazin. Whenever I could, I'd tune in to their shows and broadcasts.

I must also acknowledge the authors of two books I found invaluable in understanding the lives and achievements of a pair of Packer giants. I bookmarked nearly every page of David Zimmerman's book *Curly Lambeau: The Man Behind the Mystique*, and did the same in those sections of David Maraniss' *When Pride Still Mattered: A Life of Vince Lombardi* covering Lombardi's ten years in Green Bay. While I'm at it, allow me to give a last nod to Jerry Kramer's splendid *Instant Replay* and Fuzzy Thurston's *What A Wonderful World*.

*Life After Favre* would not have happened without the willingness of scores of football fans, and even a few non-football fans, to speak with me, to share stories, impressions, and some basic biographical details. It would be a very different book without Santiago Gardner, Jon Neuhaus, Skeeter Stolt, Derek Peterson at the Broke Spoke, Saints fan Jerry Everett, Paul and Carol Radloff, Ryan Glasspiegel, Dan and Cheryl Nielsen, Lambeau shovelers Scott Reek and John Koeller, and Rick "Ray Nitschke" Roystan. Likewise, I can hardly imagine the book without Mariann Watson, Tom Van Calster, and Becky Van Kauwenberg from the Stadium View; Jason Vanden Heuvel and Peter Burkel from the Quality Inn; Tammie, Randy, and Steve from Kesley, Iowa; Tom Fosha and Hal Prichard from Leonardville; Ruth Blanchard, Mrs. Evans, and Dixie Williams from Napoleonville; Kathy Neuhaus of the Neuhaus Tailgate; the Limburger brigade at Baumgartner's (Brian and Doug Barr; Mike, Scott, and Ed Lauer); Steven Strasser from Fort Drum; Scott Schwartz from Tailgate Row; and Judy Rank from Al's Hamburgers. To all of you, great thanks.

Great thanks as well to Bob Fisher, Judith Murphy, Sarah Neuhaus, Brett and Mary Roystan, Elizabeth Quijada, Fred Rauch, Judy from Mabel Murphy's; Theresa Hanson from the Badger Hole in Bloomer, the Van Straten brothers and their families, Bill Honey and Sue, Terri Swiboda, Bob Glasspiegel, Baumgartner's owner Chris

Soukop, patrons Nathan Phillips, Paul Barrett, Andy Wilkie, and Michael Connolly, A. J. Hawk's Aunt Joan, Deb McAllister from the Quality Inn, Larry Schemenauer and Randy Swoboda from the Shady Pine Bar in Tilden, Rob and Marlene from the Cajun Corner Cafe, the good people at the Napoleonville Public Library, Gina Lacoste, Sammi Banks, Brad Hay, and Dave Lacoste from the Broke Spoke, and Sheila Downing and Stacy from the Stadium View. I'm equally grateful to a number of people who were kind enough to speak with me but whose comments did not end up appearing in the final version of the narrative. So thank you Janet Stark, Teresa Jossie, Kay Larson, Suzie Schrank, Mary Wodack, Cari Merchant, Christina Kotchen, Gina Katchuba, Steve Rank, Trent Graham, Dan Ronin, Terry from Mabel Murphy's, Cowboys fans Robert Riojas, David Rubini, and Katherine Johnson, Colts fans William Brown, Gene Grider, and Chrissy Collesano, and Texans fan Ted Caryl. And for the warm Nelson's Landing welcome, thank you, Kelsey Bruna.

Last but not least, I want to thank Barry Horn and Jean-Jacques Taylor of the *Dallas Morning News*, Bob Sturm of 1310 Sportsradio in Dallas, Cowboys blogger Fred Goodwin, Kathy Pories of Algonquin Press, Jamie Santo for the terrific editorial work, Mary Kruser for her hospitality in St. Paul, Paula Powers for her hospitality in Los Angeles, Seth and Clara Pincus for their hospitality in New Orleans, and Robert and Audrey Loggia for providing so writer-friendly an environment as this project was conceived. And finally, for the support, guidance, inspiration, and wit over the past few years, I want to express my deep thanks to Matt Menard, Anne Sanow, Paula once more, Mark Bryant, Mary Ann Salerno, Sarah Walker, and Gary Hart.

# BIBLIOGRAPHY

I BEGAN READING BOOKS on the Packers, on pro football, and on Brett Favre upon my arrival in Wisconsin in early July 2008 and tried to keep on reading all through the season, partly to expand my knowledge base and partly to see how other writers handled football stories. Below are the volumes I took in during this rewarding immersion, one that continued through January until I had to quit trying to balance reading books and writing and go to all writing.

Blount Jr., Roy. *About Three Bricks Shy of a Load: A Highly Irregular Lowdown on the Year the Pittsburgh Steelers Were Super But Missed the Bowl*. Little, Brown and Company, 1974.

Butler, LeRoy with James J. Keller. *The LeRoy Butler Story: From Wheelchair to Lambeau Leap*. JJK Sports Entertainment, Ltd., 2003.

Cameron, Steve. *Brett Favre: Huck Finn Grows Up*. Masters Press, 1997.

Davis, Jeff. *Papa Bear: The Life and Legacy of George Halas*. McGraw-Hill, 2006.

Fatsis, Stefan. *A Few Seconds of Panic: A 5-Foot-8, 170-Pound, 43-Year-Old Sportswriter Plays in the NFL*. Penguin Books, 2008.

Favre, Brett with Chris Havel. *Brett Favre: For the Record*. Doubleday, 1997.

Favre, Deanna. *Don't Bet Against Me! Beating the Odds Against Breast Cancer and in Life*. Tyndale House, 2007.

Feinstein, John. *Next Man Up: A Year Behind the Lines in Today's NFL*. Little, Brown and Company, 2005.

Gruver, Ed. *The Ice Bowl: The Cold Truth About Football's Most Unforgettable Game*. McBooks Press, 1997.

Gulbrandsen, Don. *Green Bay Packers: The Complete Illustrated History.* Voyageur Press, 2007.

Hapka, Thomas with Erick and Adam Rolfson. *Letters To Brett Favre: A Fan Tribute.* Kitter House Press and Two Brothers Holding Corp., 2008.

Harlan, Bob and Dale Hoffman. *Green and Gold Moments.* KCI Sports Publishing, 2007.

Hornung, Paul. *Golden Boy: Girls, Games, and Gambling at Green Bay (and Notre Dame, too).* Simon & Schuster, 2004.

Kertscher, Tom. *Brett Favre: A Packer Fan's Tribute.* Cumberland House, 2006.

Knoke, Curt (photography) with Bill VanLannen (essays). *Green, Gold and Proud.* Triumph Books, 2005.

Kramer, Jerry and Dick Schaap. *Instant Replay: The Green Bay Diary of Jerry Kramer.* Doubleday, 1968. New edition, 2006.

Lewis, Michael. *The Blind Side: Evolution of a Game.* W.W. Norton and Co., 2006.

Lombardi, Vince with W. C. Heinz. *Run to Daylight.* Prentice-Hall, 1963.

MacCambridge, Michael. *America's Game: The Epic Story of How Football Captured a Nation.* Random House, 2004.

Maraniss, David. *When Pride Still Mattered: A Life of Vince Lombardi.* Simon & Schuster, 1999.

Paolantonio, Sal. *How Football Explains America.* Triumph Books, 2008.

Pearlman, Jeff. *Boys Will Be Boys: The Glory Days and Party Nights of the Dallas Cowboys Dynasty.* Harper, 2008.

Thurston, Fuzzy and Bill Wenzel. *What a Wonderful World: Fuzzy Thurston, A Story of Personal Triumph.* Self-published, 2006.

Vacchiano, Ralph. *Eli Manning: The Making of a Quarterback.* Skyhorse Publishing, 2008.

Wolf, Ron with Paul Atner. *The Packer Way: Nine Stepping Stones to Building a Winning Organization.* St. Martin's Press, 1998.

Zimmerman, David. *Curly Lambeau: The Man Behind the Mystique.* Eagle Books, 2003.